Dreaming in Canadian

Faiza Hirji

Dreaming in Canadian
South Asian Youth, Bollywood,
and Belonging

UBCPress · Vancouver · Toronto

20 19 18 17 16 15 14 13 12 11 10   5 4 3 2 1

Printed in Canada on FSC-certified ancient-forest-free paper
(100% post-consumer recycled) that is processed chlorine- and acid-free.

Library and Archives Canada Cataloguing in Publication

Hirji, Faiza
  Dreaming in Canadian : South Asian youth, Bollywood, and belonging /
Faiza Hirji.

Includes bibliographical references and index.
ISBN 978-0-7748-1798-1

  1. South Asian Canadian youth – Ethnic identity. 2. South Asian Canadian
youth – Social conditions. 3. Muslim youth – Canada – Social conditions.
4. Motion picture industry – India – Bombay – Social aspects. I. Title.

FC106.S66H57 2010	305.235089'914071	C2010-904722-2

Canadä

UBC Press gratefully acknowledges the financial support for our publishing program
of the Government of Canada (through the Canada Book Fund), the Canada Council
for the Arts, and the British Columbia Arts Council.

This book has been published with the help of a grant from the Canadian Federation
for the Humanities and Social Sciences, through the Aid to Scholarly Publications
Program, using funds provided by the Social Sciences and Humanities Research
Council of Canada.

UBC Press
The University of British Columbia
2029 West Mall
Vancouver, BC V6T 1Z2
www.ubcpress.ca

For my parents, whose courage and faith brought us here.

Contents

Acknowledgments

Many people, not all of whom I have the room to acknowledge here, contributed to the completion of this book. In particular, this work could not have been possible without the interviewees in Toronto, Ottawa, and Vancouver, who were kind enough to make time for me and to share their ideas. Their contributions were invaluable and moving. I hope that I have done justice here to their insights.

Karim H. Karim has been a great friend and mentor throughout. Daiva Stasiulis, Josh Greenberg, Yasmin Jiwani, Minelle Mahtani, and three anonymous reviewers also provided valuable advice and encouragement, as did Emily Andrew, my editor at UBC Press. A number of other people provided advice throughout the conceptualization and writing of this book, including – but not limited to – Maria Bernard, Jigna Desai, Rajinder Dudrah, and other participants at the 2006 South Asian Popular Culture Conference, as well as an anonymous reviewer for the *Journal of South Asian Popular Culture*.

Financially, I benefited greatly from the generous support of the Social Sciences and Humanities Research Council of Canada, Carleton University, the Ontario Graduate Scholarship Program, the Joint Centre of Excellence for Research on Immigration and Settlement, McMaster University, and the Aid to Scholarly Publications Program. I thank all of these organizations for making it possible to complete this work over the past seven years.

I appreciate the patience and encouragement all of my family and friends offered during this period, particularly my husband, Rahim, whose translations, companionship, and constant support helped to make watching these films a pleasure, and my parents and sisters, whose own experiences of migration shaped both this work and my life.

Finally, I would like to acknowledge the journals and their publishers that have granted permission to reproduce portions of previously published articles. Passages of this book, particularly in Chapter 2, were published in "When local meets lucre: Commerce, culture and imperialism in Bollywood cinema," *Global Media Journal–American Edition* 4, 7 (Fall 2005), http://lass. calumet.purdue.edu/cca/gmj/index.htm. Other passages, especially in Chapter 7, appeared in "Change of Pace? Islam and Tradition in Popular Indian Cinema," *Journal of South Asian Popular Culture* 6, 1 (2008): 57-69; for more information on this or other Taylor and Francis publications, please see www. informaworld.com.

Note on Transliteration

Words and names in Arabic, Hindi, and other languages recur throughout this work, presented differently in various sources. For direct quotations, I have retained the spelling used by the cited author. In other cases, I have chosen the spellings that appear to be the most standardized, although I recognize that native writers and readers of each language may not see these as the most exact renderings. As much as possible, I have attempted to maintain consistency in spellings of film titles, actor names, and religious and cultural terms in order to simplify the reading of this text.

The participants in this study were kind enough to provide me with names and spellings of their favourite movies. In a few cases, I have found alternate spellings that I believe to be the standard spellings and have thus utilized these rather than the ones provided. Many of the movies cited throughout this study have either been released under English titles or can be translated, and where possible I have provided these English names in parentheses following the Hindi title. However, in some cases, the title merely refers to the name of a character (e.g., *Veer-Zaara*) or may be interpreted in a number of different ways. In the first case, I have usually refrained from adding any explanation unless the character's name may signify an additional meaning (e.g., the title *Fiza* refers to the heroine but can also be translated as "Air" or its various synonyms). In the second case, I have offered the translation I believe to be the most apt, but this is generally based on information provided by other sources, including academic works, Web-based databases such as the Internet Movie Database, and more informal references such as friends or family.

Dreaming in Canadian

Introduction:
How Canadian Are You? Mapping
Nationalism, Media, and Self

Visible-minority immigrants are slower to integrate into Canadian
society than their white, European counterparts, and feel less Canadian,
suggesting multiculturalism doesn't work as well for non-whites,
according to a landmark report. (Jiménez 2007, A1)

It's not that Canadians don't see racism; in the CRIC-Globe and Mail
survey, two-thirds said they believe it is still a problem. But University
of Victoria sociologist Francis Adu-Febiri said young people ... will
be less willing to accept it as the status quo. "They were born here,"
he said. "They see themselves as involuntary minorities [unlike their
parents] and full Canadians." (Valpy and Anderssen 2003, A6)

In 1998 my sister returned home after viewing a Bollywood movie in one
of the local theatres. In Vancouver it was fairly common at that time to
watch popular Indian movies in specialized theatres, but it was extremely
rare in our family. Although our ancestry is Indian, my parents and my older
sisters were born in East Africa and had called Canada home since 1974.
Born and raised in Vancouver, I couldn't identify sufficiently with another
nationality to really understand why people so often asked the inevitable
questions: "Where are you from?" "What is your nationality?" "What is
your ethnicity?" "What is your background?"

Our Indian heritage was not something we considered often; indeed, although we all spoke or understood certain Indian dialects and carried on a
few South Asian traditions during weddings or prayers, such as wearing
henna or burning incense, we did not consider ourselves Indian. Unlike
some of my aunts and uncles, we rarely watched Bollywood films and in
fact had difficulty understanding them, as even my parents were not – and
still are not – conversant in Hindi. Moreover, we found the stories to be
absurd for the most part, littered with unrealistic action sequences, featuring

unattractive heroes, and showcasing questionable production values, un-focused pictures, abrupt changes in setting, or overly dramatic acting. The few Indian movies that I remembered from my childhood were either black and white, with the heroines wearing saris and the heroes sporting mus-taches, or bright and garish, with the characters trapped in 1970s fashions. Raised on a steady diet of *Charlie's Angels, General Hospital,* and *Dynasty,* with an admittedly limited frame of reference for Indian cinema, I thought that these mainstream American amusements were far superior to anything that Bollywood could produce. The song-and-dance sequences that everyone else enjoyed meant nothing to me – I couldn't understand the words and found some of the slow-moving melodies depressing, as I did many of the films themselves. Long, melodramatic, and filled with the romantic angst of star-crossed lovers, often capped off with an untimely death, they made little impression on my youthful mind. At the urging of relatives, we had watched one or two films at home and had found them mildly enjoyable, but for the most part we preferred the viewing material of our friends, shows such as *Beverly Hills 90210, Friends,* and *ER.*

On this particular day, however, my sister came home full of enthusiasm. She had watched a film that, she assured me, I would love. The storyline was overwhelmingly romantic; the acting of Shah Rukh Khan, Kajol, and the film's child star was heartwarming; the songs were beautiful; and this film, she told me, wasn't like the ones we had watched in our childhood. Despite her shaky grasp of Hindi, she and her non-Indian viewing companion had understood the plot without difficulty. Moreover, there was, she sug-gested, something modern about this particular film.

The film was *Kuch Kuch Hota Hai (KKHH;* 1998), and as my sister had com-mented, it did indeed contain nods to modernity. Having received a copy on VHS, we screened it at home, dependent on my mother's tentative trans-lations for a better understanding of the dialogue and even the title. Since none of us understood Hindi fluently, several years passed before I confirmed that the title translated as "Something Happens."

Something did happen that day. Although I had never felt the slightest temptation to engage with Bollywood films before then, I did recognize in *Kuch Kuch Hota Hai* a film that I could relate to – at least partly. The plot was still unrealistic and there was broad slapstick humour, but the action se-quences were gone. Both the hero and the two heroines were attractive and appealing. As they metamorphosed from teens to adult women, the two lead actresses began wearing saris and salwars, but in the early scenes they wore jeans and miniskirts. The uniformity that I remembered (rightly or wrongly) from my childhood was gone: the tightly wound hair, the dark hair and dark eyes, and the conservative fashions had given way to more diversity, with the presence of light-eyed, fair-skinned actresses countering the classic aesthetic of dark eyes, hair, and skin. Shah Rukh Khan, already a

Bollywood icon by that time, also looked different, wearing Western suits, speaking a combination of Hindi and English slang, and engaging in familiar pursuits such as basketball. Only later would I question the reason for this shift – at the time, I merely enjoyed it. For young people like me, with a South Asian heritage and a North American upbringing, such a film provided the best of both worlds. The production values had improved and the settings did not seem foreign – indeed, only later did I realize that the rolling hills and camp playgrounds were practically and purposely generic. The songs were typically melodramatic but enjoyable, and they merited repeat listening.

I didn't know it then, but I was displaying a tendency that was common among young people of South Asian origin living in the diaspora. For many people of my generation, the turning point had actually been the 1994 film *Hum Aapke Hain Koun* (*HAHK;* Who Am I to You?), a Bollywood blockbuster that moved away from the violent gangster movies and tragic melodramas that I remembered and instead depicted two happy, middle-class families who moved together through the major rituals of life such as marriage, birth, and death. *Hum Aapke Hain Koun* and its subsequent imitators included lavish depictions of Indian weddings, frequent costume changes, and the usual song-and-dance routines, although the spectacular aspect had been stepped up significantly.

I had not seen *HAHK* and, at that time, had no interest in doing so. *Kuch Kuch Hota Hai*, however, captured my imagination. It was Indian – but modern. The heroine might have switched from denim and skirts to modest saris once she grew up, but the hero wore brands I recognized, such as DKNY. These characters were still different from my own friends and relatives, few of whom wore richly embroidered Indian clothes or participated in Hindu rituals – but not as different as their predecessors had been. As Hansen (2005, 250) points out in an analysis of Bollywood's reception in South Africa, "part of the thrill of *KKHH* was that it presented images of a supposedly Indian form of modernity that many local Indians felt comfortable with, and that it displayed female beauty and elegance."

The attempts to make films such as *HAHK* and *KKHH* modern and interesting to youth living in the diaspora were deliberately thought out by producers who recognized that migration was a fact of South Asian life with real consequences. First-generation migrants might have felt nostalgia for the fashions and music seen in Bollywood films, but the second generation, raised outside of South Asia, might not have been able to identify with characters dressed in Indian clothes or speaking Hindi. By the 1990s the diasporic market was becoming increasingly important to Bollywood film producers. With the astonishing worldwide success of the film *Dilwale Dulhania Le Jayenge* (The Lover Takes the Bride, 1995), Bollywood began increasingly to market its wares to young people living outside of India.

In itself, *Kuch Kuch Hota Hai* did not turn me into a Bollywood devotee – in fact, I never really did become one, not in the truest sense. However, it represented a kind of turning point for me. From that time onward, I became increasingly curious about the ways that Bollywood could influence its many viewers and about the ways that Indian media might influence popular culture.

I was no regular viewer of Bollywood, but I was now more familiar with it, and I started to see how aspects of Bollywood were becoming widespread. My mother had told me stories of growing up in Tanzania and being discouraged from wearing Indian clothes, as doing so attracted the ire of the local population and made integration ever more difficult. On settling in Canada, she and many of her contemporaries often continued this policy of blending into mainstream society as much as possible, shunning traditional Indian clothes at work and at home. Even though Indian clothing attained trendy acceptance from time to time, many of the women in our community avoided it except for special occasions, trying to indicate the extent to which they had assimilated. By the time *KKHH* was released, however, Indian clothing was becoming more widely accepted by Canadian women of South Asian origin, including those of my mother's generation. In fact, Indian "culture," whatever that might mean, was becoming attractive to a wide audience and could now be embraced to a certain degree without stigma, although that culture had been hybridized through the marketing apparatus of fashion designers and pop stars. Madonna had apparently discovered it, bringing her version to the masses with the song "Shanti/Ashtangi"; other celebrities soon followed suit.

Indian clothes and jewellery were acquiring a certain cachet, although they continued to be viewed as exotic or unusual. It was now possible to find the kind of look that appealed even to someone like me, previously an avowed enemy of Indian fashions. The garish colours and bright sequins that I remembered from very occasional trips to Vancouver's Main Street in the 1980s or early 1990s were still there. Now, however, these existed alongside the possibility of more fitted tailoring, softer shades, and even some items that could have doubled as outfits for a non-Indian social gathering. It took me some time to realize that perhaps my newly discovered interest – which remained mild compared to that of many of my contemporaries – stemmed from the fact that those fashionable items were less noticeably Indian than before and more in line with a North American ideal that was familiar to me.

As I entered my twenties, when my siblings, other relatives, friends, and I had to start considering how we wanted to mark major rites of passage such as weddings, births, and funerals, I found myself noticing, more and more, the extent to which we had to decide between cultures. Questions arose for this originally South Asian, quasi-African, officially Canadian woman to consider. What did one wear to a wedding – sari or dress? For one's own wedding, which cultural rituals actually counted as Indian/ Muslim/Hindu/Christian, and which ones did I and the groom even understand? When selecting names for a baby, should we be influenced more by the desire to affirm cultural identity than by the desire to provide a name that sounded Anglo-Saxon, thereby improving the odds of mainstream acceptance and correct pronunciation?

Initially, I could produce answers to these questions, but I was never quite satisfied with my responses. As I moved throughout various regions of Canada during my graduate studies and research, I found that many young people of South Asian origin were grappling with similar questions of identity and belonging, regardless of what part of South Asia they were descended from or what religion they practised. Just as I had, these youth were producing responses that were ambiguous, dependent on a number of factors, and in flux. Raised to believe that cultural and religious issues were black and white, with fixed responses, some of us had come to believe that there were few right answers to the questions we were posing. Hybridity, migration, and evolution had occurred in the time of our ancestors and were certainly taking place in our own time, influencing our interpretations of faith, nationalism, and community.

As a budding scholar of international communication, I had maintained a recurring interest in popular Indian cinema, fascinated by various suggestions that the industry offered a source of national pride to audiences with Indian heritage, that its influence was widespread and helped to maintain diasporic Indians' sense of connection to home, and that Bollywood was alternately a stalwart defender of local/Indian culture in the face of American media imperialism, an example of globalized media that incorporated product placement and actors whose appearance was increasingly European, and/ or a suppressor of alternative films and dialects that existed apart from Bollywood/Hindustani dominance. Increasingly, however, as I engaged in more discussions of identity and observed confusion about the concept among other young Canadians of South Asian origin, I began to feel that the link between Bollywood and identity construction was worth examining, given that Bollywood offered one of the more consistent windows available into the world of South Asia.

I was not entirely unique in terms of the disinterest and disconnect that had defined my youthful relationship with Indian cinema, but my experience was also not commonplace. Many young Canadians with ethnic origins similar to my own had been raised with popular Indian cinema, either in the background or front and centre. In some cases Indian films had provided the aesthetic and music that shaped their homes, family gatherings, and clothing choices. In others, Bollywood was an occasional presence. Regardless of which was the case, I observed several instances among my peers and relatives where families seemed to use Indian films as their barometer of what was fashionable, appropriate, or culturally authentic, all the more fascinating since many of the people involved did not have the same ethnic, religious, or class background as the characters in the films.

Although the link seemed difficult to establish clearly, I began to wonder whether Bollywood was providing a key component of identity construction for young people in Canada whose ancestry was South Asian. In particular, as a Muslim who researched questions around Islam and media, I was especially interested in understanding how Bollywood might affect a sense of identity and community for young Muslim Canadians of South Asian origin. A Muslim presence was not new in Canada, but a string of incidents allegedly linking Islam to terrorism in the late 1990s and early twenty-first century had raised recurring questions about young Muslims' ability to find a sense of belonging and integration within this country.

Involuntary Minorities? Young Muslim Canadians of South Asian Origin

Official statistics and our own observations suggest to many Canadians that the country is becoming increasingly multicultural, its foundational Aboriginal-French-English composition giving way to an enormously diverse group of people, including immigrants and their children. The belief that globalization is transforming most countries, Canada among them, contributes to a perception that migration is on the rise and that the developed world will never be the same. This may well be true, although it overlooks the reality that Canada's history is more pluralist than some might acknowledge and that migration is a constant fact of world history.

Similarly, the anxiety that some seem to feel in Canada over the question of immigration leads to many authoritative pronouncements about the future of the country and its citizens (see Bissoondath 2002; Reitz and Banerjee 2007). Particular attention has recently been devoted to the broad category of youth, not only because those who occupy that category constitute the workers and decision makers of the future but also because they are younger and presumably adaptable, have often spent more time in Canadian educational institutions than have their parents, and are thus more apt to be fluent in English or French, to understand Canadian cultural norms, and to possess the necessary training for a productive life in Canada. If the young cannot be integrated, one might suggest, there is little hope that any immigrants can be incorporated fully and meaningfully into Canadian life and the dream of multiculturalism is unmasked as mirage and myth (Jiménez 2007; Reitz and Banerjee 2007). As the epigraphs to this introduction demonstrate, a considerable amount of time has been spent exploring the situation of these youth, yet there are – as I had suspected from my own experience

– no simple answers to whether or not immigrant or minority youth feel a sense of belonging and citizenship in Canada.

A few broad-based studies do exist, such as the cross-generational examination of immigrant life by Reitz and Banerjee cited in Jiménez (2007) and the *Globe and Mail's* series on "The New Canada" summarized in Valpy and Anderssen (2003), as well as the work of the contributors exploring racism, mixed-race identity, and confusion over belonging in Lee and Lutz (2005). Elements of these works, including questions of how to define or achieve a sense of identity, are relevant and have been enfolded into this book, which focuses on the identity construction of young Canadians of South Asian origin, with particular emphasis on Muslims.

Following the kind of informal observations previously described, I went in search of young people for this study, asking them to articulate their identities in nationalist, ethnic, and religious terms and to relate the formation of these to their use of mass media, specifically to Bollywood cinema, a popular Indian export with strong themes around patriotism and religious piety. Their comments in these areas are assessed within a theoretical framework that is unfurled in the opening chapters, covering perspectives on the South Asian diaspora, on constructions of nation, nationalism, and citizenship, and on Canadian multiculturalism. The focus then shifts to identity construction and the role of media in this process, with particular emphasis on the significance of tradition, nation, and faith in Bollywood film. The final chapters discuss the primary research itself and the findings.

The choice of young Canadians of South Asian origin with an emphasis on Muslims stems from a belief that this group is particularly well placed to address intersecting tensions within and challenges to what is sometimes defined as Canadian culture, despite that culture's amorphous and plural nature. South Asians rank among Canada's largest and most visible ethnic minority groups, and Muslims practise Canada's second-largest religion. Despite their high numbers relative to other minorities, however, many events have reminded South Asians and Muslims on more than one occasion that they occupy a marginal position in the overall Canadian population. Karim (1997), Razack (1998), Khan (2000), and Jiwani (2006) all document a long history of stereotyping of these groups, a history that became even more significant following 11 September 2001, when fear of terrorism began to be elided in the media and in policy discourse with a fear of certain religious and ethnic groups, particularly the two under study here (see Siddiqui 2006). Polling data collected months after 11 September suggesting that Canadians were uncomfortable with Islam and with Muslims (cited in Blanchfield 2002; Sevunts 2002; Walton and Kennedy 2002) illustrated that South Asian Muslims occupy a rather uneasy place in Canadian society, despite Canada's ostensible commitment to pluralism and diversity and despite the fact that both South Asians and Muslims have been part of the Canadian cultural and religious mosaic for many years.

This anxiety over the presence of South Asians and Muslims has only been accentuated by events around the world and at home, including rioting by immigrant youth in the suburbs of Paris, the stabbing of Dutch filmmaker Theo van Gogh by a Muslim man, and the arrest of South Asian Muslim youth in Britain and in Canada for alleged terrorist activity. Events of this kind have taken place during a period when several countries, including Canada, have debated the importance of multiculturalism and flexible policies on immigration and citizenship, particularly in the wake of crises such as the 2006 evacuation of dual citizens from Lebanon during that country's conflict with Israel (Worthington 2006; Aubry 2007; Campbell 2007; Brender 2009). Such events, however, also followed others that had placed the spotlight on Canadian Muslims and/or Canadians of South Asian origin, including Quebec's attempt to limit the practice of *hijab* (veiling), synonymous with the headscarf worn by some Muslim women, as well as use of the kirpan, the knife that some Sikhs consider part of their faith (see Khan 1995; Gagnon 2006; Ferguson 2007). Although this is less relevant in terms of cultural practice, young South Asians have also been the subject of special police task forces and government reports as the City of Vancouver has grappled with the problem of rising crime and violence among South Asian men.

In many respects, then, South Asians and Muslims are not only minorities but also minorities who are sometimes presented in the press or in policy as inherently problematic for their refusal to adapt to mainstream norms. This is not to suggest that South Asians and Muslims do not integrate into Canadian society, conducting themselves as citizens, workers, and neighbours; they can and do. It is, however, to suggest that Canada's official commitment to pluralism and diversity does not guarantee that all of its minorities are completely free at all times to practise their religion and express their ethnicity, and it also highlights that Canadian Muslims of South Asian origin have special challenges before them. Increased political and media attention do not seem to have mitigated these challenges. In some cases, it may have augmented them, accentuating Muslims' and South Asians' difference from the mainstream, presenting a few individual viewpoints as the perspective of the majority, and simplifying religions and cultures rather than explaining them more thoroughly so as to increase public understanding (see Karim 2000).

Muslims and South Asians living in Canada belong to tremendously diverse groups. Muslims who are South Asian can be equally diverse, although they may be particularly marginalized as public attention turns toward an image of Islam that is associated with Middle Eastern countries, as one participant of Pakistani origin pointed out to me during this study. However, the opposite also holds true: diasporic South Asians of different religious backgrounds may identify more strongly with Muslims who are marginalized than with other minority groups, especially if they are mistaken for Muslims, which did happen in North America following 11 September. In short, they are people who are visibly marked as different, whose cultural practices have been subject to intensive observation and judgment, and who represent a high level of internal diversity, as discussed in subsequent chapters.

Hence, for a number of reasons, these young people present an interesting case for study in the Canadian context, although this work does take into account concerns expressed in other countries over ways to integrate immigrants, particularly Muslims. In some places this concern has expressed itself through a pronounced degree of attention to some Muslim women's practice of veiling or covering themselves, whereas other countries have struggled to contain what they see as the violence and extremism endemic to alienated Muslim men. Many of the cases that have attracted attention have involved youth, and this has raised anxiety levels as governments ask whether their policies on integration or assimilation have failed them. Canada is no stranger to such worry. Since Canada's requirements for human capital, stemming from its declining rate of natural increase, make it unlikely that the flow of immigration or the reproduction of new generations will cease, there is an ongoing question in the minds of educators, politicians, and interested citizens about the best way to merge the disparate elements of a diverse society, and more and more often that question locates itself in relation to minorities such as Muslims and South Asians (Karim 2003; Gardner 2006; Diebel 2007). The way that young Canadians of South Asian origin construct identity and sense of self directly impacts their ability to engage positively in civic life as students, workers, parents, professionals, and voters. In other words, it influences their very status as citizens, people who feel they belong in Canada. This study thus aims to examine the ways that young people belonging to these groups identify themselves and the factors that lead to these forms of identification, specifically mass media and, in particular, the complex, hybrid form of cinema called Bollywood.

Seeing the Self: The Role of Media in Identity Construction
Over the past few years, some scholars (Nandy 1983, 1995; Bhabha 1994; Karim 1998; Kraidy 1999; Khan 2000) have begun to reinterpret notions of cultural resistance and purity, theorizing that these ideas may be more complicated than previously assumed. Accepting that traditional, straightforward resistance to assimilationist pressures may be a thing of the past, these theorists have turned their attention to the survival strategies employed

by immigrants and their children as they struggle for acceptance in their adopted countries but insist on retaining a foothold in the communities of their birth. For example, members of a diaspora may live thousands of miles apart but share interests in indigenous media such as film.

In the case of South Asians, media such as popular Indian films entertain members of the diaspora, but they also serve an important purpose, offering a vision of South Asia and South Asian culture to those who may never have visited a South Asian country but who seek some sense of cultural heritage and have no alternate means of satisfying that need. Here, I have centred my study on the interpretation of Bollywood films partly because of their consistent focus on issues of nationalism, identity, tradition, and integration into different cultures and partly because of their astonishing audience reach. As Desai (2005, 62) points out in a summary of her own study of Indian film and its reception by South Asian Americans, various media can be seen as formative in the identity of youth, but the role of film in the diaspora is particularly noteworthy: "I maintain that film is unique in the ways it constructs a shared South Asian diasporic identity. Indian films have a significant impact on second-generation South Asian American youth, even on those who seldom watch films, because they provide much of the vocabulary for understanding culture, authenticity, the nation, and cultural difference."

South Asian Muslims' readings of Western films are also of interest because there is a clear sense of nationalism and cultural affirmation found in many of those as well. Likewise, there are non-Bollywood films that address issues affecting South Asians; some speak of the diaspora and are marketed to audiences living there. These are frequently made by diasporic filmmakers living in North America or Europe, but some are co-produced with Indian companies and may demonstrate some overlap with Bollywood films. Other films, such as the 2009 Oscar winner *Slumdog Millionaire,* may include nods to Bollywood but utilize entirely different narrative and production techniques. Defining Bollywood films is often a tricky process, as noted by participants here. The Bollywood moniker is often applied to films made in Mumbai, formerly Bombay, but only some of those films may fit the standard Bollywood formula, which produces cinema that is usually glamourized and globalized. As Gopal and Moorti (2008, 4) explain, the origins of the term cannot be identified with great certainty, but some suggest that Bollywood is a relatively recent name referring to a contemporary, global phenomenon, whereas Hindi cinema may refer to a domestic industry. Explicitly political or socially conscious Indian films may not really fit into the Bollywood mould, given their more weighty subject matter, although they do have familiar elements such as song-and-dance sequences. As it is used here, the term "Bollywood" generally refers to popular Indian films, usually produced in Mumbai, with an emphasis on themes of nation, family, and faith. Admittedly, this usage is oversimplified, although it is even narrower than that adopted by participants, some of whom employed "Bollywood" as a catch-all term for any cinema with Indian themes or elements of Indian production. Some also saw Bollywood films as very similar in some ways to Hollywood films, a description rejected by Prasad (1998).

Prasad (1998, 43-44, 136-37) demonstrates that Hollywood and Bollywood are in fact quite distinct from one another, not least in terms of the fluidity of categorization found in popular Hindi cinema. Despite their clearly commercial focus, Bollywood films are very different from those produced in Hollywood. This is due partly to the target audience of South Asians and diasporic South Asians. Marketing to this audience demands a strategy to fulfill a cultural need, both for those living in India and for those whose early years in countries such as Canada may have been marked by a sense of cultural alienation and hence an inability to blend in. In recent years, particularly since the mid-1990s, some Bollywood producers have begun restructuring their work with extra attention to the experiences of audiences living in the South Asian diaspora – hence the hybrid feel and incorporation of Western logos in films such as *Kuch Kuch Hota Hai*.

This apparent willingness to engage with the perceived concerns of immigrants from South Asia highlights Bollywood's defining characteristics as well as its embedded contradictions. As Prasad (1998) notes, Indian film encompasses numerous categories, including a middle-class cinema that is distinctly less glamorous as well as the more glossy Bollywood. Nonetheless, even Bollywood's commercial productions may have socio-political implications: the industry often engages with imperialist tropes, eschewing foreign influences and simultaneously courting them while offering its own form of domination, which silences regional or somehow Othered voices (Pendakur 2003, 24-27). Its dual identity can be seen in its frequent attempts to portray American culture while pointedly referencing an East-West dichotomy. For the most part, it asserts independence from cultural imperialists while simultaneously neglecting the diverse forms of Indian culture and language in favour of a homogeneous, glossy, pan-Indian identity. It valorizes global consumer culture, as seen in its attempts to court revenues from the diaspora, but also points these viewers back to religion and tradition as all-important guides. All of these factors are significant in the current study. The intersection of religion and ethnicity within Bollywood content, and how this is read by its potentially marginalized viewers, is a focal point of the research here. Although others have studied the importance of South Asian film in the lives of its viewers, very few have examined this importance through firsthand interaction with those viewers. The exceptions that exist (Gillespie 1995; Durham 2004; Desai 2005) do not place Bollywood viewing within the Canadian migratory experience. Unpublished research by Jiwani (1989) in Vancouver and more recent work by Khan (2009a, 2009b) are among the few exceptions and are cited in this study.

Most important, however, although a number of studies have investigated issues of Indian culture and Hindu rituals in film, only a few (Rai 2003; Ghuman 2006; Khan 2009a, 2009b) have seriously examined the complicated portrayal of Muslims in an industry that constantly seeks to homogenize the India shown in its films. The role of Islam in Bollywood content is worthy of discussion given the complex history between Hindus and Muslims in South Asia and the high level of interest in understanding Islam and ways to represent it. Further benefit may be gained from gathering input from young Muslims at a time when they are most likely to be seeking ways to better understand their identity and their place within various communities. If media offered within the diaspora fail to satisfy these youth, the transnational nature of electronic mass media allows for many other possibilities, from the political to the popular to a complicated combination of the two. These minority youth may thus engage with media to make sense of a multicultural society and to help reconcile the various worlds they inhabit.

Symbiosis in Another Form: Nationalism and Media

Although the young adults in this study spoke of the role that Canadian institutions and North American media had played in shaping their identities, many also pointed to the formative role of travel to their ancestral countries, usually India and Pakistan. A training ground for many engineers, computer experts, and healthcare professionals, India has joined other third-world countries in watching those talented individuals move away. The colonizer no longer needs to come to India – Indian subjects move willingly to the United Kingdom, the United States, Canada, and other places in search of a new life. For the Indian government, there is the perception of a net loss. Its citizens may have found new upward mobility, but despite funds sent home or visits back to the mother country, not all the proceeds from remittances and tourism are available to the Indian government. In 2002 India responded to the challenge posed by the loss of human capital, extending the option of overseas citizenship for the first time. Moving away from a stalwart position on the necessity of residing in India exclusively, it has offered non-resident Indians the ability to come back home, as it were. This is an offer with definite limits, of course. It is made only to diasporic Indians living in specific countries and provides a different form of citizenship, one that could eventually be upgraded and whose implicit purpose appears to be promoting investment from a group assumed to be affluent and constructed in government discourse as people who still feel attached – which is to say obligated – to home (see Kalam 2007; Singh 2007).

At the same time that the Indian government has had to devise a more flexible strategy, film too has taken on a new life, whether by coincidence or as a result of global and economic pressures, particularly policies of economic liberalization introduced in the early to mid-1990s. This is true on two levels: non-Bollywood films made within and marketed to the South Asian diaspora, such as *Monsoon Wedding* (2001), *Bend It Like Beckham* (2003), and *Water* (2005), manage the neat trick of being not completely Indian and yet just Indian enough. The rise of such films and their filmmakers, diasporic talents of South Asian origin such as Gurinder Chadha, Mira Nair, and Deepa Mehta, was perhaps inevitable as the South Asian diaspora grew larger, stronger, and more mature. The real surprise, perhaps, lies in the concurrent trans-formation of Bollywood films, with their tried-and-true formulas of romance, song-and-dance intervals, and overwhelming Indian pride. Film is hardly the only medium involved in nationalist efforts, but it is one of the most effective.

In various ways – by controlling or commissioning production, by cen-soring content, by providing financial or official support – governments may signal what types of media are acceptable and should be watched. Pakistan has attempted to protect its own national identity by filtering the amount of Indian films entering the country, but as participants in this study ob-served, citizens sometimes have their own ways of deciding what media to watch, a decision that is greatly assisted by technologies such as black-market satellite dishes. India is no stranger to protectionist or paternalistic tech-niques, censoring the popular film industry through the Central Board of Film Certification, although it is not otherwise linked to the industry as an official sponsor (Pendakur 2003; Engber 2005). Nonetheless, there has been a distinct cohesion in the nationalist, return-to-the-roots narratives favoured by Indian politicians (Kalam 2007; Singh 2007) – particularly since the 2002 establishment of citizenship for Indians overseas and the 2004 establishment of a Ministry of Overseas Indian Affairs – as well as in those narratives that circulate through various Bollywood films about coming home, such as *Swades* (Our Country, 2004), whose storyline suggests that even the most successful Indian American will find the greatest happiness in India. Many of these narratives demonstrate the growing importance of the diaspora in policy and in media, to the extent that some of the film discourses, Desai (2005) suggests, are finally moving away from anti-diaspora sentiment and toward greater acceptance of diasporic communities.

Beginning with pivotal films such as *Dilwale Dulhania Le Jayenge* (*DDLJ;* 1995), a massive domestic and international success, Desai (2005, 61) detects a change in the tone of major filmmakers: "Almost without exception NRIs [non-resident Indians] are now portrayed as sometimes wealthier than In-dians in India but no different culturally from them. Indianness is now determined less by geopolitical location than by the performance ('mainten-ance') of cultural and 'traditional Indian values' that encapsulate the 'real India.'" I concede this point to an extent and certainly understand Desai's assertion that Bollywood film has evolved in many ways in respect to its treatment of diasporic Indians. At the same time, however, there are clearly many aspects of representation in Bollywood films that do not speak to the realities of the diaspora or to living in countries outside of South Asia. Bollywood films may indeed be willing to speak to non-resident Indians, but the majority do so in ways that inaccurately depict the realities of living in countries that are loosely categorized as Western – usually translating as Canada, the United States, England, and Australia. Bollywood has shown a definite reluctance to depict people who are of South Asian origin but who have been born and raised elsewhere. There are exceptions, as in the case of *DDLJ* and the later *Kal Ho Naa Ho* (Tomorrow May Not Come, 2003), but they are few and far between. Where they occur, they are frequently negative, as evinced by even earlier examples such as *Hare Rama Hare Krishna* (1971), where migrants lapse into hedonistic and rootless lifestyles.

Heavily nationalist discourse in popular Indian cinema is nothing new and has not receded noticeably in contemporary film, where subjects are expected to be overtly pro-Indian, to preserve their beliefs, and to respect traditional rules of Indian/Hindu culture, such as deferral to parents and other elders. The nature of nation does appear to have changed in some ways with an increased emphasis on Hindutva, described by Khan (2009a, 87) as "a linear narrative of Hindu supremacy" promoted by Indian nationalists. Such narratives mean that Bollywood's pro-Indian/Hindu stance is one that increasingly refuses to acknowledge India's historical pluralism and the facts underlying intercommunal conflict. Mishra (2002) suggests, however, that some of the rigid patriotic commentary may be softening as part of Bollywood's effort to market to the diaspora. The film *Veer-Zaara* (2004) went so far as to promote a Hindu-Muslim, Indian-Pakistani romance that dwells continually on the unity of South Asia and its peoples.

However, as I note in later chapters, discourses around Islam and Pakistan have become increasingly exclusionary, with images and narratives that bear a strong resemblance to long-standing Orientalist archetypes about Muslims. Ironically, although Said (1978) popularized the term "Orientalism" in reference to negative discourses constructed by the West about Islam and the East, or "the Orient," the same tendencies seem to have been imported into Bollywood, a setting where the presence of Muslim writers and actors does not appear to have resulted in fewer exoticized or superficial portrayals of Muslims. In the Orientalism described by Said, a certain amount of ignorance and fetishizing of the unfamiliar was at work: here, this seems less likely to be the cause. It is difficult to isolate the cause with any certainty, but the extreme politics of right-wing, Hindu-nationalist parties such as the Bharatiya Janata Party (BJP) may exert some influence and may certainly draw on pre-existing Orientalist stereotypes with great effect.

The identity promoted in certain Bollywood films, then, is nationalist to the point of denigrating any and all potential threats to the nation, from neighbours such as Pakistan to foreign influences such as the United States and England. It is generally Hindu and often middle class, and it also offers images of the nation that are gendered in significant respects. In a genre whose storylines often centre largely on romance, marriage, and procreation, women are invested with the responsibility of maintaining cultural rituals in order to teach them to children, thereby ensuring the safe continuation of the traditions that define this imagined India. Although these women can now be seen in educational and professional settings, and sometimes declare their independence, it is frequently the case that they are eventually led to marriage as the ultimate act of importance in their lives, with the assumption that they will be raising children and looking after their husbands. That the protection of women, especially mother's, is an overriding theme in many such films suggests that the nation is feminine, nurturing, and a space of nearly inevitable return.

Young Muslims of South Asian Origin in Their Own Words
With all of the above in mind, I set out to interview young Canadians of South Asian origin to obtain their impressions about nationality, ethnicity, religion, media, and the purported portrayals of themselves found in Bollywood cinema. My primary emphasis was on Muslim Canadians, but for comparative purposes interviewees included Canadians of different religious backgrounds. The details of the interview process are elaborated on in a later chapter; in brief, I spoke to participants in Toronto, Vancouver, and Ottawa, taking into account the diversity of these cities, their prominent South Asian and/or Muslim populations, and – for Toronto and Vancouver – their positions as nodes in a widespread South Asian diaspora. Vancouver, a relatively small city when viewed on a global scale, has nonetheless been the source of several South Asian members of Parliament at the federal level, a South Asian Muslim senator (Mobina Jaffer), and the country's first South Asian provincial premier (Ujjal Dosanjh, who later served as a federal cabinet minister). Toronto boasts the country's largest population of South Asians and demonstrates enormous plurality.

I interviewed Canadians between the ages of nineteen and thirty, building on the previous, personal observation that these years, despite representing a wide range of experience, mark a period when ideas about identity and adulthood have already been explored to some extent but have not necessarily solidified. Certainly, identity is also explored at younger ages, but one's earlier notions of identity may still be nebulous and strongly influenced by parental input. The participants in this study – who were undergoing or finishing education, beginning careers, and/or entering or cementing serious relationships – were well positioned to address questions of belonging, integration, or nationalism, as they had already undergone relevant experiences as citizens and as minorities in Canada. They were also likely to think of the future, their place in various communities, and how their own lives could be interpreted in relation to those of previous or future generations. Additionally, these young people possessed the acumen to convey their opinions in ways that were thoughtful and significant.

As I discuss in the final chapters, a distinct consistency emerged between my findings and those of Maira (2002), Durham (2004), Desai (2005), and Haji-ar-were (2006), arising through issues such as cinema's socializing role, the consumerist, imperialist, and sexist implications of enjoying popular cinema, and a sense of nationality and belonging that is complicated and uneasy. Findings from one study to the next must take into account various factors. The most important commonality may lie simply in the finding that Bollywood does appear to be influential; it does elicit a reaction even from those young people who would prefer not to acknowledge it. Bollywood can be, in some respects, an acquired taste: its length, its language, its format, and its rather heavy-handed storytelling are not for everyone. However, as participants in Gillespie (1995), Maira (2002), Durham (2004), and Desai (2005) have indicated, Bollywood film is unique in its impact. Even those young people who do not admire it in any pronounced way have opinions on it. Informants' comments were often framed in relation to their own social positioning, not only in Canada but also as members of a diaspora. They referenced the way these positions had changed, and they explained how upbringing, education, peers, and other media all combined to frame their interpretations.

These interpretations of Bollywood's dominant messages demonstrated a slippage between opposition and enjoyment that was simultaneously perplexing and understandable. Few young people whom I interviewed felt they were receiving everything they needed from any of the media to which they had access, but they dealt with this lack in different ways, combining various media forms, applying informal knowledge to the reading of texts, or accepting that complete fulfillment was not possible. Their resistance to assimilation, then, came to take on far more meaning than previously anticipated. I employ the word "resistance" as a reference to theories surrounding second-generation immigrants who choose not to assimilate completely into the host society, resisting any temptation to join the mainstream. Certainly, as the participants here described, and as Gillespie's (1995) and Handa's (2003) studies also suggest, the temptation to blend in, to downplay difference, ethnicity, and faith, strongly exists, as does the desire to belong within cultural communities. Resistance in this case, then, involves a delicate balancing act: even those individuals who struggle most ardently to retain a sense of their origins and cultural difference are unlikely to engage at every stage of their lives in an unwavering repudiation of the host society. Resistance is complicated and laden with ambiguities for those who must live in a society while juggling competing demands for national, ethnic, and religious authenticity. In this book, resistance, and the difficulty of enacting resistance in a straightforward manner, comes to signify a number of issues: Bollywood itself, as a counterpoint to Westernization/Americanization, has exhibited a form of resistance to cultural domination but has also emulated American media in some respects. Similarly, the viewers interviewed here recognized that the act of consuming popular Indian cinema could signify resistance to dominant North American media, but they also indicated that this was not a wholly empowering act (for related findings on reception of the film *Fanaa,* see Khan 2009b). Most important, in light of the aims of this research, resistance did indeed have a nuanced and complicated meaning for the participants in terms of identity construction.

Resistance: How Much and What Kind?

As indicated in articles from Valpy and Anderssen (2003) and from Jiménez (2007), as well as in studies by Maira (2002), Handa (2003), Hoodfar (2003), Durham (2004), and Desai (2005), first- or second-generation immigrant youth living in a diaspora remain a source of preoccupation at a number of levels. Common to all of these works is an interest in identity: What is the identity claimed by these youth, and why? How do they construct that identity and then maintain it? The young people in this study could be defined loosely as youth, but they also fell into a liminal category in terms not simply of their ethnicity or nationality but also of age, which meant that they both corroborated the findings in earlier works on youth and added to it, providing a developmental arc that indicates what may follow the stages identified in Gillespie (1995), Maira (2002), Handa (2003), and Durham (2004). Unlike Durham's (2004) teenage respondents or Maira's (2002) university ones, these young adults spanned more than one category. Some were still completing school, one had already started a family, and the rest were old enough to consider seriously the ways that their past could create a bridge to their future, allowing them to move out of a childhood defined by seemingly simple influences and into an adulthood marked by a diverse pantheon of cultures, interests, and people. Their occupation of such transitional space might explain their deep engagement with the topic of identity. Identity was neither static nor the same for everyone, although there were some definite common denominators, including an acknowledgment of marginalization, racism, and stereotyping in media and society.

Transcending the Bell Jars: Identity, Belonging, and Understanding

> We children of immigrants often seek to return to the country that our parents have left behind. I have made my own wanderings through Malaysia, through Hong Kong and China. We know there is something to be recovered, we want to open what our parents have closed, we are

> *ever curious. I make these journeys not because I hold onto the belief*
> *that there is another place and culture in which I might be more at*
> *home, but because I place my trust in empathy, in what Michael*
> *Ignatieff describes as the possibility that "human understanding is*
> *capable of transcending the bell jars of separate identities." (Thien*
> *2003, A13)*

The individuals in this study spoke articulately and sometimes poignantly about learning how to live with multiple identities, and they provided analyses that suggested their experiences with difference had shaped them in meaningful ways. Critics such as Bhabha (1994) have identified the possibilities provided by inhabiting what has been dubbed the "third space," a place that embodies the realities of being neither here nor there, and have suggested that this is a space of infinite potential for creativity and change. This is not always the case, of course, for the third space can also signify loneliness and alienation.

The following chapters open a discussion of issues such as these, focusing on film, diaspora, nationhood, hybridity, community, and citizenship. Although the respondents discussed these concepts in their own words, their comments did speak very much to the realities of globalization and responses to deterritorialization, the pressures placed on diasporic young individuals to construct and protect community, the role that media can and do play in the formation of identity, and strategies for survival in a society that is increasingly marked by hybridity and diversity, characteristics that triggered fear for some but hope for others. As their comments indicate, the participants here adopted their own methods of learning about others, applying active interpretations to a variety of media. As Thien (2003) posits above, such second-generation immigrants are aware of their place in the world and retain an interest in that world.

1
East Meets West – and Everything Else: Living La Vida Loca in Bollywood

Although Bollywood is hardly the only film industry in India, it is one of the most powerful, the most commercially successful, and certainly the most contradictory. It consciously mimics some American norms and contains other aspects of Western culture, yet it also repudiates the same, suggesting the superiority of Indian culture and of India as the only really desirable location for the authentic South Asian. In its avowal of nationalism and cultural tradition, it presents a significant challenge to American domination of international film and culture. At the same time, however, Bollywood itself plays the role of attempted imperialist by primarily marketing Hindi-language films to an enormous community characterized by a high level of linguistic diversity and by working to promote a kind of Hindu, Hindi-speaking, middle- to upper-class, pan-Indian identity that ignores the specificity of various regions and cultures. This lack is addressed partly by specific regional cinemas, as seen in Bengali and Tamil film production, but Bollywood rarely acknowledges Indian diversity.

Identity, in fact, is one of several recurring themes in Bollywood movies, some of which focus on frothy romantic comedies but an equal number of which emphasize the importance of Indian nationalism and Hindu tradition. Indeed, although Bollywood does have a certain formula, it is not monolithic. Some Bollywood films exist strictly for entertainment, built around romance, comedy, and music, whereas others are more serious in nature. Some popular Indian films, such as *Swades* (Our Country, 2004) and *Lagaan* [Land Tax]: *Once upon a Time in India* (2001), tend to blend romance with discussions of national identity, poverty, and resistance to colonizing influences.

The treatment of identity is also a source of contradiction, offering mixed messages about the ability and obligation of viewers to retain an authentic Indian identity, with authenticity often linked to physical residence in India and adherence to Hindu values. These themes, and their potential implications for non-Hindu viewers who do not live in India, are discussed in detail in the following sections and chapters. Whereas diasporic audiences and their reception of themes of nationalism, religion, and diaspora are examined in the final chapters, this chapter offers an overview of popular Indian cinema, its operations, its evolution, and its content. For ease of discussion, Bollywood cinema is often discussed as a whole in this book, but as noted above, there are many differences between films and between film categories. Some of these distinctions were noted by the participants, who commented on their respective preference for or disinterest in the more serious representatives of Bollywood film.

Creating a Monster? Behind the Bollywood Scenes

At the same time that Bollywood struggles to portray an authentic sense of Indianness, it also comes under fire for lacking its own sense of self. Bollywood films have been accused of mimicking selected Hollywood tendencies in terms of production, writing, and marketing (Nayar 2003), and indeed there are marked similarities. Plots are borrowed routinely from popular Hollywood films, even if they are then tailored for an Indian audience; these plots are sometimes dotted with a similar patriotic undertone and with glancing references to a nationalist politics; a parallel star system flourishes; distinct writing and production formulas underpin major films; there is often considerable emphasis on cross-marketing film-related merchandise, such as soundtracks and fashions; much of the film's budget may be poured into star salaries, special effects, and costumes; vast revenue can often be recouped outside of the country where the production was based; and major releases are now as likely to show New York or London in the background as they are to feature Mumbai or New Delhi, reducing – although not eliminating – the disparity even between settings. Indeed, as taboos around the depiction of overt sexuality continue to collapse, some of the most notable distinctions between Bollywood and Hollywood are crumbling into apparent nothingness. All the same, some remain, such as the prominence of family, stories that may draw on Hindu epics, influence from various forms of Indian theatre, poetry, and dance, and as Prasad (1998, 107) notes, an emphasis on tradition.

Additionally, Bollywood films possess other characteristics that distinguish them from non-Indian films as well as from other Indian movies. Pendakur (2003, 24, 26) notes the multilingual nature of Indian film production, as well as the many different venues for studios and processing, including Madras, Hyderabad, Bangalore, Mysore, and Tiruvananthapuram. Commercially, however, Bollywood films – which take their moniker from Bombay, the former name of Bollywood's production centre Mumbai – are dominant, and although fears of cultural imperialism from American films abound, Bollywood has its own patterns of cultural domination, primarily offering Hindi-language films to a diverse community whose languages include

Bengali, Telugu, Kannada, Malayalam, and Tamil, among others. Although regional-language films can claim a following within their own communities, Hindi-language films, "which make up about 20 percent of the total production, have captured the all-India market and have reached out to Indians settled in Africa, Middle East, South East Asia, North America, and Australia" (Pendakur 2003, 27).

The use of Hindi (a modified, hybrid form) can perhaps be explained by the fact that it was declared a national language after Independence, even though it is native to only five northern states (Virdi 2003, 18). Language aside, even regional "markers of costume, dress, and culture are either erased or deployed arbitrarily, and elements from different regions are mixed to figure as signs of cosmopolitan culture that account for a particular type of kitsch" (Virdi 2003, 2). Dwyer (2000, 110, 120) does single out the different cultural influences on Indian cinema, from Urdu writing, which found a rare venue where it could flourish commercially, to Punjabi actors and their ideals of beauty (i.e., tall and fair-skinned), but she also acknowledges the degree to which Punjabi and Muslim participants in the film industry have attempted to minimize any regional or religious markers (120-21).

The pan-Indian gloss applied to Bollywood movies may upset some, but as a commercial strategy it has paid off handsomely. It is estimated that roughly 10 million people a day purchase tickets to see a Bollywood movie, some of whom will return repeatedly to view a favourite movie (Gokulsing and Dissanayake 1998, 10, 14; see also Rajadhyaksha 1996, 2000). Despite producing more films a year (believed to be around 900, but figures vary) than any other country, including the United States, India typically does not export its films at the same rate. Indian films, reflecting the country's diversity, may come from various regions, including Mumbai, Chennai, Kolkata, Karnataka, Kerala, and others. However, Bollywood films, mainly produced in Mumbai, are the ones that have significant international recognition and a global market (Ogan 2002, 212). In many cases, costs incurred in the production of Bollywood films are primarily recouped through the overseas market, rather than within India, due to "the growing market of non-resident Indians, or Indian expatriates, nostalgic for all things Indian" (Mann 2001, F3). Exporting Indian films is not a new practice, but the areas of greatest popularity have shifted along with geopolitics. In the 1950s stars such as Raj Kapoor gained enormous audiences in places like the Soviet Union with Russian-dubbed releases such as *Awaara* (1951) (Pendakur 2003, 40), but this popularity waned as the Soviet territory began to break apart. Former Prime Minister Jawaharlal Nehru, although he was not particularly a fan of such films, was convinced that maintaining good relations with the film world was necessary when he saw "the political advantages of Raj Kapoor's popularity in the Soviet Union and elsewhere" (Dwyer 2000, 98).

African, Arab, and Latin American audiences still maintain a long-standing enjoyment of Indian cinema, and audiences can generally be found in countries that have become home to South Asian migrants (Pendakur 2003, 40). The financial significance of this diasporic audience is enormous, with hit films such as *Dilwale Dulhania Le Jayenge* (The Lover Takes the Bride, 1995) reportedly earning 200 million rupees internationally, a substantial figure even when viewed against the film's domestic gross of 500 million rupees (Pendakur 2003, 42).

Perhaps partly in recognition of this global market, and owing to a belief that the new generation of viewers has different requirements, Bollywood cinema has demonstrated some recent changes in its operations. In an industry populated by hundreds of different producers, some of whose projects are fuelled by substantial investments from criminal organizations, costs have crept up steadily over the past two decades. Increased economic liberalization has paved the way for more foreign imports, including films, television programs, and the ubiquitous MTV, offering alternatives to young viewers that Indian film directors argue must be countered through productions offering "visual exuberance with eye-popping images and renditions of sounds to draw this generation of audiences into the theaters" (Pendakur 2003, 33).

The producer Yash Chopra, no stranger to this thought process or to the lure of a foreign audience, has already set up distribution offices in the United Kingdom and New York City (Pendakur 2003, 43-44), and he has released films that target diasporic audiences and, as Rachel Dwyer argues, "set a new cool, urban visual style for Hindi films" (cited in Larkin 2003, 175). Similarly, in 1999, Sony Entertainment Television opened an office in New Jersey to market Indian films in North America, staging a New York premiere and advertising its films in diasporic newspapers and television programming (Pendakur 2003, 44). *Kabhi Alvida Naa Kehna* (Never Say Goodbye, 2006), Karan Johar's controversial film about infidelity, enjoyed a gala showing at the Toronto Film Festival, and *Guru* (2007) marked a Bollywood first by holding its world premiere in Toronto. In turn, South Asian audiences have demonstrated their desire to see such films, visiting South Asian-owned theatres in places such as New York, Chicago, Los Angeles, Toronto, and Vancouver.

Within India, movies have often been seen as promoting nationalist or religious beliefs, to the extent that British colonial powers once saw fit to censor the film industry rigorously. Indian film, then, despite its strength in centres such as Chennai, Kolkata, and particularly Mumbai (previously Madras, Calcutta, and Bombay, respectively), has been profoundly affected by the vestiges of colonial practice governing cinema, and it reflects, in some ways, the political turmoil that has characterized India at different times in the nation's history. Notions of censorship still exist in Indian cinema, but as the economy has liberalized, so have the themes and depictions in that industry, with producers adjusting their ideas to what they believe the audience wants to see. Increasingly, this audience is considered to be middle class, to be at least partly diasporic, and to have some knowledge of Hindi or English. English, then, can be found more frequently in some Bollywood films than can any number of regional Indian dialects, which remain marginalized by the mainstream film industry. One of the greatest sources of conflict within the industry and its accompanying music sector is the linguistic diversity of India, a pluralism that fails to be reflected in the majority of Bollywood films. This neglect has prompted speakers of minority languages to mount fierce opposition to the dominance of Hindi (Oommen and Joseph 1991; Dickey 1993; Gokulsing and Dissanayake 1998; Dhareshwar and Niranjana 2000; Rajadhyaksha 2000).

However, if there is fragmenting at the linguistic level, there is also a universal appeal in terms of sound and song. Music is a key element of Indian cinema, as is dance. Almost all Bollywood movies tend to incorporate musical sequences, a characteristic that has been enormously influential in determining an individual film's popularity and the profits it can generate (Bhimani 1995, 127, 316; Pendakur 2003, 119-44). Although other film industries, such as Hollywood, produce musicals, Bollywood does not make a similar attempt to reconcile the divergent elements of "narrative and spectacle. Instead, song-and-dance sequences were and are used as natural expressions of emotions and situations emerging from everyday life" (Gokulsing and Dissanayake 1998, 21; see also Prasad 1998, 136). Many different forms of South Asian music co-exist in these movies, including the *ghazal,* usually identified with a Muslim/Urdu tradition. Although its popularity has fluctuated and, indeed, the popularizing of such a classic form has attracted criticism, the *ghazal* remains prominent in Hindi films and on their accompanying musical CDs (Dwyer 2000, 41).

Song-and-dance sequences in Bollywood are crucial for conveying emotion, for offering catchy or heartrending tunes that capture the viewer's attention, and for subtly expressing sexuality, which was once impossible to depict openly in Indian film lest it provoke the disapproval of the all-powerful censors, who were notoriously strict in ensuring that Indian films did not promote sexual licentiousness or any other type of potentially corrupting activity. This is less true now, but for many years a belief prevailed that it was impossible to show kissing or anything explicitly sexual in an Indian film (see Prasad 1998, 88-127). Such sights still remain rare, particularly in the films featuring the most popular stars (Chopra 2005). Even in the absence of censorship, the desire to keep Bollywood content family-friendly has contributed to the use of romantic dances rather than open love scenes. Characters come close to kissing, dance intimately, and daydream about one another in these escapist sequences, which often involve serial costume changes, a luxurious set, and a sense of being removed from reality. Songs and sound are among the more compelling elements of Hindi film, with the introduction of sound in 1931 touted by some as the reason for the rise of Indian cinema's popularity and the failure of Western cinema to secure the Indian market (Chowdhry 2000, 13). Interestingly, the popularity of music in Hindi-language film can be credited partly to its incorporation of Western rhythms, although these sounds do not mask the presence of other influences, such as folk traditions (Barnouw and Krishnaswamy 1980, 73; see also Pendakur 2003, 121, 126-39).

Although linguistic minorities remain largely unheard, filmmakers outside of Mumbai fare little better. Lesser-known producers compete with dozens or hundreds of others for financial resources and access to smaller potential markets, and nearly all Indian filmmakers are alert to the potential competition presented by foreign films, particularly American ones. Indians who do not speak Hindi, the primary language of Bollywood cinema, can and have made an argument that Bollywood films tend to ignore local ethnic differences in favour of a homogeneous portrayal of India. This portrayal is easier to produce given the financial restraints on smaller film-production centres in India. Gokulsing and Dissanayake (1998) have tracked a significant increase in the number of films being created in centres outside of Mumbai and in languages other than Hindi (see also Prasad 2000, 145), yet few of these productions have offered a serious challenge to Bollywood's dominance. It is also worth noting that these smaller industries, or even Pakistan's Lollywood (so called because of its base in Lahore), often do not seem to have the same grip on the South Asian imagination as does Bollywood.

Bollywood's strength was further asserted when the dreaded American imports finally arrived in India. After India took out a loan from the International Monetary Fund in 1991, Washington and the Motion Picture Export Association of America placed increasing pressure on then-Prime Minister P.V. Narasimha Rao to allow dubbing of Western films into Hindi and to permit direct imports, a pressure to which he eventually succumbed (Alessandrini 2001, 321). Despite fears that the import of foreign films, combined with the increasing cost of making Indian films and challenges from television, would destroy the Indian film industry, it only grew stronger (Alessandrini 2001, 321-22). Popular Hollywood films do not generally perform well within India, unlike massive Bollywood successes such as *Dilwale Dulhania Le Jayenge* and 1994's *Hum Aapke Hain Koun* (Who Am I to You?) (Rajadhyaksha 1996, 28). Hindi films that borrow liberally from Hollywood storylines are far more common, and more likely to experience success, than are American films brought into India. Although the extraordinary popularity of a Hindi-dubbed version of *Jurassic Park* raised hopes in the United

States of finally capturing the stubbornly elusive Indian market, several dubbed American films released subsequently demonstrated little or no appeal to the Indian masses (Sidhva 1996, 49), who seem to prefer the version of America most often found in Bollywood, one where hedonistic tendencies can be detected.

Although major Bollywood blockbusters are still relatively chaste, a number of more recent movies contain overt sexual references, feature heated scenes, and make reference to premarital pregnancy, adultery, or steamy affairs. Such material was not completely absent from previous films, but the depictions have become more pointed and explicit, and although certain expressions of sexuality do still meet with the expected punishment, a few characters now manage to live happily following their premarital affairs. Bollywood films also now incorporate – or emphasize – a number of features that appear to be nods to watchers who are non-resident Indians. Subtitles, of course, are now de rigueur in most Bollywood films, but the characters have become increasingly prone to adding English phrases at random. This may be seen as further evidence of Bollywood's nonchalance regarding barriers of language or dialect – it may also be seen as a game, although confusing, attempt to meld East and West, leaving no viewer out in the cold.

Similarly, there is a definite movement afoot to portray Bollywood heroes and heroines as the epitome of sophistication in their physical appearance. Rich or poor, the main characters usually have access to a number of different costumes, but these are not exactly what they used to be. Saris, achkhans, salwars, and lenghas still dot the landscape, as extravagant and appealing as ever, but they are usually now presented in turn with increasingly revealing sundresses, jeans, and halter tops. Of course, the global flow of goods and the exposure to other cultures through travel and media mean that clothing practices can change from one generation to the next. In fact, it may be worth noting that scanty costumes can be found in some of the earlier films, although these were sometimes donned by non-Hindu characters or disparate characters coded as somehow Other. In the same way that it has now become far more common for diasporic Indians to wear Indian clothing and accessories in their host countries, there is no need to assume that resident Indians live in a static world where chaste costumes of an earlier era remain reified.

However, it is puzzling that many of the so-called Western clothes depicted in these films appear to be revealing or glamorous in a way that is unlikely to be seen in everyday life. The vampy clothing of many female stars in today's Indian films seems best calculated to display toned midriffs and inevitably fair skin, a departure from the days when modestly dressed, relatively dark-skinned, dark-eyed women were more likely to be seen. Light-eyed, fair-skinned, and sporting miniskirts and tube tops, these young women appear to be catering to a different audience than did their predecessors.

This may be due to any number of factors, but one possibility is that directors targeting a global audience may assume that diasporic viewers are most likely to embrace those Indian stars who appear, essentially, a little less Indian.

The irony is poignant: although India, as the exoticized former colonial subject, may be perpetually misunderstood and exploited for commercial gain, the vision of the colonizer – past or potential – is equally skewed in popular Indian cinema. Influenced, perhaps, by the fact that Hollywood television shows and films depict characters in revealing clothing or increasingly explicit sexual situations, Bollywood producers insert similar sequences but even take them further on occasion, dressing women in ways that seem out of place or surprising. Despite its apparent shift toward globalized norms, Bollywood also continues to draw on some of the same influences it has always used, such as the two great epic stories *Ramayana* and *Mahabharata*, classical Indian theatre, folk theatre, nineteenth-century Parsi theatre, and musical television (Gokulsing and Dissanayake 1998, 17; see also Booth 1995, 169; Pendakur 2003, 103). Both traditional Indian themes and a capitalist, globalized modernity underpin many Bollywood films; as Prasad (1998, 107) notes, "the construction of 'tradition' is part of the work of modernity." Chakravarty (1993, 55) notes that Hindi cinema is the ideal vehicle for presenting old myths with a new veneer, reminding audiences that Indian culture can continue to thrive even in times of change and globalization. No matter how strong the foreign influence, it cannot truly injure "all institutions of our traditional culture that are now under severe threat – the joint family, patriarchy, the traditional qualities of the image of the Indian woman, and also, the nation," an observation echoed by Nayar (1997, 86), who notes that Western life may be incorporated into Bollywood only in superficial ways, not in any sense that would affect the filmic depiction of family ties and togetherness.

The influence of *Ramayana* and *Mahabharata* can be seen not only in plots that feature this kind of familial devotion but also in these plots' emphasis on divine intervention, sacrifice, and the fulfillment of dharma, "one's 'sacred duty,' a code of conduct that is appropriate to (and expected of) each individual depending on his or her social rank, stage in life, or kinship ties" (Nayar 2003, 81). Individual fulfillment is not always the goal of these characters, each of whom is acutely aware of his or her place within family and society. This idea of a greater good is present in many Bollywood films, but its treatment is generally different in more contemporary films, where sudden changes of heart and miraculous events may lead to happy endings, a stark departure from the bleak politics of earlier films.

All about India: The Evolution of an Industry

There is little question that the content of Indian films has markedly changed, at least in terms of those films that are most popular. The industry is so undeniably prolific that it is not possible to discuss many of the best-known films in any great depth. Although specific films are examined briefly later in this chapter for their depiction of particular topics, this section provides an overview of major themes in mainstream Indian cinema, with later chapters offering more detailed consideration of questions of nationalism, diaspora, and globalization in Bollywood film. It is currently the case that topics such as romance, marriage, and family anchor most of the major Bollywood hits, but at one time Bollywood was distinguished for mixing romance with questions of social justice and political commentary. As Thoraval (2000, 49) notes, serious dramas have more or less gone out of style, supplanted by purely entertaining features.

Certain stories do recur, and screenwriter Javed Akhtar has suggested that most Bollywood narratives can be traced back to "ten master plots" derived from Roman, Greek, and Hindu mythology. He names stories about lost and found items, vendettas, and of course romances, arguing that most of these stem from classic myths (cited in Kabir 1999, 34). Stories about love are frequently found in popular Indian films. In the late 1980s politically infused tales of marginalized young men began to disappear, giving way to an abundance of romantic young heroes who are spiritually devout, possess extraordinary filial piety, and are hopelessly in love. These stories usually have some kind of happy ending, in contrast to the older, more tragic strain of the genre, where hero and heroine alike suffered enormous travails only to be separated in the end, sometimes by death. The contemporary emphasis on heroes, rather than on heroes *and* heroines, is no coincidence.

Although female characters are infused with enormous symbolism and generally represent the salvation of the nation and the successful transmission of positive values, many of the best-known films are distinguished by the hero's role. Pendakur (2003, 145) notes that in Bollywood male stars are better-paid and receive better stories. In the 1970s, viewed by some as a kind of golden era in popular Indian cinema, Amitabh Bachchan shot to fame as a brooding young anti-hero whose female leads were sometimes abused as he vented his rage at a society characterized by injustice and inequality.

Indeed, Bollywood's preoccupation with gender and sexuality is so marked that it is almost impossible to ignore. Catering to an audience whose members are presumably raised to believe that marriage and reproduction are the ultimate goals, Bollywood films rarely address the issue of homosexuality in a serious or explicit way. Where films do incorporate homosexuality, this is often in the form of transvestites who are the butt of jokes; the strong bonds of masculine friendship (referred to as *dosti*) are often emphasized, but any connection to homosexuality is usually glossed over. Men and women are called on to unite and to do so in marriage, as relationships outside of marriage are dishonourable and shaming to one's family. Although both partners are required to contribute to the marriage and to the creation

of children, Hindu society and Hindi film place greater domestic expectations on women. Pendakur (2003, 146) suggests that many ideas regarding
appropriate gender-specific behaviour are drawn from *Manusmriti*, "considered the pivotal text of Hindu orthodoxy ... Ideas from Manu resonate in
the daily lived experience of people as well as in their consumption of popular
cinema." Dwyer (2000, 26) quotes some of these ideas: "Her father guards
her in childhood, her husband guards her in youth, and her sons guard her
in old age. A woman is not fit for independence (Manu 9.3)."

Bollywood keeps raising the bar for young women, asking them to be all
things to all people. Female characters often combine bright minds with
beautiful bodies and a demure, respectful attitude to elders. Whereas sweet
virgins once stood in stark contrast to alluring seductresses (often explicitly
coded as Christian to explain their irreligious activities), the modern female
star must combine the qualities of both, offering spunky assertiveness that
in no way detracts from her ability to metamorphose into a suitable wife,
one who generally "wears more conservative clothing and follows tradition
to behave as a 'respectable' daughter-in-law or a married woman" (Pendakur
2003, 151). As Zara, a participant from Toronto, pointed out, both conservatism and sexualization can pose a problem for women:

> When you do have newer films like *Namastey London* [2007] or *Salaam Na-
> maste* [2005], they attract such a backlash. The role of women is not really
> evolving. They might put women in miniskirts or modern clothes and say
> that she's modern now, but is that modern? I would say not.

Maira (2002, 171) describes a feminine ideal of light skin and overt sexuality
(see also Nayar 2003, 74), an ideal that must also offer some indication that
this sexuality is intended to be expressed fully following marriage. Although
fair skin has long been prized in much of Indian society, new requirements
for slenderness are more recent and may demonstrate some influence from
global media.

One feature that has not changed is the use of these major stars to attract
audiences, such that celebrity-studded blockbusters sharply distinguish
themselves from lesser lights in the waves of films entering the Indian and
diasporic South Asian market every year. Bollywood operates on a clear ce-
lebrity hierarchy, and magazines and websites that track the activities of the
stars help to promote the films. Features in the movies that have changed
include the growing use of English mixed in with more commonly used
Hindi (possibly due both to the predominance of English in the South Asian
diaspora and to its increased use among the Indian middle class), the increased appearance of non-Indian settings, and an amplified emphasis on
consumerist pleasures in many of the newer films, including lavish dress,

enormous homes, and expensive cars. Many of the major rituals in Bollywood cinema are accompanied by costume changes, sometimes in conjunction with musical routines. Following the release of a major film, it is common to find similar fashions and CDs of the movie's music widely available within the diaspora.

These costume changes and song-and-dance sequences, often mixed into a meandering, derivative script that is marked by improbable coincidence, miraculous acts of salvation, and some degree of predictability, combine to offer a form of film that is often dismissed as escapist. Regardless of the perceived negativity associated with the notion of escape or fantasy, some commentators have greeted such charges with a shrug, arguing that these films are at least partially designed for Indian film audiences whose lives contain limited pleasures (see Chakravarty 1993). Nonetheless, Bollywood producers do often find themselves on the defensive, particularly when their work is weighed against that of the so-called "parallel cinema," a more artistic stream of Indian film (Pendakur 1990, 248) that has focused on tackling taboo subject matter and winning worldwide recognition for its serious treatment of issues. Although these films account for only 10 percent of India's cinematic output, they are central to artistic attempts to "capture a segment of Indian reality" (Gokulsing and Dissanayake 1998, 23), and their makers sometimes add to criticisms of Bollywood as superficial and outdated (Baghdadi and Rao 1995, xii, 34, 46, 76, 113).

As noted, Bollywood films may also address cultural and political issues, although in a way that is different from the parallel cinema. The nationalist, capitalist, or sexist ideologies that underpin much of contemporary Bollywood cinema may send strong messages, even if they appear in the guise of an epic love story. Certainly, popular Indian films have also explicitly addressed political and cultural issues, notably in earlier classics. Pendakur (2003, 99) explains that British censorship during the pre-Independence era prevented selected scenes and films from being shown, but "screen writers circumvented the censors by using coded language in dialogue, which the audience understood and admired. Instead of locating stories about corruption and nepotism to indict contemporary political regimes, the writer would place the film in some distant past." Kumar (2002, 50), expressing some disappointment with Bollywood's current treatment of globalization and nationalism, points to films that "offered criticism of the nationalist project and its skewed modernity," such as the 1950s films *Do Bigha Zameen* (Two Acres of Land, 1953), *Jagte Raho* (Stay Awake, 1956), and *Pyaasa* (Eternal Thirst, 1957). In these films, Kumar argues, it was possible to detect commentary on divisions of class, gender, and geography in a country that touted its status as a modern democracy. Of course, Bollywood does still present films that discuss pressing issues, such as poverty and terrorism: one example is the low-budget thriller *Aamir* (2008), in which the lead character is suddenly removed from a comfortable existence and forced to follow the orders of an extremist group, taking him into the slums of Mumbai. However, Kumar may well be correct in suggesting that critical, hard-hitting films are increasingly in the minority, particularly if the political winds have shifted away from socialist groups such as the Indian People's Theatre Association and toward the Bharatiya Janata Party (BJP) and Hindu nationalists.

Films such as *Mother India* (1957) may have enforced the gendered nature of nationalist ideology, but they certainly spoke powerfully about poverty, corruption, and despair. In *Mother India* the character portrayed by the actress Nargis comes to represent the nation as a mother whose various trials drive her son to angry action, including a physical threat against a young woman. Despite maternal love, Nargis' character acts to subdue this violence against woman/nation and the natural social order by killing her son, an iconic moment in Indian cinema and one re-enacted in a variety of films calling on women to make difficult choices between personal feelings and social obligation. *Mother India,* an enduring classic, remains one of a handful of Indian films to be nominated for a Best Foreign Film Oscar – the others are *Bandit Queen* (1994) (Dwyer 2000, 130) and *Lagaan* [Land Tax]: *Once upon a Time in India* (2001).

Stories of star-crossed lovers mixed with those depicting the new nation and its various tensions. The emphasis on the political became only more noticeable with the rise of stars such as Amitabh Bachchan in the 1970s, when Indian cinema began to address unemployment and inequality in a society where youth had been raised to expect more. The anger that Bachchan's characters displayed toward the political system, corruption, and inequality spoke strongly to the nation, and his films during that period became some of the best-known of all time.

The action scenes found in these earlier films and some social commentary remain, but they are generally less common now than storylines centred on star-crossed lovers. When more serious issues do arise, they are rarely addressed in a way that threatens the societal status quo. Discussing, for instance, the question of gender in the enormously popular *Hum Aapke Hain Koun (HAHK)*, Chatterji (1998, 5-7) suggests that the film replicates patriarchal norms embedded in an affluent, conventional lifestyle that every urban Indian family would see as ideal (see also Gokulsing and Dissanayake 1998, 75-79; Virdi 2003). In discussing *HAHK*, Alessandrini (2001, 323) opines that Bollywood entered a new era by dispensing with questions of social justice and subalterns. It is interesting to note that whereas some participants in the current study specifically cited films that dealt with history or social issues, others pointed to a film such as *HAHK* as holding special meaning for them. Several commented on the importance of family and the rituals around weddings and births depicted in this film, perhaps pointing to the fact that they could see South Asian identity performed on screen. Others also indicated that they saw *HAHK* as heralding a new type of film altogether – one that was more modern, fun, and interesting. None offered any explicit commentary on the open promotion of consumerism and Western products (such as Cadbury or Pepsi) found in this film, which would come to set the standard for future blockbusters, although Tariq, an Ottawa participant, did comment negatively on the formulaic production of such films:

> I enjoyed *Hum Aapke Hain Koun* and whatever else, but I also felt like it was the beginning of the teen-flick era of Bollywood, and I think to this day they're still following that same formula, which really becomes bothersome to me because there's no originality and it's just the same thing over and over again.

As Tariq noted, *HAHK* has indeed been viewed by many as a turning point in popular Indian cinema, a revival that allowed entire families to enjoy movies in a way that threatened no one and supposedly benefited everyone. A story of marriage and family – essentially, the entire movie consists of an ill-fated love story between one couple and a slowly unfurling courtship between another – *HAHK* "reinforces India's cultural heritage" through its depiction of various rituals, including engagement, marriage, and *mendhi*, the traditional tracing of decorative patterns on the bride's hands using henna (Gokulsing and Dissanayake 1998, 44). Religious traditions are also affirmed in this movie, as in so many others, providing a backdrop of divinely determined justice (Gokulsing and Dissanayake 1998, 62, 70). *HAHK* also heralds an era in which movie characters almost always represent a form of national identity that is largely upper-caste, upper-middle class, Hindi-speaking, and Hindu (Alessandrini 2001, 323).

Other movies that followed and matched *HAHK*'s success, such as *Kuch Kuch Hota Hai* (Something Happens, 1998) and *Kabhi Khushi Kabhie Gham* (Sometimes Happy, Sometimes Sad, 2001), are also careful to combine homage to the consumerist dream with respect for perceived Indian values and culture. In other words, family conflicts are avoided or else resolved by the end of each movie, marital harmony prevails in a way that allows the male head of the family to retain (most of) his authority, and Indian culture is celebrated in many ways, including the dances, traditional costumes, and religious festivals or ceremonial events. *Kuch Kuch Hota Hai*, which was notable for the fact that its popularity with South Asian fans helped it to enter top-ten lists in the United Kingdom, has been described as "a bubble-gum romance in which clean-cut students sport American designer clothes and live by traditional Indian values" (Lakshmanan 1999, W3). There is a cultural conflict presented by this juxtaposition, which may speak to the composite existence of diasporic viewers.

Indeed, the notion of diaspora looms large in present-day Bollywood films; certainly, themes of migration, movement, and exile from home are not new, but they tend to have more of a presence in films from the mid-1990s onward. Some of these films, such as *Pardes* (Foreign Land, 1997), a story of a young woman's painful discovery that America's promise is shallow and unfulfilling, are relatively serious and speak explicitly of identity and asserting one's values; others, such as *Kabhi Alvida Naa Kehna* (Never Say Goodbye, 2006), may not significantly speak to issues of diaspora, but they feature jet-setting characters or ones who live in places such as London and New York, rendering them perhaps more familiar to audiences in the South Asian diaspora.

It is difficult to identify one singular theme that defines contemporary Indian films: escapism exists side by side with more serious movies, including those I mention in a later analysis as well as those cited by participants. However, the escapist movies do continue to be the most popular, with a consistent emphasis on family and relationships. Diasporic experience is not a universal theme, but the recognition of diasporic audiences' spending power does seem to be a major factor in the ways that Bollywood cinema has attempted to become more cosmopolitan and sophisticated. Whether or not it succeeds is a question that provoked open skepticism from the participants in this study. Certainly, its vision of an upper-class, well-dressed diasporic population is not representative of the South Asian labourers, service employees, taxi drivers, and working poor in the diaspora who exist side by side with moneyed professionals. Despite its limitations, however, there is no question that Bollywood is keenly aware of the diaspora and feels it cannot afford to ignore that dispersed audience.

2

Theories of the Wandering Soul: Interpretations of Diaspora

The sense of uprootedness, of disconnection, of loss and estrangement, which hitherto was morally appropriated by the traditionally recognized diasporas, may now signify something more general about the human condition. (Cohen 1997, 196)

All Around the World: Displacement and Dispersal

The notion of diaspora is undeniably central to current studies of Bollywood, but in a larger sense diaspora is also pertinent to many of the current inquiries occupying news headlines and policy reports about the perceived problem of individuals who do not fit into the so-called host society. There is also a question as to whether or not the participants in this study can be legitimately addressed as members of a diasporic audience. Age-old patterns of immigration and of displacement have created dispersed communities of people around the globe, a phenomenon that has been especially notable in recent decades as migration becomes more frequent, partly due to the needs of emigrants but also due to the needs of host countries, many of which are now dependent on immigration to maintain their populations and competitiveness as birthrates decline. This phenomenon is also significant in part because of perceived outcomes: in the past several years, problems such as planned terrorist acts, riots, and complaints about *sharia,* a form of Islamic law, and about cultural practices have seriously troubled the foundations of self-proclaimed tolerant nations, with political pundits blaming any related or resulting social unrest on the inability of some immigrants to integrate.

Pro-assimilation discourses suggesting that recalcitrant minorities must blend into the host society as much as possible are hardly new. Yet these commentaries are interesting and perhaps problematic due to the change in the population being discussed. No longer are these policy makers or journalists necessarily addressing new immigrants. In France, the Netherlands, and Canada, the events that have caused those societies to question their policies and beliefs around pluralism and acceptance have revolved chiefly around young second-generation immigrants – members of the Muslim or South Asian or Middle Eastern diasporas, to be sure, but citizens and long-time dwellers in the countries where they have been accused of burning cars, committing murder, and planning terrorist acts.

Whereas some may associate diaspora with immigration and resettlement, there is a less clearly defined middle ground for the children and grandchildren of those who left their countries and started anew. This is in part because the notion of diaspora is so difficult to define. Some theorists are content with loose definitions, recognizing any globally dispersed ethnic group as a diaspora. However, writers such as William Safran (cited in Cohen 1997) and Cohen (1997) have made game – although slightly different – attempts to offer specific criteria for the identification of diasporas. Cohen largely endorses Safran's original explanation of diaspora, in which the members or their ancestors have been dispersed from some central point to at least two foreign places, have formed collective memory or myth around the homeland, do not expect to be fully integrated into their new host societies and hence occupy a separate position, idealize the homeland and hope to return at some point, work to maintain or further the interests of the homeland, and retain a sense of kinship and solidarity with that homeland.

The notion of diaspora is hence both complex and contested, partly because there exist, as Cohen (1997) suggests, different forms of diaspora but also because diasporas are often in a state of flux. This complexity explains, to a certain extent, why apparently dissimilar configurations may be referred to as diasporas. It also explains why the term is sometimes used interchangeably with others that refer to the dispersal or movement of peoples (e.g., exiles, transmigrancy, deterritorialized nations). A diaspora may consist of some exiles, who have been forced to depart their home country due to political unrest or persecution, as well as some transmigrants, who may have left home in search of greater opportunity but continue to "maintain multiple relationships ... that span borders" (Basch et al. 1994, 7). A diaspora may also be linked to a deterritorialized nation whose members have been similarly removed, through circumstance or choice, from the actual physical territory they consider home, but diaspora is not necessarily synonymous with any of these terms. Although there are some commonly recurring characteristics that can be associated with the notion of diaspora, there is no essential model of what a diaspora is or should be.

Diasporas can represent the outreaches of imperial power, the dispersal of persecuted or harassed communities, or the spread of workers to regions where they are needed. Although the circumstances under which these types of dispersal occur may have changed throughout the decades, these basic models are still found today. In some cases, due to familiarity with a colonial language or school system, the colonized may find themselves departing for the "home country," the nexus of imperial power. In other cases, the reasons for departure may be even more mundane: as Sun (2002) suggests, once exposed to a foreign way of life, people may contemplate how that life could be better and more interesting than their native way of life, and they may consider departing their countries or cities in search of it. It is also true that diasporas may be formed out of necessity – due to wars, political unrest, or restrictive regimes. Similarly, economic interests continue to play a role in the movement of people, although such migrants may experience different levels of mobility and affluence.

These tendencies toward continual movement are facilitated, if not encouraged, by the evolution of media technologies. Diasporas have often been reliant on media to retain a sense of internal cohesion and closeness among their members, but the type of media used can vary. Gillespie (1995) documents the use of Indian dramas to educate Punjabi youth living in the United Kingdom about their culture and history; indeed, Indian films play a role in the formation of community and identity among any number of Indian expatriates (Nandy 1983, 1995; Mitra 1999; Ray 2001, 2003), and other examples exist of the way media can be used to provide news from a home country or from others living in the diaspora, thus offering a sense of culture that cannot necessarily be accessed in the host country and creating a common place for meeting or discussion. This function is similar to that offered by newspapers and novels, as examined in Anderson's *Imagined Communities* (1983).

Indeed, diasporas are imagined communities in that they may consist of people who have never visited the so-called homeland or who lack any ambition to do so. Tsaliki's (2003) discussion of a Greek virtual community is specific not so much to a connection with Greece as to a more nebulous, overarching sense of Greekness that may be held by second- or third-generation immigrants, in the same way that Ray's (2001) doubly displaced Fijian Indians living in Australia do not all retain a sense of belonging to India as a country but rather maintain a commitment to some hybridized form of Indianness.

In short, there is no essential and universally recognized definition of what constitutes a diaspora, but in a sense it is characterized by what it is not: it is not a nation in the same structured way as a legal polity, but it does contain elements of nationalist feeling. It is not necessarily a community of exiles, but exile may be part of the diasporic experience. It is an imagined community in the sense that it is very often, like the communities described by Anderson (1983), held together by media, although the media being used may vary and may hold more importance in some diasporas than in others. These media may be independently utilized by individuals or may be tools of the nation-state. Indeed, although some diasporas may arise without the assistance of a steering hand or cause, there are cases where the state works consciously to establish or maintain this notion of a community that retains its links to the homeland. In the case of India, Bollywood does seem to operate – intentionally or not – in conjunction with a state-mandated project to attract non-resident Indians (Kaur and Sinha 2005). Diasporic bodies can challenge the existence of some states, but they can also provide important economic and political benefits, a fact recognized by a number of governments. As migration increases, as travel becomes more accessible, or as conflict creates new generations of displaced groups, the idea of diaspora continues to evolve, with different examples constantly emerging.

Some diasporas are defined by a continued sense of connection and loyalty to "the old country," even if the old country no longer exists or never existed as the migrant now recalls it (Cohen 1997, ix). Immigrants who feel alienated from the nation-state(s) in which they now reside may find the embers of patriotism for their homeland rekindled. Khan's (2000) study of female Muslim immigrants in Canada finds that whereas some of her subjects react to discrimination by attempting to assimilate into the larger Canadian population, masking as many markers of cultural difference as possible, others assert their Islamic, South Asian, and/or Arab identities more fiercely than ever before (see also Hoodfar 2003). Moghissi (2006) agrees that diasporas are often formed and maintained in response to a sense of alienation from the host society, which may be hostile to attempts at integration. If members of diasporas find themselves subject to racism, they are more vulnerable, she cautions, to manipulation by politically motivated extremists who use religious identity and community to attract disenfranchised youth. This is not to suggest that such a response is common, but it is possible, as is retreat into an ethnic community and isolation from the mainstream. Hence stronger ties to ethnic or religious communities may be consciously and positively claimed not in response to a desire to pay homage to places left behind but in reaction to feelings of displacement, ostracism, and discomfort (for similar findings, see Gilroy 1993, 112; Sun 2002). Several participants in this study noted that their search for identity was tied to an awareness of their difference, and their turn toward media in this sense is hardly unique.

With reference to the black diaspora, Hall (1994) affirms that marginalization helped to create a sense of a larger community with an understanding of its history and origins, and he adds that this realization was achieved at least partly through the mediating effects of cultural texts such as film. After all, "transnational bonds no longer have to be cemented by migration or by exclusive territorial claims. In the age of cyberspace, a diaspora can, to some degree, be held together or re-created through the mind, through cultural artifacts and through a shared imagination" (Cohen 1997, 26). Thus a strengthened sense of nationalism does not mean that transmigrants are more determined than ever to return to the homeland. Rather, they seek other means of asserting their identities alongside the more conventional ties that the home and host countries may impose (Karim 2003, 9). Hall (1994, 402) dismisses the conventional idea of dispersed peoples and nostalgia for an ethnically pure past in the definition of diaspora, pointing instead to the "recognition of a necessary heterogeneity and diversity," "a conception of 'identity' which lives with and through, not despite, difference."

Ray (2003, 31) points out that it is no longer really possible to view territorial nations as entities clearly delineated from diasporas since the latter can be "networked to the homeland culture to such an extent that the traditional divide of outside/inside loses much of its analytical purchase" (see also Mitra 1999). In Ray's discussion of Fijian Indians living in Australia, the repeated migration of these individuals does not remove the significance of the original homeland, but a shared ethnic identity also does not completely bind dispersed Indians into a nostalgic group. Appadurai (1996, 172) echoes this, pointing to the dialectical relations that underpin the existence of diaspora: "For every nation-state that has exported significant numbers of its populations to the United States as refugees, tourists, or students, there is now a delocalized transnation, which retains a special ideological link to a putative place of origin but is otherwise a thoroughly diasporic collectivity."

Admittedly, defining "a thoroughly diasporic collectivity" is a challenge, as Clifford (1997, 249) agrees: diasporas "are ambivalent, even embattled, over basic features. Furthermore ... societies may wax and wane in diasporism." Although diasporic communities may well be formed by those who physically relocate, second- or third-generation immigrants may also consider themselves members of an ethnic diaspora. Others may consider themselves part of a diaspora on the basis of religious feeling, even if they do not necessarily claim belonging to a diaspora that coalesces around ethnicity, race, or nationalism.

Despite having been raised in a particular country or countries, individuals may have been raised with evocations of a homeland and may associate themselves with those. In the arena of religion, Mandaville (2001) points out that a diaspora can sometimes function as the very space that inspires a desire to connect more intimately with religious or ethnic traditions. At the least, it may serve as a place, geographical or otherwise, in which knowledge can be pursued and accepted wisdom can be questioned. The concept of diaspora is particularly pertinent in the case of religions such as Islam, as Muslims cannot claim any particular homeland. For the young Muslims of South Asian ancestry in this study, their ethnic origins had occasionally separated them from Muslims of Arab or other extraction, but there was a fragmented, nebulous entity to which they felt some allegiance, and this factored into their readings of Indian cinema, their use of media, and their beliefs regarding themselves and their identity.

Radhakrishnan (2003, 129) agrees that a diaspora can be a place of promise if utilized correctly. In this analysis, identities and history cannot possibly be left behind, nor should they be: "The diaspora is an excellent opportunity to think through some of these vexed questions: solidarity and criticism, belonging and distance, insider spaces and outsider spaces, identity as invention and identity as natural, location-subject positionality and the politics of representation, rootedness and rootlessness." Desai (2004, 23), while acknowledging the potential for a diaspora to be a space of creativity and invention, nonetheless warns against heralding diaspora and its possibilities with unmitigated optimism, suggesting that "the dangers of diasporic studies can be summarized as a valorization of migration without attention to citizenship and the nation-state, an emphasis on the global at the price of the local, and consequently, a subsumption of race to political economy."

This process of coming to terms with competing identities is also mapped out in other works relating to diaspora, where the variety of possible reactions to living in a diaspora becomes obvious: Naficy (1993) and Sreberny-Mohammadi and Mohammadi (1994) note that people living in a diaspora can mobilize politically on behalf of their perceived homeland, whereas others may jettison any sense of obligation to those left behind. To some young people, the notion of cosmopolitanism comes easily, facilitated by financial privilege and a global imagination; for others, as Brah (1996), Gillespie (1995), and Handa (2003) document, the experience of movement and settlement may lead to conflicting emotions over their community's role in a larger society and over mutually acceptable ways to conform to cultural standards of behaviour. Brah (1996), Gillespie (1995), Nandy (1983, 1995), and Ray (2001, 2003) all depict a more complex and politicized coming-to-terms than the positive one described by Handa (2003) in her study of youth settled in Canada. Yet her work seems to glide over some of the crucial questions of diaspora that do indeed preoccupy even the second and third generations.

The Sweet Hereafter? Living or Leaving the Diasporic Experience

> While diaspora may be regarded as concomitant with transnationalism, or even in some cases consequent of transnationalist forces, it may not be reduced to such macroeconomic and technological flows. It remains, above all, a human phenomenon – lived and experienced. (Braziel and Mannur 2003, 8)

This book focuses particularly on young individuals who may be considered members of South Asian or Muslim diasporas, despite the fact that they may not be familiar with all of the characteristics of diasporic living described by Safran (cited in Cohen 1997) or Cohen (1997). Some are immigrants who came to Canada at a young age, whereas others are the children of immigrants. Although the participants in this study are Canadian-born or have lived in Canada most of their lives, diaspora nonetheless remains a highly relevant concept to nearly all of them, even if they are unable to articulate a clear definition of the term. As descendants of immigrants, they are conscious of their ties to other countries, to other cultures, and to a past that does not include them but affects them in meaningful ways.

Studies of diaspora have often tended to look at the experience of those who actually move, the people who physically disperse and thus form or contribute to a diasporic entity. For the young people in this study, most of whom are second-generation immigrants, it is not necessarily the case that they have ever been to South Asia, or that they have undergone the experience of immigration firsthand. Yet they may be conscious that such movement underpins their existence and their current situation. Reitz and Banerjee (2007, 539) have sought to uncover whether second-generation immigrants have a sense of Canadian identity, pursuing this inquiry by asking their informants about their citizenship and their ethnic or cultural identity. The answer regarding citizenship was clear; the second answer surprised Reitz and Banerjee because "Canadian" was rarely the reply. In light of my own findings, this is perhaps not very surprising. Although my own participants are Canadian, very few would deny that they have a membership, however tenuous, in a larger, not necessarily cohesive, community.

For these participants, connections to the South Asian diaspora are not necessarily the same as those made and maintained by people for whom the experience of displacement has been more direct. The young informants in this study may well have family living in another country, and they may embrace aspects of that country's culture and consider it a second home or a place of great meaning. However, for most of the participants, and perhaps for many others in a similar situation, this is not a place of return. Never having left this supposed homeland, these young adults do not display the same nostalgia that some of them have witnessed in their parents and other relatives. This may be particularly true for those raised in families where multiple migrations have taken place, such that the connection to South Asia is both remote and mysterious, despite the fact that their appearance readily identifies them to others as South Asian. Tariq, a participant in Ottawa, offers an attempt to summarize this entangled history that captures its attendant confusions:

> I think what happens with us a lot of the time is we're just divided. It's like, India's supposed to be home, or Pakistan's supposed to be home, but Canada's home. But then, Canada's not really home, and I think we ultimately

get really screwed in the process, because we're sitting at this transitional stage where yes, Canada is home, but then is India or Pakistan really home?

This situation presents diasporic interests different from those described by Kumar (2002), where an immigrant leaves behind family and friends in the belief that he or she will return soon, only to find the host country a place where – however bewildering that place may initially be – he or she can pursue different dreams and hopes. Soon the host country becomes the place of permanent residence, and the homeland becomes the place for infrequent visits and the recipient of guilt-ridden telephone calls and un-fulfilled promises of return. For these immigrants, living in a diaspora can mean poignancy and the grief of being torn between competing commit-ments that can rarely be resolved successfully. In Bollywood cinema, this conflict is simplified: the South Asian diaspora is frequently a space where one goes to improve oneself, only to discover that such improvements are merely superficial when compared to the richness of knowledge found in the homeland.

The experience of diaspora is significantly different and exceedingly com-plex for the young adults in this study. The notion of migration is largely something that has been communicated to them through oral history. They are aware of holding a heritage derived from a place outside of Canada, and in some cases they may be quite knowledgeable about it. However, the dif-ficulties they have undergone, if any, are not the same as those experienced by first-generation immigrants. They live in the only home country they have ever known – they have not been separated from it. For the most part, their views of their ancestral country or countries are not tinted with long-ing to return permanently or with existential angst. Their understanding of the places that weaned their parents may be based simply on familial stories, or on gleanings from media, or on occasional visits. They may maintain ties with friends and relatives but rarely with the same intensity displayed by some first-generation immigrants. For the most part, the knowledge that they came from somewhere else opens up the desire for knowledge about places of origin and history, but it does not necessarily portend a sense of loss. They live, as Tejaswini Niranjana puts it, "in translation," viewing the world through multiple perspectives and attempting to convey a sense of this multiplicity to others (cited in Costantino 2008, 132).

Thus the question arises of whether these young people are members of a diaspora. Some would agree that they are, yet others would not. The no-tion of diaspora is so nebulous, and the experience of diaspora so varied, that there is no definite answer. For the purposes of this study, I regard these individuals as members of a diaspora; at the absolute minimum, they are engulfed in a diasporic consciousness, but I think they may well be positioned as part of a diaspora that takes pains to acknowledge them. Even though they may not all experience a longing for return, many are conscious of some allegiance to other South Asians or to those who share their religious background. Some maintain ties to the country of their birth or their parents' birth through visits, communication with loved ones, exchanges of goods, and staying abreast of current trends in fashion and media. These links may assume superficial forms at times, but they do exist and do shape the lives of these individuals in meaningful and lasting ways.

Few are as relentlessly peripatetic as the economically privileged individuals described by Ong (1999), flitting easily from one place to the next, yet they experience greater ease of movement and a wider range of options than the rural peasants discussed in Sun's (2002) work. They do rely on diasporic media for education, but they are absorbing the reverse of the images seen by those peasants. Whereas Sun's subjects may build imaginaries of diaspora through film and television, the individuals in this study rely on the same in order to absorb imaginaries of a so-called homeland.

For them, diaspora may not materialize exclusively through the auspices of mass media, but these certainly open up possibilities that might not otherwise exist. Although travel to India, Pakistan, or elsewhere is a possibility that many of the participants have pursued, it is not a constant possibility. Individuals living in a diaspora often rely on communicative devices to stay informed of what is happening in the place of origin, if such it can be called. There is little question that media producers are quite aware of the existence of a diasporic audience, and they take pains to address this group. Some media produced for the South Asian diaspora are written in Hindi or Punjabi, but there are many that incorporate English to varying degrees, and a number of websites cater specifically to the English-speaking members of the diaspora, such as TheIndianStar.com or mybindi.com. These media serve different purposes, but they all speak to the significance of the diasporic population, a significance acknowledged by the Indian government both in its recent extension of overseas citizenship to non-resident Indians and in its staging of Pravasi Bharatiya Divas, an annual event held in India to celebrate the achievements of diasporic Indians. Although adults who participate may be exhorted to remember their obligations to India, youth may also be enrolled in programs enabling them to become better acquainted with Indian culture, history, and religion. The Indian diaspora is certainly not the only one discussed in this study, but it is significant and highly relevant on a number of levels.

Different Diasporas: India, Pakistan, and the Colonial Legacy

> *Who is an N.R.I. [non-resident Indian]? The one who goes back – with many suitcases instead of that single one that he or she had brought on the first journey. The tourist citizen. (Kumar 2002, 21)*

One must, of course, be careful to avoid the trap that Desai (2004, 5) identifies in her own clarification of terminology. South Asia, she notes, is often identified as India, perhaps because the latter is so dominant in media production. In fact, the region encompasses great diversity, spanning places as varied as Bangladesh, Bhutan, India, the Maldives, Nepal, Pakistan, Sri Lanka, and Tibet. People from all of these regions, scattered around the world, can be considered a kind of "Brown Atlantic" (31), in which the members have been labelled differently (South Asian, Asian, Indian, black) depending on the norms of their host countries (6). In this particular study, all of the participants can trace their origins back to South Asia, most often India or Pakistan, but they may be two or three generations removed from that region or may have complex relationships to it, as in the case of one young woman whose parents moved from India to Pakistan following Partition and became fervent Pakistani nationalists. Several individuals are of Indian origin but their parents were born in East Africa and migrated from there to Canada, so even the parents have had little direct contact with, or experience of, South Asia.

Aside from its size, this diaspora is also overwhelmingly diverse. India is home to numerous languages, cultures, and religions, some of which have overlapping characteristics and some of which are diametrically different. This diversity is reflected in the Indian diaspora, perhaps one of the largest in the world, with roughly 20 million people spread out over dozens of countries. Statistics compiled by the Indian government in 2001 suggest that in thirty-nine of those countries, an overseas Indian population (including both Indian citizens and people of Indian origin) numbering 20,000 or more can be found. In Canada, of course, this number is considerably higher, with over 850,000 people of Indian origin, or 2.8 percent of Canada's population of roughly 30 million. Canada has the eighth-highest number of overseas Indians, following Malaysia (1,665,000), Myanmar (2,902,000), Saudi Arabia (1,500,000), South Africa (1,000,000), the United Arab Emirates (950,000), the United Kingdom (1,200,000), and the United States (1,678,000) (High Level Committee on the Indian Diaspora 2001). Whereas early Indian emigration could initially be attributed most often to labour flows – the need for cheap labour in more-developed countries was a fit with the high population and relative underdevelopment in India – it now occurs for a variety of reasons.

As members of a former British colony, Indians were exposed to the English language and variants of the British educational and political systems. Although many welcomed the end of official colonialism, marked by India's independence in 1947, the British presence in India had significant consequences, including Partition, the division of the country based on religious lines. In an attempt to rectify religious conflict between the Hindu majority and the Muslim minority, British rulers gave each group its own country, leaving India a Hindu-majority nation while carving out a portion for Muslims in the new nation of Pakistan. Left in countries wracked by political unrest following Partition, with limited opportunities for economic or social advancement, some Indians and Pakistanis opted to leave and find out whether peace and prosperity could be located elsewhere, a pattern that would continue over the following decades. Not surprisingly, given their familiarity with the British, many saw the United Kingdom as a different kind of motherland. If the United Kingdom seemed like an inappropriate option, countries such as the United States, Canada, and Australia also had some degree of familiarity, given their use of English and – in the latter two countries – their own traces of British administration. These same countries also became the recipients of multiple migrants, Indians who initially sought new lives in places such as East Africa or Fiji, only to encounter even more political or social problems. Persuaded or forced to leave by political, social, and economic factors, such migrants continued their pattern of movement by settling in ever-more-developed countries.

At the same time that South Asians were integrating into their new societies and obtaining citizenship and employment, India itself was changing. Although it remains a country with considerable poverty and vast disparity between classes, it has produced a large number of qualified professionals, particularly in fields such as information technology and medicine. These professionals often, although not always, move elsewhere in search of a high income, a more luxurious lifestyle, or simply better educational opportunities for their families. The loss of these professionals is what the Government of India's revised policies on overseas citizenship are intended to address. Although it is a limited form of citizenship, restricting rights on voting, for instance, it is nonetheless an acknowledgment of the fact that India tends to export many of its greatest human resources. With the loss of such talent comes a concomitant drain on the economy, even after factoring in remittances and the considerable revenues generated by non-resident Indian tourists and visitors purchasing expensive garments and jewellery for extravagant events such as weddings and festivals.

For producers in India, there are distinct advantages in marketing to the diaspora. Fashion, jewellery, magazines, newspapers, television, music, and film, the subject of this study, are often exported to the diaspora. Bollywood indicates in a number of ways that it recognizes the importance of the diaspora, incorporating English into its dialogue, adding subtitles in a number of languages, and addressing themes that it considers relevant to Indian diasporic life. Members of the Indian and Pakistani diasporas subscribe to many of these efforts by purchasing DVDs, satellite dishes, and CDs that allow them to stay current in viewing movies and television programs and in listening to popular music, often the music associated with new hit films. Many forms of media help members of the Indian and Pakistani diasporas to maintain their connections to one another and to the so-called homelands, and film is one of the most powerful, offering images of places that may exist in no other form for viewers.

These places may literally occupy no space in the existence of diasporic individuals. Some have never been to India; others left it so long ago that their understanding of it is both mediated and frozen in time. Braziel and Mannur (2003, 9) cite the specific case of Ismaili Muslims who emigrated to East Africa, the Caribbean, and North America from Kutch, Sindh, Katiawar, and Gujarat in the nineteenth century, establishing themselves so firmly in their new countries that in the present day some of their descendants "do not necessarily accord much importance to connections with South Asia, making questions of looking back to India as a homeland irrelevant, or at best, inappropriate." Since a number of the participants in this case are in fact Ismaili Muslims, this assertion bears more interrogation, as noted in the following chapters.

However, Braziel and Mannur's point is well taken: multiple migrants, even if they do have origins somewhere in South Asia, do not necessarily identify strongly or singly with that region. There are, of course, other ways that diasporic immigrants may come to feel dissociated from India or Pakistan – that is, as these countries actually exist. Having left many years ago, they may prefer to maintain their distance in order to preserve the image they still recall. Kumar (2002, 173) recounts the experience of his aunt and uncle, who emigrated to the United States well in advance of any of their relatives or peers. Isolated for many years and living an existence more difficult than they had imagined prior to emigration, the two do not return to India for even an occasional visit, yet Kumar's aunt tells him that she can still see it in her mind's eye. Kumar hesitates to tell her that "the India she had known was no longer there. It had changed." Ultimately, he opts to help maintain her illusions once he realizes that the place "they left behind had been precious. They liked to believe it was still all intact. It was *they* who had not changed. They had lost so much that they wanted to hold on to what was left of the past" (174, original emphasis).

As evidenced by the commentaries of participants in this study, this is by no means a unique incident. The desire to preserve the past and to observe an idealized image of India from afar is one that several interviewees have witnessed in their own parents, grandparents, and other relatives. Most recognize the extent to which this is a common feature of diasporas: the strain of occupying multiple worlds is only slightly less pronounced when one country is settled mainly in the imagination. Although it may seem obvious that change would have occurred in a place left behind so long ago, the temptation to fossilize the past is strong for individuals who may occasionally struggle with the challenges of a new country and culture.

Radhakrishnan (2003, 128) remarks on this temptation and its possible consequences:

> Very often it is when we feel deeply dissatisfied with marketplace pluralism and its unwillingness to confront and correct the injustices of dominant racism that we turn our diasporan gaze back to the home country. Often, the gaze is uncritical and nostalgic ... We can cultivate India in total diasporan ignorance of the realities of the home country. By this token, anything and everything is India according to our parched imagination: half-truths, stereotypes, so-called tradition, rituals, and so forth. Or we can cultivate an idealized India that has nothing to do with contemporary history. Then again, we can visualize the India we remember as an antidote to the maladies both here and there and pretend that India hasn't changed since we left its shores. These options are harmful projections of individual psychological needs that have little to do with history.

Obviously, not all individuals living in a diaspora glamourize the past and the notion of a culture more meaningful than the one they currently inhabit. Much of the focus thus far has been on the Indian diaspora, a place where history may be interpreted or recreated selectively, as in debates around Partition or the 1984 Golden Temple massacre, in which a large number of Sikhs, including both soldiers and civilians, who had occupied the holy shrine were killed in a firefight with the Indian army at the order of then Prime Minister Indira Gandhi. Within diasporas, then, tensions around class, caste, and power remain.

Diaspora is by no means a space so virtual, so postmodern or hybrid that it negates all economic, political, or social struggle. Rather, it is a space where these struggles fragment and may acquire new meanings. As the following chapter makes clear, this condition of living in a diaspora or multiple diasporas, even as members removed from the physical act of migration, has a distinct effect on the identity construction of participants in this study. The notion of having some connection to people or places outside of Canada affects their choice of media, their perspective on global events and media, and their sense of self. In contrast to suggestions that first-generation and second-generation immigrants tend to place too much importance on their places of origin, this study's findings align with research that highlights the impossibility of ignoring the country of residence (Gillespie 1995; Ray 2001, 2003; Kumar 2002; Karim 2003). Living in a diaspora is not as simple as holding onto the past or forging a new future. It is an uneasy tightrope walk between the two. Within that slender, virtual space, identities and societies can be negotiated; Bhabha (1994) suggests, in fact, that this place of betwixt and between may be the best arena in which to create change. As Beck (1994,

2000) notes, remaining static is rarely an option in societies transformed by migration and capital flows, all connected by a politics that is unquestionably global. Within this framework of connectivity and reflexivity, the rootlessness Cohen describes at the very beginning of this chapter can be, and sometimes is, replaced by a determined effort to weave together competing identities and loyalties, creating a new hybrid culture in a space whose very unfamiliarity allows for possibility.

3
Karma Chameleon: Citizenship, Identity, and the New Hybrids

Our daughters consider themselves members of a number of global
cultural clubs, as yet perhaps not fully aware of the complexity of their
inheritance. The new hybrids, they feel at home in many locations in
the global cultural ecumene. (Sreberny-Mohammadi and Mohammadi
1994, 193)

The Ties That Bind: Citizenship and Belonging

The subject of diaspora is one that often becomes entangled with questions
of citizenship, nationalism, and identity, and these were questions that the
participants and I explored in this study, trying to establish what factors,
including media, might have helped them to arrive at an understanding of
self. These questions are, I think, especially important when members of
certain ethnic and religious groups are sometimes challenged to define
themselves by offering fealty to one nation. Diasporas and diasporic identities present conceptions of community and nation that offer alternatives to
the more conventional understanding that a country is bordered within a
clearly defined nation-state. Membership in a diaspora is often presented as
a rejection of the citizenship associated with nation-states, with such rejection occasionally metamorphosing all the way into cosmopolitanism, a kind
of global citizenship. Questions of citizenship and multiple forms of belonging did arise throughout this study and appeared integral to identity construction. Kumar (2002, 178) notes that a "seasoned traveler" who moves
between cultures can also be seen as a "global soul" whose unique standpoint
allows for translation and understanding of these very cultures, echoing
Tejaswini Niranjama's concept of "living in translation," where the transla-
tors may balance too many cultural elements to belong anywhere easily yet
just enough to inhabit multiple spaces and to explain one culture to another
(cited in Costantino 2008, 132). This chapter delves further into this belief,
investigating the question of whether diaspora complicates traditional
understandings of citizenship by offering different spaces and affiliations

to individuals, and also looks at the way that a sense of national identity may be formed or affected within a diaspora.

As it is currently conceived in much of the Northern world, citizenship requires a commitment to join a particular national group whose borders are defined by a legal set of practices and regulations. Inclusion in this group is often valorized above membership in any other community, which may be problematic for citizens whose race, gender, or class marks them as different/inferior and thus renders their status marginal within the nation (see Thobani 2007). It may be similarly problematic for those who have meaningful ties elsewhere and do not consider themselves to be exclusively bound to the nation-state. Indeed, for members of diasporic communities, this presents a particularly troubling conflict, as the notion of belonging to one collectivity may be constructed as necessarily singular in dominant legal or political discourse, ignoring the fact that in actual practice citizens are aware that they belong to overlapping communities.

This visualization of the nation is entirely different from that noted by Van den Bulck and Van Poecke (1996, 160), among others: "Nationhood, or the identification with a nation, is based on a perceived or ascribed common history (possibly including territory) and culture." Clearly, the idea of common histories, territories, and cultures – often based on notions of shared or similar ancestry – is increasingly problematic at a time when many citizens are embroiled in migratory flows that may provide them with different histories and competing cultures, all juxtaposed against a backdrop of what Manning (2003, xx) calls ephemeral territories: "We continue to be in a state of flux whereby the homes we construct remain ephemeral."

Diaspora Dreams and the Call of the Collective

Unlike the more recognized legal ties of a nation-state, the pull of a diaspora is embedded in a sense of cultural, historical, and social unity: "In broad terms, culture may be viewed as the symbolic construction of the vast array of a social group's life experiences. Culture is the embodiment, the chronicle of a group's history" (Brah 1996, 18). This is not to say that a cultural sense of allegiance is lacking in the national collectivity, but it is more often the case that a culturally grounded and less formally political sense of affinity binds together members of a diaspora, sometimes unwillingly. In the case of the respondents in this study, they are marked as South Asians, even those who have not been to the so-called homeland and those whose closest connection to this homeland resides in the mediated construction found in Indian films. A lack of acceptance in the nation-state of residence, or a consistent reminder of one's ethnic or religious origins, may serve to emphasize the sense of belonging to the diasporic collective. Naficy (2001, 14), in fact, suggests that "diaspora is necessarily collective, in both its origination and its destination."

Although the lure of belonging to a collectivity is a powerful one, the requirements of fealty may sometimes, rather perversely, impinge on individual rights at the same time that a sense of self-identity is fostered. This limitation is visible not only within the nation-state but also within more nebulously connected and defined groups. Khan (2000) documents the disparate cases of Muslim women in Canada who handle the challenge of belonging to a Muslim community while living in a non-Muslim country in various ways. Some disavow their religious and/or cultural heritage in favour of a secular, so-called modern lifestyle but are nonetheless haunted by an identity that follows them wherever they go, marked by their skin colour, accent, or beliefs. Others are punished for attempts to embrace what they see as Western ideals of liberation; transgression of familial and cultural norms may result in ostracism or shame. These Muslim women, however, are equally punished by the non-Muslim community that initially counselled their rejection of the Muslim collective in favour of the "Canadian" secular collective. On seeking affirmation from those same non-Muslims, who often represent supposed havens such as women's shelters, the women in Khan's study find that their problems are dismissed or constructed as resulting from their cultural identity (see also Jiwani 2006). Similarly, the young Muslim women studied in Hoodfar (2003) report experiencing a constant refusal on the part of some Canadians to try to understand their religion and culture(s), while other Muslims try to dictate cultural or religious norms that these women feel have little basis in a real understanding of religious texts. Their attempts to negotiate movement from one collectivity to another, or to belong simultaneously to both, places them in a state that Abdolmaboud Ansari calls "dual marginality" (cited in Naficy 1993, 131). Ahmed's memoir (1999) points out that this experience is not limited to women of a certain class or in a particular country: living as an academic in the United Kingdom and in the United States, she was constantly aware of the pressure on Muslims and other minorities to renounce membership in their religious and cultural collectives if they wished to be treated as intelligent and worthy of respect.

Collectivities and Consequences: Negotiating Individual Identity

Living in any kind of collectivity, then, should not elide individual difference – rather, it should celebrate it. As Cairns (1995) argues and as Benedict Anderson implies (cited in Mandaville 2001, 12-13), a polity must offer its citizens a certain degree of protection and rights in order to attain the sense of patriotism and loyalty that Carens (2000, 166) alludes to in his definition of conventional citizenship:

It is expected, both empirically and normatively, that people will feel a strong sense of emotional identification with, and only with, one political community, namely, the state in which they possess legal citizenship ... The conventional view does not deny that people may have other important forms of collective identity besides citizenship, and that these other identities may influence the political ideas and activities of citizens. Nevertheless, people are assumed to draw their primary *political* identity from membership in the state. (emphasis in original)

The traditional formulation of citizenship described by Carens suggests that political affiliations should, in a sense, overwhelm socio-cultural ties, but this is less commonly the case among diasporic communities, whose members maintain ties both to a transnational community and to the nation-state in which they reside. Assuming that loyalties to one's ethnic or religious community can never be different from yet equal to a sense of political identification with a nation, social conservatives suggest that diversity strikes at the very heart of democracy, an accusation that Kymlicka (2001, 31) characterizes as "the opening of a new front in the 'multiculturalism wars,'" in which minority rights are considered a threat to "long-term political unity and social stability" (for one example of such criticism, see Bissoondath 2002).

These dangers are further emphasized when nation-states that have lost citizens to migration attempt to stake a claim to those same individuals, encouraging them to maintain ties to their original homes through investment, political involvement, and/or new forms of citizenship. There may be some participants in this study who do subscribe to a form of diaspora that is largely territorial; certainly, the Indian government is working to convince some young people of South Asian origin that their roots are precisely in India. For others, as Sassen (2006, 414) goes on to suggest, it may be possible to identify a "renationalizing of membership politics" where a weakened nation-state articulates itself in new ways: "Use of religion and 'culture,' rather than citizenship, to construct membership may well be a function of the changed relationship of citizens to the state and the insecurities it produces. In this regard, use of religion is not an anachronism but a formation arising out of particular changes in the current age." The use of religion and culture is key, and in all likelihood it does express a kind of insecurity vis-à-vis the state. However, this use does not necessarily supplant citizenship. The factors Sassen names are significant, particularly in understanding the way some states and industries envision the positioning of these young people, but ultimately, as second-generation immigrants, they live in a complicated space that may straddle several forms of diasporic consciousness.

Breaking down the "Ghetto Walls": A Politics of Pluralism

All the others who succeeded in this country did so only by changing.
They became someone else. (Kumar 2002, 247)

In the age of mass migration and the Internet, cultural plurality is an irreversible fact, like globalization. Like it or dislike it, it's where we live, and the dream of a pure monoculture is at best an unattainable, nostalgic fantasy, and at worst a life-threatening menace. (Rushdie 2005, A27)

The possibility of cross-border inclusivity, multiple affiliations, and community ideals is what gives weight to Bissoondath's (2002, 98) pronouncement that the "individuals who form a group, the 'ethnics' who create a community, are frequently people of vastly varying composition. Shared ethnicity does not entail unanimity of vision." The truth of this has already been discussed and is further demonstrated in later chapters that offer a more detailed examination of South Asians and Muslims in Canada, but this statement also skims over the possibility that the "ethnics" to whom Bissoondath refers are able to share a vision with others depending on the issue at stake. It is this model of civic engagement, where activism is not mandated by national or even ethnic lines but instead by commitment to particular issues, that affirms Ferguson's (2002) conclusions regarding youth and citizenship.

Ferguson suggests that fears of disengagement are entirely valid if the histories and identities of different individuals are not acknowledged in educational and political institutions (see also Harzig and Hoerder 2006, 43). However, Ferguson (2002, 6) adds that maintaining ethnic identity will not cause these individuals to experience more interest in what takes place outside Canada – this state of affairs already exists. Moreover, as Ujimoto (1990, 211-12) notes, second- and third-generation immigrants are unlikely to dismiss the natural concern that first-generation immigrants feel for their country of origin; instead, they sometimes acquire even more interest in the cultural identity that eludes them in their adopted country (see also Patel 2006, 159). Since these young people consider a responsible citizen to be a citizen of the world, not simply of the nation-state, there may be some truth to Sreberny-Mohammadi and Mohammadi's (1994) prediction that the exilic wanderings of people such as themselves represents a transition stage – the next generation is more cosmopolitan, more accustomed to the idea of operating in different transnational contexts.

A new reality of local and global pluralism is ill-served by arguments that diversity and true citizenship are inherently opposed. In Bissoondath's (2002) analysis – and in a number of similarly conservative political and media commentaries around the question of minority citizens – immigrants and visible minorities have a pronounced responsibility to assimilate by leaving behind signs of difference, including language or cultural beliefs, in favour of the host society's language, culture, and attitudes. Canadian policy on immigration and pluralism often suggests that the country is a cultural mosaic, wherein specific cultural practices and identifications may be maintained. Kahil, a respondent in Ottawa, appeared to have this policy in mind when he was asked whether nationality, ethnicity, and religion are linked or completely separate. He replied thoughtfully,

> I think there's a linkage because ... I think especially being Canadian is well-defined by the fact that you can maintain your religious identity, your ethnic identity, and that's what makes one Canadian.

In fact, Canada's notions of diversity and tolerance often seem to carry hints of mythology. Despite boasting about the country's openness and acceptance, Canadian citizens sometimes revolt against what they consider to be excessive nurturance of difference at the expense of all-Canadian fealty. The 2006 arrests of eighteen young men in the Toronto area accused of plotting terrorist attacks, all of whom were reportedly Muslim and/or South Asian, and the government-sponsored evacuation of dual citizens from Lebanon are merely two events that have given rise to public criticism of policies regarding multiculturalism, dual citizenship, and immigration (see Patriquin 2006). Writing in the *Toronto Star* as part of a series on multiculturalism, Munro (2005, A27) notes a poll by the Strategic Council finding that nearly nine out of ten Canadians "believe that immigrants should be encouraged to integrate into broader Canadian society rather than maintaining their ethnic identity and culture." If such findings signal an increased tendency to endorse a politics of assimilation, this may explain commentaries such as that offered by Desai (2004, 165), who suggests that Canada is far from the bastion of tolerance and pluralism that it is made out to be. "Multiculturalism assumes," she says in her analysis of South Asian migration, "that immigration is a teleology of progress in which the Asian immigrant modernizes and joins the Western (Canadian) nation, never to seek to return or re-turn to the homeland."

Similarly, in interviewing mixed-race Canadian women about their interpretation of multiculturalism, Mahtani (2004, 4) found that her participants were aware of and opposed to a common belief that being Canadian equates to possessing French or British origins. They note that "being different does not equate with being un-Canadian," an assertion echoed by my own participants, who challenged others to remember that Canada is a nation rooted in diversity. In my study, however, most young people assumed "Canadian" as an identifying label without question, noting that this was not only their birthright but also their only real option. Radha, a young woman from Ottawa, clarified the reasoning behind the inevitable question of nationality, which was also at the root of her own general resistance to answering it:

Nationality would be more Canadian – absolutely it would be Canadian, and ethnicity – the only time the question comes up, what nationality are you, they're always aiming to ask where your family is from, right? They're looking for the answer Pakistani or Indian. Even though I know that I'm Canadian and my nationality is Canadian, absolutely, you realize what type of answer they're looking for.

In recognition of the same motivation, some of Mahtani's (2004, 4) participants exercise a political choice by adopting "the identification of Canadian as an empowering label." This choice is fraught with the tension that accompanies any attempt to insert oneself into a society that does not recognize claims to inclusion. Rather than renounce the present, then, new strategies must be forged in order to reconcile difference.

The Mists of Time: Beyond and between Nations and Nostalgia

> *Diaspora space is the intersectionality of diaspora, border, and dis/*
> *location as a point of confluence of economic, political, cultural, and*
> *psychic processes. It is where multiple subject positions are juxtaposed,*
> *contested, proclaimed or disavowed; where the permitted and the*
> *prohibited perpetually interrogate; and where the accepted and the*
> *transgressive imperceptibly mingle even while these syncretic forms may*
> *be disclaimed in the name of purity and tradition. Here, tradition is*
> *itself continually invented even as it may be hailed as originating from*
> *the mists of time. (Brah 1996, 208)*

Writing as early as 1963, Glazer and Moynihan observe that fantasies of cultural pluralism are "as unlikely as the hope of a 'melting pot'" given that language and culture are difficult to retain after the first generation, let alone the second (13). For the most part, it seems unlikely that language and culture will have been transmitted, untouched and unaltered, from one generation to the next when a change in environment has taken place. The immigrant interviewees in Murji and Hébert (1999), whose insights are discussed further in the next chapter, touch on the extraordinary swiftness with which their Indian dialects were replaced by English in Canada. On arrival in Canada, they felt compelled to acquire proficiency in English, even though their focus on doing so gradually resulted in the loss of their mother tongue(s) and hence in a subsequent loss for their children, similar to the second-generation participants interviewed here. In the cases Murji and Hébert (1999, 8) describe, this loss is met not only with acknowledgment and mourning but also with a form of compromise, in which language is consciously retained in certain rituals but removed in others (see also Costantino 2008; Hiebert and Ley 2006). Perhaps not surprisingly, linguistic education and retention are significant aspects of the appeal of Bollywood film, even when the language being learned and maintained is not one that the individual would identify as native to his or her family.

This indicates the many factors that come to bear on the construction of cultural identity. Not only do Canadians of South Asian origin contend with the dominance of English (or, less commonly, French), but their own languages can also be moved subtly to the periphery when some South Asian dialects come to be accepted as the closest to normative. The young people interviewed by Maira (2002) fight to retain their specific languages, but nonetheless some cultures and languages emerge as dominant in a society that can perhaps accommodate only so much difference. Even when one makes the best possible effort to resist the erasure of culture by sheltering oneself from the outside world, it seems unusual that no influences from that world would seep in. Yet this does not suggest that all ties to the cultural past are erased automatically as the years pass. "At any given time," states Brah (1996, 18), "a group will inherit certain cultural institutions and traditions, but its acts of reiteration or repudiation, its everyday interactions and its ritual practices will serve to select, modify, and transform these institutions." The resulting forms and institutions sometimes come to be known as hybrid, or in Ulf Hannerz's conception, creolized. As Mandaville (2001, 94) explains, the "defining feature of creolisation for Hannerz is the confluence of widely *disparate* cultures which interact in the context of a centre-periphery relationship" (original emphasis).

The notions of hybridity and creolization have often alarmed those who believe that culture can be clearly delineated and preserved and that any form of change or injection of other elements may signify contamination. As Mandaville (2001) notes, the meaning of hybridity has undergone some transformations of its own: "It was originally seen to represent a loss of purity, an authenticity compromised by the insertion of an alien element which tainted the whole" (90), but it eventually assumed a rather different meaning as a method for producing "stronger, richer offspring" (91).

There is some merit to the notion of cultural preservation given the ongoing loss of languages, artistic production, and rituals by groups around the world. However, even when individuals are determined to hold onto the cultural practices that they associate with their place of ancestry or with their religion, they may – in fact, almost certainly will – confront fragmentation within their own communities regarding the correct practices, particularly given that their culture, religion, or place of origin will undergo its own evolution. Indeed, Pyke and Dang (2003) detail the complex hierarchy that emerges for second-generation Asian American immigrants who may simultaneously feel a compulsion to assimilate and become "Americanized" and experience pressure to demonstrate that their heritage is not lost. In light of all this, resistance and the pursuit of a true, pure culture may at times seem the equivalent of tilting at windmills, of giving chase to enemies or goals whose existence is questionable.

It is perhaps this kind of single-mindedness that opens up certain ethnic groups to attacks from commentators who oppose multiculturalism or who suggest, like Howard-Hassman (1999), that there is a dominant Canadian ethnic identity (chiefly anglophone and Christian) that is endangered by the state's encouragement of cultural specificity. This argument is expanded on here in the discussion of findings, which indicates that participants spoke of a clear national Canadian identity, relatively separate from ethnicity, but also saw Canadian culture as the by-product of many different, syncretic cultures. None appeared to believe that culture is static and can be imported into different countries and decades without any change, a sentiment echoed by Radhakrishnan (2003, 126), who views diaspora as a space of possibility, creation, and promise: "The diaspora has created rich possibilities of understanding different histories. And these histories have taught us that identities, selves, traditions, and natures do change with travel (and there is nothing decadent or deplorable about mutability) and that we can achieve such changes in identity intentionally." Similarly, Boyarin and Boyarin (2003, 108) eschew the notion that hybridization weakens cultural transmission and preservation, positing that "diasporic cultural identity teaches us that cultures are not preserved by being protected from 'mixing' but probably can only continue to exist as a product of such mixing."

This does not imply that the practice of blending cultures to produce new ones is simple or formulaic. Instead, individual identities emerge that are fluid and imperfectly defined, existing in an in-between place that Homi Bhabha has identified as the "third space." For Bhabha, the third space is not a place of exile but one in which "hybridity is seen to be an anti-hegemonic force which seeks to force any would-be totalising narrative to come face to face with a challenge to its own supposed purity" (cited in Mandaville 2001, 93). Hybridity, then, for some postcolonial theorists, is in its own way a tool for resistance, a way of overcoming a sense of isolation or marginalization while fighting against dominant culture(s) (Shohat and Stam 2003, 14). There is doubtless some validity to this, yet I think that the work of theorists such as Hoodfar (2003) and Khan (2000), with its emphasis on the wide variety of adaptive techniques minorities employ, suggests that a process more complex than either resistance or assimilation is taking place in many cases. Even for individuals who have lived in Canada for many years, for instance, certain ambiguities may crowd into their conception of identity, even if they can state proudly and without a shadow of a doubt that they are Canadian. Resistance and assimilation themselves are far from simple, with each requiring a certain amount of decision making and acquisition or retention of cultural capital.

In this book, the individuals involved have very different lives and answer to different obligations, yet their comments indicate the extent to which they must move between worlds, adapting their behaviour as circumstances require. At times, their worlds collide, sometimes for better, sometimes for worse, but it is often the case that these young people develop chameleon-like tendencies, playing certain roles as they move from one setting to the next. This may be part of a hybrid strategy for survival, or it may indicate a type of avoidance that arises in lieu of a positive strategy for identity formation. This study examines the details of such strategies, the factors that may contribute to the choice of one over another, and the consequences of juggling worlds or, alternately, melding them.

The implications of such strategies, and the necessity for them, may be perceived differently by various citizens. Canada is a country that has promoted a policy of multiculturalism and diversity as an integral part of its national identity and appeal. Diversity in unity has been promoted by a host of prime ministers and politicians, and it has been gladly embraced by many Canadian citizens. In the case of Muslims and their integration into Canada, Husaini (1990, 98) says enthusiastically: "Canada is a unique country in the world where preservation and advancement of multiculturalism is an official governmental policy. It is Canada's ingenuity and inner security that could allow freedom of cultures and their enhancement." She adds that eventually newcomers to Canada move away from nostalgic longings for return, concentrating instead on establishing roots. Their children, at least those born in Canada, assist greatly in this process, becoming "the final tether to the new society with two concerns: one, how to equip them to face a future in their country of birth, and two, how to pass on to them their ancestral cultural/religious heritage" (3).

It may be true that these are the two chief goals, and the process of working toward these may be a fairly simple one. However, examined more closely, both raise multiple questions about belonging, civic engagement, and the reconciliation of different cultural demands. Mandaville (2001) and Brah (1996) both suggest that living in a diaspora means an awareness of other connections, although Brah is also clear that diaspora does not, as some would argue, signify primarily a desire for return to a homeland (16). Rather, "diasporic journeys are essentially about settling down, about putting roots 'elsewhere'" (182). This desire to sink roots does not always find friendly or fertile ground. In this case, it is understandable that individuals might turn to other groups or communities where acceptance is more easily offered or where pressures to integrate might be more direct or couched in familiar terms. Even when welcome arrives from the host society, there is perhaps a rather natural desire to maintain ties with those who may share beliefs, practices, and memories. More to the point for the individuals studied here, the need for connection may also arise from a wish to explore and discover aspects of heritage that are not found as easily in the place of residence.

This desire for a sense of origins, identity, and belonging is hardly unique, particularly for individuals raised in "a place of cultural fusions and confusions" (Wiwa 2005, A15), where it is hardly possible to ignore the different aspects of their personhood. In a time when communication networks, settlement patterns, and global travel expose many groups to others, it is perhaps not surprising that individuals are constantly asked about their identity and then turn those questions on themselves. Even if they have never visited the place associated with their origin, they may be identified indelibly with it, one more reason why I argue that the subjects of this book are indeed living in diaspora and may be able to speak to its ambiguities and challenges in a way that is powerful, varied, and meaningful: "When the demographic flows of people across territorial boundaries have become more the norm than the exception, it is counterproductive to maintain that one can only understand a place when one is in it" (Radhakrishnan 2003, 126).

As the following chapters explain, these participants have faced, and continue to face, complex challenges to the process of identity construction. As people of South Asian origin, most of whom are Muslim, many feel that it is almost impossible not to take any interest in their culture or religion, and many feel compelled to explain both of these to others who may hold long-standing assumptions about South Asians, Muslims, or minorities in general. Their strategies for building, reinventing, or questioning their identity can differ significantly, but they do demonstrate elements of the hybridity and creolization described here. There is no one solution for how to create belonging and nationalism in communities that are so internally fragmented and home to such myriad strands, but there can be acknowledgment of what it means to be the new hybrids. These individuals may not demonstrate the same easy sense of self and place as Sreberny-Mohammadi and Mohammadi's (1994) daughters, but they do know that their identity is about more than themselves, and few of them believe that it is possible any longer – if it ever was – to enclose that identity within the strict borders of any nation or any state.

4

But Where Are You Really From?
South Asians and Muslims in Canada

Separate and Equal? Muslim and South Asian Identity in Canada

Young adults in nearly any diaspora present an interesting opportunity for the study of identity. The choice of Muslim Canadians of South Asian origin is certainly specific, yet despite the apparent narrowness of this selection, multiple possible identities and affiliations abound. Speaking specifically of South Asian Canadians, Patel (2006, 157) suggests that they live a life markedly different from that of other Canadians for a number of reasons: "Factors such as religion, multiple identities, and the capacity to live with the contradictions and ambivalence that the enormous diversity of South Asia engenders, indicate that Canadians of South Asian origin currently function within a very different set of dynamics than do most other Canadians." At the same time, there are also numerous points of intersection and overlap between Muslims and South Asians, ones that may sometimes go unacknowledged while contributing to a sense of confusion about the ability to delineate and define identity.

Although I describe them on occasion as communities for the sake of simplicity, it is fair to say that Muslim and South Asian groups in Canada and around the world demonstrate high levels of internal diversity and may experience conflict within and between one another while also enduring external criticism. In spite, or perhaps because, of their growing numerical presence in Canada, Muslims and South Asians have often faced significant problems with integration. Highly publicized conflicts over the wearing of turbans and the practice of *hijab* (veiling) certainly contribute to the distinct view of these groups as different from "real Canadians," but at the same time, the period following 11 September 2001 has been one in which a Muslim and South Asian identity has been defined not only by difference but also by a sense of threat, particularly following the 2006 arrest of eighteen young Canadian men (often described as "The Toronto 18") accused of participating in a terrorist plot. Most or all appeared to be Muslim and at least several were of South Asian background. The result of incidents such as these, mirrored in the arrest of young South Asian Muslims in Britain, has been that South Asian Muslims now share the spotlight with Middle Easterners, once viewed as the archetypal image of a Muslim. The role played by South Asian Muslims' sense of self – or lack thereof – is one that has come under increasing scrutiny as young Muslims and/or South Asians in Britain, France, the Netherlands, and elsewhere have appeared vulnerable to a feeling of marginalization and alienation from the countries in which they live.

This chapter discusses the distinctive issues Muslims and South Asians face in the Canadian context, including historical similarities and differences imported from elsewhere, as they attempt to carve out a space for themselves. Although Muslims may be seen as forming a religious diaspora, whereas South Asians could be seen as more of a racial or ethnic group, there are various points of intersection, overlap, and melding. As discussed in previous chapters, conventional definitions may not allow for the possibility of viewing religious groups, such as Muslims, as constituents of a diaspora, yet more elastic applications of the concept might allow, as in Mandaville (2001) and Khan (2000), that Muslims do demonstrate some of the qualities (e.g., dispersal, shared memories and beliefs, the use of media for community formation and cohesion) that would allow them to be viewed as part of a diaspora. South Asians may belong simultaneously to more than one diaspora, including ones formed around religion, nationality, race, and specific ethnicity. Although diaspora does provide a unique space for the transformation of individual and group identities, this space can prove discomfiting for those who prefer the stability of perceived tradition. As Abu-Lughod (1991, 140) points out, "the self is always a construction, never a natural or found entity ... The process of creating a self through opposition to an other always entails the violence of repressing or ignoring other forms of difference." This chapter investigates the context in which the self may be constructed for the young subjects of this research, taking into account global and national factors, religious, cultural, and political pressures, and more simply the evident challenges of inhabiting a generational and geographical position where there are few trails to follow – rather, there are ones to be explored and others to be blazed.

South Asians form one of Canada's largest and most visible ethnic minority groups, and Muslims practise Canada's second-largest religion, although South Asians and Muslims alike constitute only a small proportion of the Canadian population, with nearly 917,000 South Asians and 600,000 Muslims in a Canadian population of roughly 30 million people. Both groups experienced considerable fear and isolation following 11 September 2001, when Canadian anti-terrorism legislation and anti-brown sentiment were perceived as directly affecting their communities in a markedly negative manner. Such events illustrated the fact that South Asian Muslims occupy a rather uneasy place in Canadian society as double minorities, despite

Canada's ostensible commitment to pluralism and diversity and despite the fact that both South Asians and Muslims have been part of the Canadian cultural and religious mosaic for many years.

South Asian Muslims represent a particularly interesting example of a minority group not only in the current political climate but also in larger cultural terms. Some Muslims may have experienced an increased sense of marginalization following 11 September, but it is possible to surmise that others have occupied a marginal position in the past. Those who have South Asian ancestry may have been exposed, in varying degrees, to different forms of South Asian culture, but the dominant forms of these may be strongly accented by Hinduism or Sikhism. Muslims living in South Asia may have their own strategies for adaptation, but Muslims of South Asian origin living in Canada face separate challenges in terms of their positioning within the South Asian diaspora, within the Muslim diaspora, and within the Canadian reality of a purportedly multicultural environment that nonetheless struggles to understand difference. Although this study is specific to Canada, the following sections of this chapter do attempt to provide some global context, however limited, regarding South Asians and Muslims.

Little India, Big Diaspora: South Asians Circle the Globe

> *Probably the uniqueness of Indian culture lies not so much in a unique ideology as in the society's traditional ability to live with cultural ambiguities and to use them to build psychological and even meta-physical defences against cultural invasion. (Nandy 1983, 107)*

> *The struggle for identity is not only about religion but also about national and ethnic association. (Smith 2002, 15)*

The South Asian diaspora is one of the largest in the world and encompasses a number of countries. Desai (2004) explains that although South Asia is a region containing the nation-states of Bangladesh, Bhutan, India, the Maldives, Nepal, Pakistan, Sri Lanka, and Tibet, it is also used more loosely to indicate alliances and identities both within the diaspora and in these countries (5). "South Asian" is frequently conflated with "Indian," perhaps due to the dominance of Indians in the South Asian diaspora, and is particularly apt as a descriptor for those individuals who departed India prior to Partition, when more specific national identities emerged with considerable suddenness and some confusion (6). "South Asian" manages to act as an umbrella term for these identities, creating an impression of shared identity despite a history of religious, cultural, and class-based division among and within some of the countries of South Asia.

Canada itself contains a sizable South Asian population, and among Canadians in their twenties, the largest group of visible minorities is South Asian (Anderssen and Valpy 2003, A10). Overall, Canadians of South Asian origin number roughly 917,000, representing 3.1 percent of Canada's population. Between 1996 and 2001 the South Asian population in Canada grew approximately 37 percent, a growth that outpaced even the Chinese Canadian community, which currently represents the largest visible minority population in Canada (Statistics Canada 2003a, 11). Although Muslims who could identify any South Asian origins were recruited for this study, the majority named Indian roots and several had Pakistani origins. Partly for this reason, a discussion of the Indian diaspora and the relationship between India and Pakistan constitutes a large part of the analysis here. This is also because of the undoubted influence of India within the South Asian diaspora given the size and breadth of India's diaspora, estimated at roughly 20 million people (Desai 2004, 5).

In the South Asian diaspora, as among Muslims, the nature of immigration has significantly changed. In Canada, where policy once attempted to balance the need for affordable labour with the desire to please white citizens who objected to South Asian immigration, South Asians were present in small numbers from at least the nineteenth century. However, they possessed limited rights, and by the early twentieth century the provincial and federal governments had passed laws intended to prevent more South Asian immigration, leading to the memorable 1914 refusal to accept numerous South Asians who sailed to Vancouver aboard the *Komagata Maru*. Not until the 1960s did immigration rules in the United States and Canada change enough to allow South Asians to enter these countries in substantially higher numbers.

Indian migration clearly did not commence with these waves of movement, having been preceded by the wide dispersal of Indian labourers throughout the globe, but it was a different kind of migration that began to take place. Previously, migration might have been initiated most commonly by people who moved into menial professions. The exodus of professionals to the United States caused that country and India to reconsider their thoughts on migration and difference. The colonizer may still visit the developing world in a search for cheap labour or new markets, but the real success of colonialism, the ripple effect still being felt decades after the fact, is the willingness of former colonial subjects to seek their fortunes in the urban centres of empire. Freed in theory to be master of its own destiny, India now finds that the colonial presence takes a form very different from what had previously been the case. The lure of living abroad and making one's fortune elsewhere looms large for many Indians, a phenomenon best encapsulated in the new popularity of the term "non-resident Indian," or

"NRI." Although the term is sometimes used casually to indicate a person of Indian origin or citizenship who lives outside of India, it is derived from government terminology used to refer to people who maintain a relationship – whether in name or in terms of the ability to maintain property – with India while living abroad (Shukla 2003, 10, 59).

Despite the dominance of India within the South Asian diaspora, a dominance discussed further here in examining the question of Bollywood, this diaspora is one that is marked by diversity, difference, and even conflict. Khan (2004) suggests that this has not always been the case, describing a medieval South Asia where individuals made strategic choices all the time regarding the beliefs and practices they were willing to embrace. Less preoccupied with the need to distinguish themselves from other groups than might be the case now, these South Asians sought identity through a number of sources, including their geographical positioning, their relationships with their neighbours, and their belief in folktales and oral history that sometimes placed universal importance on shrines, temples, or festivals that would otherwise have been the provenance of a particular religious group. Opposition to colonialism brought some unity, but eventually the divide-and-conquer strategies of colonizers were bound to create splintering, which was only accentuated by the 1947 Partition of India. As Hindus and Muslims moved physically and ideologically into separate spaces, South Asians around the globe began to be aware of their difference, affirming individual identities: "An increasingly complex field of affiliations began to distinguish the histories of 'Indians' from those of 'Pakistanis,' and later 'Bangladeshis,' and other South Asians" (Shukla 2003, 45).

Another layer of complexity was added by multiple migrants, those individuals who had left a South Asian country and immigrated elsewhere, only to end up moving again, either through necessity or choice. Warah (1998, 12) discusses the question of "triple heritage," a legacy handed down to several of the participants in this study, who have Indian ancestry, parents who lived in another country, and upbringing or education in the West. Due to a need for labourers to work on plantations and railways, the British sent many Indians to various colonies in the nineteenth century, including parts of East Africa and South Africa (Warah 1998, 12). Discussing the experience of Asian migrants in Africa, Warah recounts their experiences of cultural retention: Asians tended to stay "fairly insulated against the culture of the country of their adoption. Most people of Indian origin in Kenya speak their mother tongue, follow their religious rituals, eat Indian food and have some vision of what their ancestral country is like, even if they have never been there" (12). This observation aligns to some degree with Shukla's (2003, 64) commentaries on the reclamation of Indian identity by Ugandan Indians following their expulsion by the dictator Idi Amin in the 1970s:

As stateless peoples, many Ugandan Indians began to see the cultural and psychic usefulness of "becoming Indian" and submitting to the sense of a past rooted in a more abstract "homeland." Ugandan and Kenyan Indians brought to existing Indian immigrant communities a set of experiences that both complicated and buttressed pan-ethnic nationalism. The memories of multiple migrations, the histories of indentured labor, the triangulation of colonial sympathies and anticolonial resistance all broadened the discourses of Indian identity. Likewise, during this period, the presence of Indians from the Caribbean – from Trinidad, Jamaica, and Guyana – challenged the linear narratives of class ascendancy being created by an earlier generation of now middle-class Indians in Britain.

South Asians both in Africa and elsewhere in the diaspora, then, were affected by colonial politics in a different way than were Indians in the homeland, yet some similarities existed. Warah (1998, 28-30) suggests that the effects of Indian independence and Partition could be felt as far as East Africa, dividing Muslims from non-Muslims who aligned themselves either with the new India, with Pakistan, or with no place at all, as the carving up of the country confused their understanding of home, place, and borders.

Elsewhere in the diaspora, South Asians continued to put down roots, even if their position could be tenuous, as in Africa, or in more-developed countries that valued only their labour. Throughout the United Kingdom, the United States, and Canada, Little Indias – and, to a lesser extent, Little Pakistans – sprang up, suggesting "the reproduction of a national (Indian) formation elsewhere, as well as the building of an ethnic enclave within the United States or Britain" (Shukla 2003, 83). The existence of such enclaves raises some of the same questions regarding citizenship as those discussed previously, such as the following query: "Is being part of a 'little India' to be part of Britain, the United States, or India?" (Shukla 2003, 83). Although Shukla's focus is mainly on America and the United Kingdom, the same question has certainly been applied in the Canadian context. One possible answer is that it is not necessarily the case that one must choose; another answer might be that belonging to a Little India can rarely be the same as belonging to India. Rather, a Little India is a particular version of India, with some natural connections to that country as well as ones that are forged with purpose and intensity. For some, the automatic response to change is to try to find a kind of mooring in culture, a difficult task if that culture has always been experienced at a distance:

New generations of any formation always seem to elicit the prospect of disappearance and loss, and this is certainly the case with new Indian diasporic cultures. A very old question, of what is Indian, less Indian, more

Indian, and still Indian appears as the quality of Indianness becomes un-moored from nation, state, or any other mechanism of surveillance. Im-migrants from India to the United States and United Kingdom lament that their children are not "Indian" anymore, precisely when youth express desires and longings that are distinct from those consolations of their parents. (Shukla 2003, 217)

Movement may cause a desire to recapture origins that are perceived to be lost, a loss that is mourned even when the moment of its occurrence cannot necessarily be pinpointed.

These attempts to claim an identity take many forms. Shukla (2003, 233) discusses the eliding of religious identity with a sense of nationhood, point-ing to the phenomenon of Hindu youth groups whose commitment to the maintenance of culture or religion may

> often satisfy an exclusivist and nationalist understanding of Indian identity. Religion here, as more generally in the diaspora, I would argue, is a language for nation. Other religious articulations, as they might occur through Islam and Sikhism, which have active youth groups, too, may be a counterpoint, even a challenge to India, by espousing other forms of nationalism.

Others may immerse themselves in mediated forms of culture in an effort to understand whence they came, as with those double or triple migrants who have no direct connection to Indian culture and thus seek it from the easiest source:

> Many Asians in Kenya have never read an Indian classic, learnt Indian his-tory or fully grasped the philosophical meaning of the Indian scriptures. If they learn about India at all, it is from the worst source possible – commercial Indian cinema which tends to be shallow, melodramatic, and very often, a poor and distorted depiction of life in India. (Warah 1998, 48)

Warah's judgment may appear to be harsh and certainly does not acknow-ledge the social, cultural, and political undercurrents that other scholars have detected in popular Indian cinema (see Nandy 1995; Prasad 1998). Regardless, the implications of this media-assisted identity formation are discussed in the following chapters. Warah (1998, 49) adds that another way of seeking authenticity in real life is by observing strict hierarchies: "Even among themselves, Asians rarely refer to themselves as a race, but as members of the religious, linguistic or caste group to which they belong." There seems to be some evidence in this study to suggest that this level of specificity does not hold quite as much significance for younger generations, but nonethe-less they are aware that the constant establishment of difference is one means of reasserting a sense of South Asian self. They are also aware, as several participants noted in this research, that their refusal to subscribe to these notions of division may not prevent them from experiencing attendant implications in their own lives and personal relationships.

The role of nationality in creating barriers is quite evident in the after-effects of Partition, with its overtones of religious segregation. However, even among Hindus and Sikhs, there may be further segregation on the basis of a specific sect, caste, or of physical characteristics, such as skin colour. Internal hierarchies are not unique to a particular religion; Gillespie 1995, 32) notes the way South Asians of different religions attempt to maintain caste and sect distinctions in England, albeit with mixed results given the impossibility of preventing lower caste members from pursuing economic and social success outside of India's borders (see also Brah 1996; Cohen 1997, 61). Caste can mutate in the diaspora, then, but Brah (1996, 30) also cautions that it is simplistic to suggest that caste is completely static in any location, including India.

These kinds of prejudices, however, are not the only ones that divide South Asians. Politics and religion intertwine in the portrayal of Sikhs as essentially different from Hindus and frequently extremist, a depiction that is often applied to Muslims as well and can be found in several examples of Bolly-wood cinema. These divisions are based only partly on religion, with more of them attached to political acts such as the Sikh campaign for its own homeland and the violence between Hindus, Sikhs, and Muslims that ex-ploded after Partition and echoed in events such as the Hindu-Sikh fighting following the 1984 assassination of Indira Gandhi by two Sikh bodyguards, the Bombay intercommunal riots of 1993, the ongoing dispute over Kashmir, and the 2002 Gujarat riots, among others. Although many Sikhs continue to maintain their difference from other groups in India, some Indian nation-alists have attempted to overcome division by minimizing ethnic or religious difference (Cohen 1997, 62), an attempt that would likely find favour with those who argue, like Khan (2004), that careful study of South Asian litera-ture, customs, and history can uncover surprising similarities among Hindus, Muslims, and Sikhs. In theory, then, this may seem like a positive attempt to establish unity, but in practice the outcome of efforts to stoke Indian nationalism has been the ascendance of a Hindu Indian identity, both within South Asia and within the diaspora (Gottschalk 2000, 18).

"In general," Cohen (1997, 63) reports, "orthodox forms of Hinduism became predominant in the diaspora and were the principal means whereby the Indian labour diaspora was reconnected to the 'Great Tradition' of India." He goes on to cite Amarpal K. Dhaliwal's opinion that diaspora may ultim-ately be the space that resolves the differences between polarized religions and cultures: "She argues that, while the South Asian diaspora has multiple and shifting relationships with India, these do not automatically challenge the Indian nation. Indeed, she suggests that the diaspora may provide a means of resolving the unconstituted nationhood of India itself – in particular the unresolved difference between Sikh and Hindu" (136).

Despite making reference to Hindus and Muslims rather than to Sikhs, Ray (2001, 155) does emphasize that divisions between South Asians can come to seem artificial when one is faced with the challenges of displacement. The Fiji Indians living in diaspora whom he describes refused to conform to old notions of separation and hierarchy, instead going "to great lengths to fashion new hybrid diasporic realities. During the indenture period and the early days of post-indenture, both Hindus and Muslims participated in the major ritual festivals like *Holi,* the riotous Hindu ritual of reversals, and the Tazia, the Shi'a Islamic Moharram re-enactment of the martyrdom of Husain and Hassan." This may be a step in a new direction for some, but it may also signal a revival of the long-standing traditions of communal celebration and sharing described by Khan (2004) in her discussion of identity in South Asia (see also Gottschalk 2000, 36, 155-56). Khan points out that in medieval South Asia, certain practices and beliefs might have been maintained jointly by groups who would now view these quite differently. The proximity between groups living in the same villages often led them to forge complicated bonds, including ones that eventually came to be disavowed as religious and cultural groups sought to carve out a clearly delineated identity.

This kind of hybridity and accommodation can be forgotten or rejected by those who view diaspora as a space where changes must be met with stubborn attempts to recreate the past in order to resist incorporation into a different social order: "Ashis Nandy makes the point that exiles often develop a fixed and backward-looking image of their homeland. Thus, he argues that, in the Indian case, diasporic Hinduism is often more exclusive and homogenic than that in India" (Morley 2000, 49). However, this can involve several stages and many contradictions. In a sense, Gottschalk (2000, 60-63) argues, identity within present-day South Asia is defined at least partly by what it is not: Indians and Pakistanis know that their affiliations are opposed, driving them to immerse themselves in practices that will further differentiate them, while South Asians in general know that they are not westerners, a fact that can unite them rather loosely. When individuals are taken out of an area where they can at least identify some surface ethnic similarities, they may follow unusual steps to preserve a sense of self, however artificial. The same blurring of religious and cultural identities noted by Khan (2004) in South Asia can also be seen in diasporic Indian Muslims whose proximity to Hindus has resulted in the creolization of various practices in places such as Fiji: "During the indenture period, Muslims had little opportunity for religious and cultural expression of their own; they used to regularly take part in Hindu festivities and folk cultural gatherings" (Ray 2001, 169).

There is no clear and distinct answer to whether the diaspora will help South Asia to evolve or whether it will merely preserve and even feed existing rivalries. It does seem possible to say that the differences perceived among South Asians are not always evident to outsiders and hence that in the di-aspora South Asians may be grouped together, a tendency demonstrated by the evolution of a vocabulary to describe all of them equally. A superficial level of unity can be encompassed in such descriptors as the term "desi," used loosely to apply to any number of South Asians living in the diaspora. "Desi is a chameleon-like word," explains the Masala Trois Collective in their book *Desilicious* (2003, 13), "evocative more than descriptive, adopted most comfortably by young South Asians who appreciate the irony of naming a mind-bogglingly diverse number of cultural communities, spread across continents, using a word that simply suggests home." In particular, the term "desi" is often used in reference to youth, a fact noted by Malkani (2006, A15) in his analysis of the way desi identity in Great Britain can be South Asian and British without any contradiction or compromise:

> Our desi identity feels more like a youth subculture than an ethnic identity. (The word desi is derived from Sanskrit for "countryman," but among the young its meaning is closer to the hip-hop slang "homeboy.") As a subculture, the desi scene is as British as punk rock or acid house, and therefore less fundamental and more porous than an ethnic identity – but without being any less South Asian.

Malkani notes the new diversity within Britain and its acknowledgment of a desi culture that can fuse the disparate influences of places as far apart as London and Mumbai. It is within places such as this, offers Desai (2004, 31), that one can examine migration in all of its complexity and in relation to "dominant discourses on modernity, capitalism, and the nation. The Brown Atlantic, located in the heart of the beast, provides a foray into understanding negotiations of South Asian transnationalities with U.S. imperialism, British colonialism, and global capitalism." As Beck (2000) has indicated, it is impossible to study local spaces that are seemingly new, pluralistic, and modern without understanding that locality maintains a symbiotic relationship – what Beck labels a kind of reflexivity – with the global. And neither Malkani's Britain nor Desai's America is immune to the interaction between city and world, village and diaspora. There may be a desi culture spread across all of these, but it differs in whatever nooks and crannies it occupies, and it is by no means organic, simple, or static. Indeed, some of the young people interviewed for this project noted the intermittent trendiness of so-called desi culture and the implications of its commodification and mainstream popularity.

Malkani's (2006, A15) version of the Brown Atlantic locates both diversity and unity in the person of youth, making only implicit reference to the forces of capitalism or imperialism. Yet in his description of acculturation, as explained by his interview subjects, it is clear that culture is linked to a number of other factors: "The boys and girls I interviewed would describe assimilated 'coconuts' (brown on the outside, white on the inside) not in terms of ethnic characteristics but of street-savviness and gender: they were either 'saps' (uncool), 'ponces' (effeminate) or 'batty' (homosexual)." Those who insisted on maintaining a strict observation of Indian culture, at least as they understood it, were linked to impressions of hypermasculinity, whereas those who gave in to the temptations of assimilation were lacking in strength and virility.

Several aspects of this observation are worth interrogating. First, neither assimilation nor cultural assertion is entirely unproblematic; the young people interviewed by Malkani saw issues with both. Second, contrary to narratives of immigration that suggest generational change, the youth did not demonstrate simply one technique in response to perceived challenges to culture. Even among the youth, there was vast difference. Gender also melded with cultural retention in a way that is hardly unique to South Asians in Britain, yet in Malkani's study there is a far more explicit link made between gender and sexuality and between gender and culture than any suggested so far in the present discussion. This link, however, is not far removed from traditional discourses by colonized people, in which women serve as fragile purveyors of indigenous culture, while the strong masculine force protects female/national/cultural space. This connection between gender, culture, and sexuality reasserts itself repeatedly in Indian cinema, especially popular Indian cinema.

This relationship evokes the term "intersectionality," which Desai (2004, 26) explains was first used by Kimberlé Crenshaw as a way of explaining the "simultaneity of multiple differences in the experiences of women of color." Although that usage is certainly applicable here and in following chapters, the broader version, focusing on the analysis of layered aspects of difference and power relations, offers an excellent way of examining the contradictory positionality of Malkani's interviewees, as well as the ones discussed here. Rejecting assimilation as a form of selling out or emasculation, Malkani's youth nonetheless understood that there was some element of posturing or exaggeration associated with the assertion of cultural identity and authenticity. The intense resistance to assimilation indicates the extent of its temptation. If this were not so, there would be far less attention, not to mention antagonism, focused on this question.

Gillespie's (1995) and Handa's (2003) studies seem to imply the importance of this temptation, or presence, even in the lives of their young participants, most of whom seemed to exist in an interesting state of hybridity. Modern, well adjusted, and generally integrated into mainstream society, these young people nonetheless occasionally turned up their nose at those who insisted on the public display of culture. Gillespie's (1995, 180-97) examination of Punjabi teenagers in the United Kingdom finds internal discrimination at work among South Asians, who describe a social hierarchy in which recent immigrants or highly traditional Punjabis reside at the very bottom, their Indian origins too clearly marked by their clothing, hairstyle, and manner-isms, a finding very similar to that of Pyke and Dang (2003), whose Asian American respondents established their social groups based on strict categor-izations of youth as Americanized or whitewashed. One of Ali's (2003, 148) participants used his interview time to emphasize that he was Bengali, indicating his aversion to being considered Pakistani, a distinction that may have stemmed, Ali suggests, from his awareness that "Paki" is a common and devastating racial slur. Likewise, Handa's (2003, 82-89) South Asian female subjects, residing in Toronto, were vehement that they did not endorse ra-cism and that they supported the notion of a multicultural society, yet their comments regarding Indians who are "typical" or "fresh off the boat" clearly demonstrated the perception that a divide persists between South Asians who are more assimilated to Western culture and those who are not. In a sense, then, these young women appear to demonstrate cultural racism to-ward their own peers: "Cultural racism assumes a situation in which the nation and the citizen are in a binary relation to the alien, foreigner, and immigrant, who are collectively defined as 'the other'" (Agnew 2007, 14).

Handa's participants offered their observations despite appearing, at least to Handa's eyes, far more comfortable with their culture and selves than she could have imagined being only ten or twenty years before. To a certain extent, then, as Desai (2004, 12) suggests, the influences of colonialism still persist in the South Asian diaspora, even in a country such as Canada – the site of Handa's research – where different identities are expected to flourish. What has changed, perhaps, is the means by which diasporic subjects inter-nalize their beliefs about the culture to which they should belong. For those immigrants who came from South Asia during or soon after colonialism, it is perhaps not surprising that there is an unconscious belief in the superior-ity of English-speaking, fair-skinned individuals dressed in Western clothes; although opposition to colonialism brought about its demise, deep-seated impressions about class and race may have lingered and been difficult to dispel. For the youth in Gillespie (1995), Handa (2003), and even this study, those beliefs may be fostered in the new environment, a natural by-product of living in an arena where one is not a member of the majority. Even when whiteness is not representative of the majority, as in one highly diverse English neighbourhood examined by Ali (2003) in her study of mixed-race children, young people still grapple with their multiple identities. One young girl described her parents, both British-born, as Indian rather than English/ British, perhaps because she understood that questions about nationality are often questions about origin and relative belonging. Such answers, remarks Ali, demonstrate "the way in which affiliations to the 'myth of common origin' continue to be transmitted across generations through ethnic markers" (136).

Certainly, differences do exist between and within the generations. As waves of immigration continue, there is no unified process by which all immigrants come to a specific and obvious understanding of identity and ethnicity. There is little validity to "nationalist constructions of belonging that link racialized and gendered bodies and space in seamless tales of bloodlines and family to the land" (Desai 2004, 18). Nonetheless, there do seem to be some confused remnants of these narratives in the comments of the young men to whom Malkani (2006) spoke. There is perhaps no aspect of identity that is irrelevant in this study or in any other similar investigation. Gender, race, ethnicity, religion, class – all of these and more combine to create a complicated understanding of personhood and where one stands within a community.

Still Waiting for the Green Peril? Islam as World Religion

Religion can be viewed both as a way to overcome difference and as a way to accentuate it, depending on the context and circumstances. The emphasis in the media and by some academics on Islam as a supposed motivator for acts of terrorism around the globe (for examples, see Pipes 2001; Wente 2001; Pipes and Hedegaard 2002) might lead some to believe that Islam is a strong religious and political force. In reality, even though Islam does bind together roughly one billion people around the world, it is by no means a way of creating political or social unity, and the vast disparities in methods of practice also ensure that the religious bonds can be tenuous. Although the phrase "Muslim world" is bandied about regularly in the press and occasionally in political speeches, the fact is that Muslims in Canada, or around the world, are no more united or homogeneous than any other religious group. Globally, they are widely dispersed, with large concentrations in countries such as Indonesia or parts of the Middle East, accompanied by growing numbers in North America and Europe. These shifts into the latter have caused some consternation as countries in the global North struggle to accept the reality of a Muslim presence that has moved within their borders, as opposed to the days when colonial forces occupied Muslim-dominated places such as North Africa.

Smith (2002) notes that former colonial powers have had their expecta-tions turned upside down, having initially believed that their move out of colonial territories would be the first step in a process of modernization and economic independence for peoples once colonized. Instead, facing political unrest and lack of opportunity, some Muslims began a type of reverse migra-tion, moving to the very countries associated with imperialism. Possessing some degree of assumed familiarity with the language and culture of former occupiers, however fleeting, these immigrants arrived in places such as Germany, France, and England, where the visitors and the hosts alike as-sumed that their stay would be fleeting, a temporary sojourn in search of economic prosperity that would end with a return journey. Instead, many of the immigrants settled down, producing second generations of children who came to view the new country as their home, forcing everyone con-cerned to confront the reality of a permanent Muslim presence, one that has spread to points farther west, such as North America. Some would de-scribe this process of dispersal as the formation of a religious diaspora, whereas others would question the possibility that such an entity might exist. A religious diaspora, like an ethnic or national one, is necessarily di-verse and decentred, but this condition is further exacerbated by a lack of state connections. There is, practically speaking, no real homeland, point of return, or gathering place for most Muslims.

Despite universal acceptance that Prophet Muhammad was the final prophet of Allah, and that Allah is the only God, Muslims follow a number of different beliefs, leaders, and practices. In some Canadian centres, Shia Muslims – the global minority – may have relatively strong representation compared to their position in the Middle East, South Asia, or even the United States (MacFarquhar 2007). Ismaili Muslims, for example, are well represented in cities such as Vancouver and Toronto, and they identify themselves as Shia, despite the fact that other Shia and Sunnis sometimes disclaim them – as well as Sufis and Ahmadiyyas – as pseudo-Muslims who do not follow the same practices as other Muslims.

Islam's influence is perhaps most visible in parts of the Middle East and Asia, including India, where religion is sometimes portrayed as a divisive force in spite of the fact that many Indians once shared the same religion, and a significant number continue to demonstrate overlap in terms of their practices and rituals. Waves of proselytizing forces moved through the sub-continent after the Prophet's lifetime, converting a large number of Indians to the Islamic faith. It is perhaps for this reason that Hindu rituals can still be seen at times in the cultural practices of South Asian Muslims, despite the apparent perception of difference. Khan (2004) suggests, in fact, that the purported division between religious groups in South Asia is one that has been exaggerated, providing a false picture of the hybrid religious and cultural practices seen historically in South Asia. She offers a historical commentary on the ways that various religious groups interacted in South Asia, celebrating some of the same festivals and worshipping at the same sites. This intertwining of various sects was so complicated and mysterious to colonial administrators that they did their best to categorize each group as simply as possible, with the result that individuals eventually came to realize their difference and the behavioural expectations placed on them.

Nonetheless, the confluence between different religious and cultural groups did persist to a certain extent and can be seen repeatedly throughout this study, and it is still relatively pronounced in Canada. Although Canada is home to a steadily growing and very visible South Asian population, it also possesses a relatively young Muslim population whose numbers show no sign of declining. Between 1991 and 2001, the number of Muslims in Canada more than doubled, jumping from 253,300 to 579,600. This increase was due mainly to immigration, but the relatively young median age of these individuals – twenty-eight years old – also suggests that steady growth may take place through reproduction (Statistics Canada 2003b, 8). This being the case, it is important to investigate the role that Muslims have played and continue to play in Canadian society.

Muslims in the Mosaic: Muslims, Diaspora, and Difference

> *I have heard my mother pointing out to her friends, with some pleasure, that the world has turned upside down and they have ended up learning their religion from their Canadian children rather than from their Muslim parents back home. (Anonymous interviewee in Hoodfar 2003, 23)*

Although her study is somewhat dated, Husaini's (1990) points regarding the history of Muslim immigration to Canada still retain considerable value. She notes changes in the nature of Muslim immigration, which commenced mainly with Turkish or Arab labourers. Karim (2002, 263) points out that historical documents indicate a Muslim presence, however small, in Canada from the mid-nineteenth century, and he also cites an official record of thirteen Canadian Muslim residents provided by the 1871 census. In the 1960s changes to Canada's immigration policy helped to diversify the class and ethnicity of newcomers, including Muslims, who began to arrive as skilled immigrants from Asia and Africa (Husaini 1990, 21-22). Despite the common portrayal of Muslims as Arabs, then, Muslims in Canada demonstrate rich internal diversity in terms of their ethnic origins and background.

Inquiring about the needs and concerns of Canadian Muslims with particular emphasis on Albertans, Husaini (1990) found that Canadian Muslims, in general, are "concerned about what they would call the 'Future of Islam.' In essence they are anxious to pass their rich and valued Islamic heritage to their Canadian-born generation, which is nurtured and educated in the secular values and outlook of Canadian society" (36). Related to this, they expressed a desire for Muslim social networks and a strong sense of community, as well as for successful means of providing religious education (52). Interestingly, their answers did not seem to indicate insularity or repudiation of a culture populated by non-Muslims; rather, they suggested to Husaini that another key concern would be "to create harmony and co-existence between Islamic values and the values of the broader society so that 'Canadian Muslims' can relate to their peers" (37). Since this is still the challenge that many Canadian Muslims take up today, wondering how to reconcile a Canadian upbringing and education with religious and cultural values that some perceive as being opposed to their Canadian experience, Husaini's study, rather than appearing stale, seems to suggest that the concerns of Muslims have not changed as much as they have intensified and, perhaps, clarified.

At the same time, Canadian society has undergone changes of its own, some with great reluctance. Although the Muslim population has grown in Canada and now shows few signs of declining, some Canadian cities have reacted to the Muslim presence by attempting to limit its reach. Isin and Siemiatycki (2002) document the problems of seeking out space for mosques in Toronto, while Khan (1995) notes the debate over permitting head scarves or other examples of *hijab* (veiling) to be worn in Quebec schools. Razack (1998, 6) suggests that the intensity of the debate over veiling and female genital mutilation, practices depicted in the media as Islamic when in fact they are largely cultural, serves to reinforce notions about "the brutalities of 'Islamic' and Asian states." Such emphasis on religion and culture as oppressors of women-as-victims refuses to acknowledge the possible context and reasons for the practices named above and also turns a blind eye to different, yet very real, forms of sexism in North American society. Proposals to introduce *sharia,* a form of Islamic law, in Ontario created such overwhelming controversy and concerns over the repression of women's rights that Premier Dalton McGuinty finally resolved the debate with a 2005 decision not to grant authority to any religious tribunals in the province (Allemang 2005). Although other religious groups, including Ismaili Muslims, have administered tribunals for years, the *sharia* case prompted widespread fears over the consequences of empowering Islamic extremists.

The case of the Ismaili Muslim community, in fact, is somewhat unique. Taking into account the high level of mainstream integration displayed by this group, Husaini (1990, 35) takes a few moments to discuss its status in Alberta, where her study was based:

> The Ismaili Muslim community in Alberta is the most organized, cohesive and motivated of all other groups of Muslims in Alberta. Except in the economic and educational sphere, they maintain an intense form of

"institutional completeness" in Breton's sense of the term. They also display a unique combination of adaptability to the Canadian way of life with total dedication to Ismaili faith and practices.

This case is particularly interesting and is raised again throughout the present study. Canadian Ismaili Muslims may come from any ethnic background, but many tend to derive their origins from parts of South or Central Asia. The earlier immigrants, many of whom arrived in Canada in the 1970s, are more likely to be of South Asian ancestry, but if they can trace their roots back to India, it is often by way of other countries, such as East Africa. The strong adaptability and cultural retention pointed to by Husaini do exist, yet this does not imply that even Ismaili Muslims feel entirely comfortable with their multiple sources of difference. Karim (2010) notes their willingness to accommodate different cultural practices within and alongside their community, embracing mainstream social and political causes while maintaining traditional rites and beliefs.

Dossa (1988) also remarks on the integrative ability of Ismailis in Canada, attributing this to their cohesiveness as a community, an observation similar to Husaini's institutional completeness. Asked about the significance of the cultural and religious institutions to which they belong, Husaini's (1990, 52) participants suggested that these organizations helped them to integrate into mainstream Canadian society, assisting them with "overcoming cultural nostalgia by meeting others, by creating social networks ... An equally large number of respondents found adjusting to this society easier because they found a familiar religious environment." In other words, the confidence these organizations provided in terms of constructing identity and community helped them to feel at ease to the point where they perceived fewer barriers to involvement in mainstream Canadian society.

Likewise, Murji and Hébert's (1999, 13) Muslim interviewees praised Canada's openness to the notion of retaining one's faith and heritage. At the same time, however, they also indicated occasional "resentment of not being identified as being 'Canadian' because of one's colour or practice, of being the other, of experiencing discrimination and prejudice." Razack (1998, 28) suggests that such discrimination is more widespread than the official state view acknowledges, arguing that multiculturalism exists side by side with a tacit "assumption that, in choosing to come here, immigrants relinquish their right to the conditions under which their cultural identities might flourish. Such an argument ... sidesteps the point that immigrants seek ... a protection that can come from maintaining their own cultural practices." Husaini (1990, 100) passes over multiculturalism's possible limitations in describing Canada as a "free, democratic, peaceful and tolerant society which, at least formally, does not pressure the incoming immigrants to renounce their cultural and religious heritage." "Living in such a conducive atmosphere for cultural preservation," she posits, "it is much easier and psychologically smoother for Canadians of different nationalities of origin to forget their original conflicts, and come together to build upon points of similarities and common loyalties."

Although it may still be the case that Canadian minorities have some freedom to express loyalties to other nations or entities, recent political events, including but not limited to the wars in Afghanistan and Iraq, have clarified the degree to which certain minorities are considered problematic in the functioning of the nation-state. The sense of global obligation felt by many Canadian Muslims to their fellow practitioners around the world came into stark relief during these conflicts, when an expression of faith came to be seen as a repudiation of a supposedly secular state and, therefore, of democracy itself. Carens (2000, 141) describes the type of scrutiny Muslims must undergo in such a situation: "One question that one encounters frequently, either implicitly or explicitly, is whether Muslims can be full members of liberal democratic societies given the strength of their communal identity. In the view of some democratic theorists, participation in the democratic process requires a capacity to distance oneself from one's identity." This separation from one's identity appears to pose considerable difficulty for many Muslims, particularly as a sense of injustice fuels their interest in matters related to other Muslims. Acknowledging these questions about Muslim loyalties, Siddiqui (2006, A17) responds to thinly veiled commentaries in the media about the need to review dual citizenship and immigration by stating bluntly, "the latest hand-wringing on multiculturalism and its first cousin, immigration, in reality is a debate about Muslims."

Whether it has been acquired recently or is the product of accumulated years of discomfort, the idea that Muslims should keep their focus strictly on Canada is one that contradicts the sense of global concern reported in Husaini's (1990, 59) study:

> Many Canadian Muslims reported that they feel a sense of obligation, empathy and responsibility not only for Muslims in their own countries of origin, but also for all those in other countries of Asia and Africa, where people are not only victims of poverty and deprivation but also of wars, foreign subjugation and displacement. They have often stated that Canada has given them a chance to acquire education and prosperity, freedom and dignity. As true Muslims and as Canadians, it is their responsibility to share their wealth, knowledge and expertise with those who are not as fortunate as they are.

Arguably, any departure from this notion – which signals that cosmopolitanism is not merely an interesting theory as much as a practice that is already taking place, albeit with an interesting ethnic twist – would weaken the foundations of a "free, democratic, peaceful and tolerant society which ... acknowledges and respects all differences" (Husaini 1990, 100). After speaking with a number of Canadian Muslims, Husaini expresses her conviction that it is possible for these citizens to continue their religious practices, engage fully with Canadian society, and maintain an overarching interest in current events and concerns around the world. Indeed, she argues, it is even desirable since the Canadian model may be the best one available at the moment, one that may serve as an example to other countries and societies (101-2).

In theory, the situation elsewhere is rather different. Although much attention is devoted by policy makers to comparing and contrasting the Canadian and American models, with a supposed emphasis on plurality in the former and assimilation in the latter, the example of Europe has its own lessons and bears further consideration. Speaking of Europe in general, Ramadan (2002) remarks on the necessity of being able to combine a thoughtful interpretation of the Muslim faith with an equally reasoned and invested concern for European practices, culture, and social justice. Britain has had specific issues with its Muslim population stemming directly from its own experience of a terrorist attack subsequent to 11 September 2001 with the bombings of the London subway on 7 July 2005. All three of the countries named here have grappled with their own understanding of the Muslim problem – and it is indeed framed as a problem in media and policy discourse – and Britain's eventual reaction has certainly aroused considerable controversy. Lyall and Fisher (2006, 6) comment on the British government's attempts to reach out to the Muslim community within its borders, suggesting that British Muslims retain unremitting hostility toward their adopted country despite these persistent efforts. This is perhaps not as surprising as it might seem at first given that high-ranking representatives at the time such as Home Secretary Jack Straw and Prime Minister Tony Blair located the source of their ongoing communication problem in an area that seems to attract persistent attention around the globe: Muslim women's clothing. Specifically, Straw decided to address the issue of cultural difference by announcing his unwillingness to meet with Muslim women who would not remove facial coverings, despite the fact that those same women interpret this form of covering as a religious obligation.

Although the religious necessity of such practices is debatable and is indeed debated within and outside Islam, the fact that they are singled out and cited as examples of Muslims' refusal to integrate into society may render unsurprising the following results from a poll of Muslims by the Pew Global Attitudes Project: "81 percent of those surveyed in Britain said they considered themselves Muslims first and Britons second. That contrasts with Spain, where 69 percent of those surveyed considered themselves Muslims first and

Spaniards second; Germany, where the comparable number is 66 percent, and even Jordan, with 67 percent" (cited in Lyall and Fisher 2006, 6). This disparity was not always quite so extreme. Lyall and Fisher (2006, 6) cite experts who suggest that previous generations of Muslims in England experienced less difficulty in balancing their Muslimness and Englishness: "Many of the first wave of immigrants were from rural Pakistan, spoke poor English and never integrated much. But the generation that is coming of age now is caught between the traditionalism of their parents and the Western ideas they have been born in to, and the result can be toxic."

Although conservative parents and the traditional mentality of older generations are sometimes cited as important influences in the radicalizing of young Muslims, this does not always seem to be the case. Cesari (2002, 41-42) describes a growing number of young Muslims in France who choose to express their identity by adhering more strictly than ever to religious rules and practices. This cohort is small in comparison to the number of Muslim youth who are flexible about religion, tending instead toward a customized approach where they embrace those rituals or beliefs that fit into their lives and whose purpose makes sense to them rather than hewing to a strictly orthodox line. In fact, when studying the reasons why young Québécois Muslim women cover themselves, a practice that can range from wearing a light headscarf to donning an all-encompassing garment, Hoodfar (2003) was startled to discover that very few of the parents of these women wanted them to veil, as the act of such covering is commonly described. Most considered the practice un-Islamic but were unable to dissuade their daughters from veiling. Whereas some daughters were motivated by their parents' strictness and felt that veiling would convince others of their modesty, hence allowing them to go out in public without encountering harassment or disapproval, others began veiling as a reaction to their sense of marginalization in Canadian society.

In the much-discussed case of the eight young men in an affluent British suburb who were arrested in 2004 for allegedly attempting to make and store explosives for a planned terrorist attack, observers have been at a loss to explain adequately the motives that might have driven these youth. The parents of two of the young men have been described by friends and neighbours as moderate Muslims, whose sons encountered a sheikh known for his extremist views. Commenting on the challenges of raising Muslim children in British society, one friend of the family offers: "Our children are born here and grow up here. But we couldn't pass the real Islam to them because we don't know it ourselves. We were too busy working 12-hour shifts to support the kids and family back home. We just didn't know there was a problem" (cited in Ghafour 2006, A16). Similarly, in other parts of Europe where assimilation is more highly touted than in places such as Britain and

Canada, Muslim immigrants who raised their children in the host society, educated them in its schools, and ensured they spoke its language(s) are now bemused and occasionally frightened to realize that their children are no more integrated than they are. Rather, they can be more isolated. In those parts where Muslims were imported to provide cheap labour, they may still be considered unwelcome as permanent residents and citizens (Morley 2000, 264), despite having the same skills and cultural capital as non-Muslims. The resistance these young people face has less to do with their continued difference from the majority than with their similarity. Speaking of French society, Ben Jelloun argues that the "more these young people react like young French people from their own social set, the more het-up the xenophobes get" (cited in Morley 2000, 264).

Results do vary, depending on the influences surrounding these young people. Cesari (2002, 42) points out that religion may provide a sense of belonging for youth "whose schools, political parties, trade unions, and professions have failed to provide a collective sense of common good." Smith (2002, 15) suggests that the creation of hybrid identities is of particular interest to young Muslims, many of whom have a vested interest in finding a way to accommodate their religion and their national identity, the latter being derived from their present place of residence rather than from any real or imagined homeland. Ramadan (2002, 163) agrees, suggesting that the notion of homeland may provide ideas as young Muslims meld parts of their experience into a new identity, but these ideas should not weigh down attempts at innovation and creativity: "The formation of such a culture is a pioneering endeavor, making use of European energy while taking into account various national customs and simultaneously respecting Islamic values and guidelines." This kind of pioneering is best done by committed young people who refuse to be exiled to the margins, instead finding new ways of existing. Smith (2002, 15) may well be correct when she opines that it "is the youth of the communities, members of the second and third generations, who are the vanguard in helping think through the positive relation of Islam to the adopted country," but for young people who lack employment or other means of self-fulfillment, the ensuing vacuum can sometimes be filled by religion. This religion can be transmitted by numerous sources, some of which may be strongly opposed to one another.

Karim (2010) notes that some Muslims, particularly intellectuals, are working toward a serious engagement with modernity, seeking to address the tensions and contradictions between perceived Muslim and Western values. Well aware that Muslim youth are questioning the traditions and mores of their elders, many of which are often explained vaguely under the rubric of religious necessity, self-proclaimed progressive Muslims have identified key priorities around social justice, Islamic feminism, and pluralism. Finding ways to reconcile tradition with modernity, and to cross generational and cultural bridges, may offer refuge to some young Muslims. Others, exposed to a more conservative brand of Islam, may seek a different kind of refuge, withdrawing from mainstream society and looking for new ways to become ever more religiously "pure." In the cases discussed by Lyall and Fisher (2006), this form of religion is often taught by imams from rural Pakistan, whose teachings may be infused with conservative understandings of religion and culture. After all, even though Mamdani (2004) notes correctly that the so-called Islamist fundamentalism so often discussed in the media is not really about religion but about politics, it is equally the case that many of the controversies and misunderstandings around perceived religious questions are better discussed in terms of their intersection with culture. This may be true of numerous cultures, but here it is the various forms and meanings of South Asian culture that are investigated for their confluence with the practice of Islam.

Double Binds, Multiple Marginalities: Muslim and South Asian Selves

> *Works that have focused on religion to the exclusion of larger social issues often project onto Indians religious identities (with particular focus on Hindu and Muslim) that appear internally singular and absolutely exclusive. Although some authors have challenged such monolithic portrayals, they often note only the internal schisms that divide a group into smaller groups and fail to consider the identities by which individuals can claim membership in multiple religious and other social groups. This tendency, coupled with the long-standing, predominant interest of Western scholarship in Indian religiosity, has mistakenly led some to overemphasize the considerable importance of religious belief, practice, and institutions in India at the expense of other important social factors. (Gottschalk 2000, 174)*

In a study by Bhimani (2003), one participant provides an account of her upbringing that is specific to an identity as a South Asian Muslim, yet the same may be applied to South Asians of other religions who are taught to regard cultural imperatives as religious dictates, ones that must be obeyed at all costs. Similarly, cultural standards may also be used to compel compliance from Muslims. Born in Karachi and living in Toronto, this young woman offers the following:

> My history as a Muslim woman is inextricable from my history as a South Asian woman living in the global North. As a child, and then as an adolescent, my principal experience of Islam was as a set of cultural taboos and

prescriptions that were presented as religious ones. My parents' views on things like dating, for example, had far more to do with their cultural identity as South Asians than with their religious beliefs, but they articulated their perceptions in religious terms rather than cultural ones. I don't think that the decision to couch their views in that particular way was a conscious one, but it was hardly an uncommon practice among first-generation immigrant families. (Cited in Bhimani 2003, 46)

The confusion between culture and religion is indeed common and has persisted over generations, perhaps most significantly in the South Asian and Muslim case given the fevered scrutiny of these groups. Although the global focus on Muslims is particularly well known, South Asians are hardly immune to racism and misunderstanding. Commentaries on Hindu nationalism, Sikh extremism, turbans, kirpans, arranged marriages, and domestic violence suggest confusion as much over what it means to be South Asian as what it means to be Muslim. Following 11 September 2001, harassment of even non-Muslim South Asians indicated a widespread misapprehension within the wider North American population of how to recognize specific ethnic and religious groups. More insidious, perhaps this perplexity reflects that the tendency to exoticize and isolate those who appear to be Other is hardly a thing of the past, persisting even in an avowedly multicultural society.

These Others, then, exist under a burning spotlight, balancing various identities, from those they create to those imposed on them. Although Naficy (1993, 131) quotes Maya Jaggi's use of the term "double exclusion" as well as Abdolmaboud Ansari's "dual marginality" to describe those who are isolated both in the host society and from the homeland, in this case double exclusion or dual marginality may sometimes only scratch the surface. At times, as with Hoodfar's (2003) study, the young people being examined may find themselves facing down a number of marginalizing and oppressing factors. In other cases, even "multiple exclusion" or "multiple marginality" may not be the appropriate terms to describe the liminality of diasporic young individuals, who are seen as alien within the host society and within the country (or countries) of origin. Certainly, the lives of South Asians in Canada are equally complex on a number of levels, and there is no general description that would cover the way all of them perceive their positionality.

For all that critics of multiculturalism vehemently insist that they simply want to see minorities leave their markers of difference behind and join the majority, there seems to be a widespread confusion over how to react when these minorities do acquire the language, education, and symbols of belonging. Rightly or wrongly, some Muslims and/or South Asians residing in Britain, France, and the Netherlands have demonstrated that despite living in those countries for years, they continued to feel a lack of accept-ance, fuelling the violent outbursts that made headlines around the world. Although the economic situation of these groups may be more positive in Canada, the participants in this study were well aware of their status as quasi-outsiders, embodied perhaps most simply and most pervasively in the nagging question, "But where are you *really* from?" Interestingly, then, it was not the minorities but the members of the majority who seemed unable to allow for the possibility of Muslims and South Asians being true members of the Canadian mosaic, struck perhaps by what Homi Bhabha has referred to as "the strangeness of the familiar" and the way in which this "renders cultural difference ... most problematic" (cited in Morley 2000, 265).

A retreat into difference is not the necessary outcome of such strangeness. However, as young Muslims and South Asians confront constant reminders of their incomplete integration into the national fabric, ranging from ques-tions about their origins to more stark signposts such as the banning of turbans and kirpans in some institutions and the prohibition against *hijab* (veiling) in Quebec schools, it is not surprising that many seek alternative forms of community and identity. Many may even consider this a natural part of their lives rather than a conscious construction, yet it does appear that individual and group identities can be maintained only with some degree of active effort:

> The cohesion of collective identity must be sustained *through time,* through a collective memory, through lived and shared traditions, through the sense of a common past and heritage. It must also be maintained *across space,* through a complex mapping of territories and frontiers, principles of inclu-sion and exclusion that define "us" against "them." At certain moments the established and normative bases of collective identity enter into crisis. (Morley and Robins 1995, 72, original emphasis)

Crisis and discontinuity, the effect of societal and historical ruptures, may drive some people further toward an active affiliation with their culture or religion. Rather than simply occupying the racial or ethnic category into which one is born, a passive affiliation, one identifies at a more meaningful level as a member of a particular group (Shohat and Stam 1994, 20).

For South Asian Muslims living in North America, Leonard (2002) argues that membership is coming to mean something different from what was previously the case. Although historical stereotypes of Muslims are often linked to images of the Middle East and Arabs, Leonard suggests that South Asians are in fact becoming the new leaders of Muslim communities in North America. The very fact that they, and their countries, do not share the same fractious relationship with North America as the Middle East has allowed

South Asian Muslims to integrate with more ease. South Asians are also more likely to have some experience of living in a democracy, however imperfect, and they are already aware of what it means to be minorities and of the political processes they must engage in if they want to increase their profile and standing. Leonard (2002, 233) names several instances where South Asian Muslims are beginning to assume control of major organizations, arguing that second-generation South Asian Muslims will contribute significantly to the creation of a diasporic community where specific identities will become less important than an "increasingly transglobal movement toward a 'modern' and meaningful *ummah* [Islamic community]." If Leonard is correct, this sudden emphasis on the South Asian role may also help to overcome linguistic difference within Muslim groups, a key aspect of compartmentalization and a primary obstacle to the interrogation and interpretation of religious texts, many of which are in Arabic.

It is clear that the mere fact of difference does not translate into an automatic desire to be a cultural standard-bearer. Yet, although there are multiple ways of approaching this difference, and of being defined by it, there does not appear to be a means of escape. Given this fact, Muslims of South Asian origin, living in a country that proclaims its pride in pluralism while nonetheless demonstrating apparent unease with this fact, may feel compelled to examine their selves further. This investigation does not always yield a definite answer regarding who they are, where they belong, or how to handle confusion, but it is a worthwhile process. These individuals live the theories of hybridity and creolization discussed in the previous chapter, sometimes consciously, sometimes less consciously, but rarely by mistake.

Muslims of South Asian origin, looking around, have been reminded that they are not necessarily understood by others, but they are also aware that they are not always understood by themselves and their own communities. Patel (2006, 158) points out that young South Asians, at least, may attempt to distance themselves from their roots in an effort to fit into mainstream Canadian culture, but ultimately, he suggests, they are likely to reclaim them, unable to sever strong ties to family and community: "Some even attempt to learn about their heritage through 'Bollywood' movies ... Racism and/or the realization that they are different lead many to begin the often complicated and challenging process of working through the issues around their dual or even multiple cultural identities, including ethnicity." As the following chapter discusses, this complicated process may be filled with numerous attempts to acquire information and education, but since these attempts are not always going to be effective or appropriate, the individuals in question must employ a number of resources in the complicated business of establishing, maintaining, and understanding identity. Murji and Hébert (1999, 10-11) point out the importance of numerous factors, including linguistic loss and competence as well as the freedom to choose those frag- ments of self and community that should be melted down into new, hybrid selves. Convoluted as this process of identity formation may be, there are few other options for people who do want to use their status as diasporic subjects to create a space for the articulation of new and meaningful identi- ties in which they can declare confidence rather than recycling the patterns and pitfalls of a history whose weight might become too great to bear.

5
Little Mosques and Bollywood Epics: Media and Identity Construction

Although many psychological and sociological factors can contribute to identity formation and to a sense of belonging and/or civic engagement, this book focuses specifically on media, partly because media can be powerful conveyors of nationalist and cultural sentiment and partly because media are so crucial to sustaining connections and collective memory for those living in a diaspora. Complaints abound at times about a dearth of mass media in Canada and elsewhere that speak adequately to the issues of ethnic minorities, but this situation has slowly begun to shift since the 2007 debut of *Little Mosque on the Prairie*. A situation comedy aired by Canada's public broadcaster, the Canadian Broadcasting Corporation (CBC), *Little Mosque* examines the cultural clash between Muslims and non-Muslims in a small town in Saskatchewan. Similarly, the Hindi-language film *Water* (2005), directed by Toronto filmmaker Deepa Mehta, marked Canada's first foreign-language Oscar nomination for a movie filmed in a language other than French.

Nonetheless, it is still much more likely in Canada that South Asian or Muslim audiences will find themselves viewing content that does not represent the racial, religious, or geographic realities of their lives, particularly given that so much media content shown in Canada is not generated domestically, coming more often from the United States. In a sense, then, Canadians of South Asian origin and/or Muslim background have limited recourse to a representative, indigenous form of media, in the national or cultural sense. The result is not that these groups eschew media altogether. Some adjust to North American media, perhaps due to the lack of other options or perhaps out of preference, while technology has provided new alternatives for those who desire programming about the Islamic faith or about South Asian cultures. Satellite dishes and pirated DVDs expand the range of options available, but at the same time, the changing face of Canada has also prompted a transformation in the making, marketing, and distribution of movies, with major theatre chains now screening Bollywood epics and other forms of cinema that can appeal to South Asians, such as *Bend It Like Beckham* (2003), *Bride and Prejudice* (2004), and *Slumdog Millionaire* (2008).

It is not possible here to examine all of the forms of media that have some element of appeal for young Canadian Muslims of South Asian origin, but subsequent chapters touch on the media that were identified by participants as major sources of interest, education, and socialization. News media, for instance, have often been targeted by Muslims and South Asians, among other groups, for misleading representations of minorities (van Dijk 1988, 1991; Jiwani 1993; Shoemaker and Reese 1996; Cottle 2000; Fleras and Kunz 2001; Poole 2002; Perigoe 2006), and there does seem to be evidence that these portrayals can have a deleterious effect on some readers and viewers, as Mahtani (2008) notes in her review of media representation of immigration and its audience reception. This chapter examines mass media, particularly visual media, with specific emphasis on their connection to the creation and maintenance of a national identity, their relevance in diasporas, and their significance when weighed against the interpretive powers of audiences.

Although the field of communication has moved well beyond the simple belief that audiences automatically absorb everything they see and hear, few would suggest that media have no effects at all. From corporations to nation-states, a number of forces harness the power of media in order to win public opinion – in the case of some nation-states, it might even be more accurate to say that they employ media in an effort to win their publics. Consistently conscious of the danger of losing their ties to their citizens, many nation-states do attempt to forge ties in a number of ways, a fascinating process in and of itself but one rendered even more layered and multi-dimensional by the fact that publics often engage in their own mediated dialogue with nations, whether in the form of states or other communities.

Borders and States: Mediated Imaginaries of the Nation
Ultimately, the role of media in constituting nations or nationalisms cannot be cleanly summarized, but undoubtedly media are fundamentally important in changing or confirming notions of identity, citizenship, or belonging within the framework of the nation-state. The political scientist Karl W. Deutsch (1966, 1969, 1974) saw nation-states as avenues for peace, prosperity, and growth on a global scale. In this vein, he averred that citizens must be loyal to the nation-state and work for its betterment, and if this did not occur naturally, then governments had both the right and the responsibility to use media to remind citizens of their national duties, even if this meant that individuals were subjected to propaganda or media surveillance. Ominous as this may sound, Deutsch clearly believed that democratic governments

would be using these tools only in the spirit of the collective good, and in his support of the patriotic collective, he bemoaned the media-sending and media-consuming habits of those emigrants to one nation-state who maintained a connection to another through letters, telephones, and other media. Such opposition to the use of media to foster connections to countries outside the "host society" is, as Karim (2003, 15) notes, frequently found in many governments where transborder links are seen as a sign of inability – or unwillingness – to integrate.

Opposition notwithstanding, those citizens who find their previous national identities impossible to abandon continue to discover and develop avenues for fostering them. Clifford (1997, 247) suggests that individuals living in diasporas, "once separated from homelands by vast oceans and political barriers, increasingly find themselves in border relations with the old country thanks to a to-and-fro made possible by modern technologies of transport, communication, and labor migration" (see also Sreberny-Mohammadi and Mohammadi 1994; Gillespie 1995; Cohen 1997; Kolar-Panov 2003). Whether or not Deutsch was correct to fear such ties, their increasing strength means that nationalism can no longer be discussed strictly within the territorial boundaries of the nation-state, if ever this was the case. More and more, the idea of the traditional and firmly defined nation-state must give way to the notion of an imagined community that is deterritorialized, nebulous, and dispersed. At the same time, the latter does not displace the former. In fact, the nation-state may even work to cultivate a sense of patriotic obligation among diasporic individuals or may go further and encourage the establishment of diasporic groups that retain political, economic, or cultural ties to the country of origin. The nation-state, at least a partial imaginary in itself, must contend with competing visions of nations and nationhood, visions that are sometimes held together by no more than the connections forged by various forms of media.

Although some nation-states benefit from the projects of transnational corporations, including media corporations, others fear the prospect of diminished relevance when the goal is to acquire consumers who will no longer be subject to national boundaries, perceived "as arbitrary and irrational obstacles to this reorganisation of business strategies. Audiovisual geographies are thus becoming detached from the symbolic spaces of national culture, and realigned on the basis of the more 'universal' principles of international consumer culture" (Morley and Robins 1995, 11). These corporate and state forces operate in ambivalent conjunction, occasionally with perfect cohesion and other times in opposition as their goals diverge. In the case of China, a country that has studied processes of propaganda with some care, "the project of the Chinese state to promote patriotism offshore would not have taken off without the Chinese Central Television ... now covering its satellite footprints" (Sun 2002, 4). The Internet, film documentaries, television dramas, and state broadcasting of global media events also bind this loosely interwoven community (Sun 2002, 5).

In some cases, the attempts to use media as agents of cohesion go beyond the national or the diasporic. The European Community must contend with varying levels and forms of nationalism, all juxtaposed against the influences of migration and global politics. Struggling to define its role and establish itself in conjunction with nationalist imaginaries, the European Community has enlisted media in the effort "to articulate the 'deep solidarity' of our collective consciousness and our common culture." "At the same time, they are asked to reflect the rich variety and diversity of the European nations and regions. There is the belief, or hope, that this cultural project will help to create the sense of community necessary for Europe to confront the new world order" (Morley and Robins 1995, 174). The central role allocated to media here is hardly unusual. As Sreberny-Mohammadi and Mohammadi (1994, 15) note, mass media used in the home on a regular basis "are far more subtle carriers of ideology than a state propaganda unit, because they infiltrate private space with an illusion of being value-free, yet establish very powerful mythologies."

Effective as some of these media may be, they must nonetheless conform to certain global and local realities. Fears of cultural imperialism aside, wholesale attempts at promoting a Eurocentric or Americanized global culture have rarely been wholly successful. Morley and Robins (1995, 63) point out that, in Europe at least, foreign programming is successful only when the home country fails to produce a viable alternative. The steady increase in the news channel Al-Jazeera's international popularity with Arabic-speaking populations despite opposition from some states (Miladi 2003) demonstrates the way cultural imperialism can be countered, as well as the occasional inability of nation-states to fight back effectively when media technologies have introduced alternatives to citizens. Ultimately, Cohen (1997, 196) concludes, nation-states wishing to address these issues must be able "to manage diversity while permitting free expression and the degree of social cohesion sufficient to ensure legitimacy for the state and its principal institutions."

The first step in managing diversity is admitting that attempts at building nation-states on a basic ethnic model are (literally) misplaced and misguided: "What the nationalists wanted was a territorializing of each social identity. What they have got instead ... is a chain of cosmopolitan cities and an increasing proliferation of diasporic, subnational and ethnic identities that cannot easily be contained in the nation-state system" (Cohen 1997, 196). Those who view the processes of globalization with trepidation, assuming that powerful nation-states will succeed in implementing widespread control, do not always realize the extent to which these nations have had to adapt to a new global politics. Some nation-states may simply be incapable of doing so; others have learned new techniques for survival and growth.

In the case of Asia, Ong (1999, 169) says, mass media offer hybrid images that blend East and West in a palatable way, painting migrant Asians as individuals who can transfer between different worlds but ultimately return to their places of origin carrying symbols of their success. Although media may assist in the kind of transformative subpolitics described by Beck (1994, 2000), they can also be used to create a new space of acceptance for those who might otherwise question their circumstances. Both Brah (1996) and Appadurai (1996) seem to suggest that even though media have always played a role in the formation and maintenance of nations – of the political variety and otherwise – this relationship has been fundamentally altered by developments in technology, such that books, newspapers, letters, and telephones cannot be seen as exercising the same effect as electronic media in the construction of nationalism. Morley and Robins (1995, 181) add that the postwar period has particularly demonstrated that broadcasting is the most significant form of media "in which the *imaginaire* of a national community is reflected and shaped ... the pre-eminent forum through which the democratic life of the nation state has been represented." Rey Chow adds a commentary on the importance of the visual when conveyed by electronic media with clarity and immediacy, allowing "entire histories, nations and peoples to be exposed, revealed, captured on the screen, made visible as images" (cited in Sun 2002, 54). These histories are then emblazoned in the collective memory in a distinct and lasting manner, as Dayan and Katz (1992) chronicle in their discussion of media events.

Beyond the technology itself, the global face of capital has also altered, affecting the ownership and reach of media. This transformed relationship also affects the abilities of nation-states to manage and connect with populations:

> In the informational age, getting strategic information to the global media – TV, film, newsprint, website – is controlled less by politicians than by media and corporate elites who regulate, for instance, the diversity and type of cultural images in 'a new galaxy of communication' ... In short, emergent publics are not merely an effect of mass media flows but rather translocal fields in which media and corporate networks compete (with each other and with state power) in the production, distribution, and regulation of particular kinds of images, norms, and knowledges across political spaces. (Ong 1999, 160)

The power of the nation-state, despite being challenged by developments in media technology, is rarely completely undermined by them. As Deutsch counselled, governments have at times undertaken strict management of media to create a sense of unity and to corral loyalties. Although "developments in satellite technology have meant that many people can bypass state-regulated mechanisms to interact with people and images from afar" (Sun 2002, 159), such developments have also ensured that propaganda can be broadcast more effectively than ever before, entering more homes and offering a compelling nationalist message (161-62).

The use of mass media to consolidate – or to complicate – national feeling and power is hardly new, as Shohat and Stam (1994) point out in their discussion of colonial cinema. Colonial powers supported the production and distribution of films that they hoped would impose imperial sentiment over the disparate peoples they governed (102), but the reverse has also been true. Filmmakers attempting to forge a sense of national unity in countries still shaking off the vestiges of the colonial era have turned to the cinema as well, only to be reminded that "the concept of the national is contradictory, the site of competing discourses" (285).

Naficy (2001, 100), studying diasporic and exilic filmmaking, agrees that nationalism is a complicated concept for peoples who have been doubly or triply misplaced. Moreover, "it is not enough," he contends, "that accented filmmakers have oppositional politics. They must also act oppositionally by engaging in alternative practices that have an 'organizing function.'" Gilroy (1993, 16) too discusses the organizing function that stems from media such as film, which has helped to establish a more unequivocal sense of black nationalism transcending time, space, and the outdated construct of the nation-state (see also Hall 1994, 401). For Naficy and Gilroy, then, media can be powerful forces for change, whereas Shohat and Stam (1994, 31) are more ambivalent about media's ability to create a sense of nation if this reinforces patterns of global domination, with more economically powerful nations or transnational organizations exerting cultural influence over weaker partners. These concerns are clearly applicable in this study, where a massive Indian film industry allows minimal breathing room for alternative forms of cinema and overshadows neighbouring industries, yet that same Indian industry also feels the pressure of competition from popular global products, such as those created by Hollywood.

A Whole New World: Media and Diaspora

If the connection between nation-states and media has grown increasingly complicated and difficult to summarize neatly, the removal of borders only renders this discussion more nebulous. In many cases, the relationship between media and nation, particularly for those living in a diaspora, can be a dialectical one, where power can shift back and forth and where the participants crucially rely on one another. Sinclair and Cunningham (2001, 11) note that both diaspora and broadcasting are based on the same model of movement and border crossings: "The concept of 'broadcasting' is based on precisely the same organically rooted metaphor of the scattering of seed, implying both dispersal and propagation." Diaspora is not solely a creation of media, but its close relationship to media rests at least partly on the fact that diasporas often use and develop media to assist in the necessary business of strengthening ties, staying informed, and politically mobilizing. At the very least, "diasporas are disproportionately advantaged by" advances in media technology (Cohen 1997, 175) and may often be leaders in technological change, adopting or developing new media to reach their widely dispersed audiences (Karim 2003, 12). Ackah and Newman (2003, 212) add that although media such as information communication technologies should not be viewed as the means whereby cohesive communities are forged out of thin air, these technologies may, and often do, assist in reinforcing relations that already exist. If these media help to strengthen cultural values and a sense of diasporic belonging, they may be seen as operating in conjunction with more territorialized forces.

In contrast, other territorialized populations compensate for their inability to travel by watching television shows depicting world cities: "Viewing representations of these places at once fulfills and stimulates – to some extent – the wanderlust of homebound audiences. Moreover, watching and identifying with characters living in faraway foreign places provides, to some extent, a mediated experience of desired cosmopolitanism" (Sun 2002, 70; for a similar analysis, see Mandaville 2001, 16). Stories of dispersal and exile, so difficult to normalize in some societies and yet such a fact of life, may come to seem more common and thus more acceptable through these media, while also introducing non-migrants to the hardships or challenges suffered by their travelling family and friends. These are the means of communication available for those whose lives are so decidedly transnational that, as Sun (2002, 159) says, "'home' is often where a television set, computer terminal, or DVD player is." Shohat and Stam (1994, 7) note that these means of communication "'deterritorialize' the process of imagining communities. And while the media can destroy community and fashion solitude by turning spectators into atomized consumers or self-entertaining monads, they can also fashion community and alternative affiliations."

Although there is a less political tinge to Mandaville's (2001) notion of travelling Islam, in which young Muslims who embrace Islam do not see the need to return to a homeland, there is a similar level of empowerment that is possible only in a diaspora. For these young people, Islam itself becomes the place they wish to inhabit (121-22), and mass media help to foster debate, discussion, and some sense of unity that may create an Islam uniquely suited to the challenges of living in a diaspora (132-35). These technologies can be appropriated by Islamist political agendas, creating the kind of conflicts

Turner (2000) hopes will dissolve in a cosmopolitan era, but they can also promote heterogeneity within the community and provide the "basis of a new framework within which Muslims might reimagine the umma [Islamic community]" (Mandaville 2001, 175).

This aligns with Appadurai's (1996, 197) suggestion that the "politics of diaspora, at least within the past decade, have been decisively affected by global electronic transformations," which provide "part of the engaged cultural and political literacy that diasporic persons bring to their spatial neighborhoods." As migration increases, cities and states gradually assume a different mien, propelled by the collision and collusion of global and local forces. Unable to untangle themselves from one another, these cities and states soon discover that "their significance resides more in their global than in their national roles" (Cohen 1997, 167). In some places, a global culture emerges and infiltrates a variety of local spaces – it may be affected by the local, but some characteristics are nonetheless the same from one place to the next. Although size may be one of the simplest factors that affects a diaspora's cultural influence, Cohen (1997) suggests that there is also something intrinsic to diaspora itself that allows its members to make such an impact on various communities: "Many members of diasporic communities are bi- or multilingual ... Often they are better able to discern what their own group shares with other groups and when its cultural norms and social practices threaten majority groups" (170). This may well be the reason, he offers, that diasporic groups often have strong representation in various forms of arts and media, as well as in more conventional areas of achievement such as business or science (170).

Media in diaspora, then, take a variety of forms. Desai (2004, 43), speaking of diasporic film, notes that diasporic media need not assume any particular politics or even a spirit of opposition. Yet, in the films she discusses, there are some recurring themes that have weight and meaning for those whose lives have been affected by a history of movement. She identifies a constant refrain around the ideas of difference, displacement, and loss. These notions certainly echo lived experience, but they also represent one side of a continuing dialogue, a conversation between those media that speak consciously to members of diasporas and those that ignore diasporas' increasingly visible presence. The emergence of a wave of diasporic filmmakers such as Gurinder Chadha, Deepa Mehta, and Mira Nair, who talk at length about culture shock, about transformations of culture within spaces and over generations, and about racism, can be attributed in part to their perception of a vacuum within media at large. Although some aspects of Bollywood and Indian culture appear to have entered the mainstream, many others have been ignored or repressed for years, leaving South Asians and Muslims living in the diaspora to consume media that do not speak to their lives and realities.

Bridging the Gap? Little Islands, Big Media

> *As Mira Kamdar has written: "India was far, far away. Airline tickets were expensive. There was no direct dial international calling, no fax machines-cum-answering machines attached to people's phones, no e-mail. We were a little island of India in a vast land of* Leave It to Beaver.*" (Kumar 2002, 168)*

Even though culture has been used at times to offer a superficial nod to inclusion in the nation-state, genuine acceptance and appreciation of the media enjoyed by minority groups can indicate a growing level of cosmopolitanness in the host society (Sinclair et al. 2001, 63). The opposite pattern occurs as well, although slightly differently, with immigrants showing interest in the host society's media "as a means of access to mainstream language and culture" (66). In her study of advertising images in India, Fernandes (2000, 616) argues that Western-based transnational corporations are finally realizing that global success depends on how well they are able to address national imaginaries and cultural nuances: "The production of meanings of the global occurs through the idiom of the nation. Moreover, this depiction of the local and the national does not attempt to mask or disguise the transnational organization of production relations." Cases such as these, resolved through an emphasis on hybridity, may indicate a growing move toward the self-confrontation Beck (1994, 5) cites as an essential by-product of reflexive modernization.

Hybridity seems to be one defence in an environment where North American and European cultures are seen as overwhelmingly influential. It is hardly possible to ignore these cultures entirely, in the same way that the global finds it increasingly difficult to ignore the local. However, unless or until a satisfactory resolution is achieved, there can be a sense of isolation or alienation experienced by those who feel that they are not sufficiently addressed by the cultural products of the society in which they live. This is particularly pertinent in the case of the young Canadians studied here, whose television and film are most often produced by the United States and thus represent neither their ethnic identities nor their national realities. Even in Canadian-made productions, diversity is hardly a given, as evidenced by Miller's (2005) historical account of Canadian television. Reactions to this may differ, but it is not surprising that the active cultivation of alternatives may be one response. Kumar (2002) suggests that the popularity of diasporic media is easily explained when juxtaposed against the lack of representation and acknowledgment that minority groups experience outside of their places of origin. Discussing Indian fiction written in English, Kumar notes the yearning of some diasporic individuals to consume this literature given that "they have not had the stories of their lives told" (26).

Although Kumar's example indicates one sense in which South Asian minorities, at least, may find a medium that speaks to their realities, it still represents a specialized niche, one that does not allow them to see themselves reflected in a mainstream setting. Growing up as members of a society in which they speak the language and attend schools, they may question why their existence is not depicted in mass media, particularly visual media such as film and television. The consequences can be severe. As Ali (2003, 34-35) notes in her study of mixed-race children, popular culture plays a key role in helping the young to understand race, ethnicity, and their own relative positionality in society, even if this understanding is imperfect or fractured. The absence of positive depictions of minorities only strengthens the tendency to see – literally – whiteness as "universal and natural" (Agnew 2007, 17), such that whiteness assumes the defining appearance and understanding of Canada (21), as it does of America and Europe.

In the introductory chapter of this book, I reflected on the aversion I once felt to images of South Asian men and women who did not look sufficiently modern; only with the passage of time and exposure to the experiences of others did I realize, reluctantly, that my aversion may have been a natural outgrowth of the fact that I had been socialized to accept images of white North Americans as the norm. I was already a minority in a society that was mainly white, and I had grown up on a steady diet of mainstream media, so I had limited access to images of South Asian women who were admired and considered beautiful. Even when I did stumble on Bollywood cinema in the 1990s and discovered South Asian actresses who had captured titles in international beauty pageants, they bore limited resemblance to the dark-eyed, dark-haired, voluptuous women that I remembered from classic Indian cinema. The greatest celebrities were increasingly slender, light-eyed, and light-skinned – which may have been what allowed me to relate to them, as they combined a South Asian heritage with the features of my childhood beauty icons – yet their features did not necessarily foster greater acceptance of my own appearance, which remains unmistakably South Asian. The constant dyeing of hair and the occasional wearing of coloured contact lenses among many of my contemporaries cause me to wonder if this lack of acceptance remains widespread.

Nonetheless, the influence of Bollywood stars still offers some alternative to the mainstream, however problematic that alternative may be. As Bollywood has become more widely accepted, there does seem to be, as I have suggested previously, a greater tendency for young women in Canada, the United States, and the United Kingdom to embrace Indian fashions and jewellery and to model themselves at times on the appearance of Indian actresses. The recent success of *Slumdog Millionaire* (2008), winner of the 2009 Academy Award for Best Picture, may also offer young women a new role model through the increased profile of the previously unknown star,

Freida Pinto, although it is worth noting that to a certain extent, Pinto meets the same beauty ideals as Aishwarya Rai and Rani Mukherjee. She is fine-boned and relatively light-skinned and that in the film she seems both light-haired and light-eyed; indeed, at several points in the movie, the camera angles and lighting seem to accentuate this appearance, although this may not be intentional.

The kind of confusion and discomfort engendered by lack of representative images in mass media is hardly unique to young people of South Asian origin. Speaking of the African American community, the rapper Ice Cube notes the damage that can be done to youth by a society whose media refuse to acknowledge minorities. Complaints of unattainable images on film and television abound, focusing on impossibly slender, young, or otherwise attractive people who do not reflect society as a whole. When that kind of unattainability is magnified, offering a vision of blondeness or whiteness that cannot possibly be replicated by the viewer, the possibilities for developing self-hatred and a negative self-image may multiply. No wonder, says Ice Cube, that young African Americans, for instance, may do their best to downplay their blackness in any way possible, trying to change their hair, eyes, or features to reflect the supposed reality captured on television and film screens across America (cited in hooks 1994, 127). Although Ice Cube is speaking of a specific group, arguably the shadow effects of such media images can also be seen in the young people in Handa's (2003) and Gillespie's (1995) studies, who proclaim pride in their identity yet sometimes seek to look as much like the majority as possible.

This effect is perhaps sharpened by the fact that it is not simply mainstream media that turn a blind eye to difference; a number of observers, as well as participants in this study, have noted that even cinema and television that attempt to demonstrate sensitivity to cultural issues can fall into the trap of presenting a homogeneous vision of the world. Dei's (2008, 19) discussion of the 2004 Oscar-winning film *Crash*, written by a Canadian and lauded for its seemingly realistic portrayal of racism, suggests that even this well-meaning film serves only to reinforce stereotypes and to foster a discourse of race relations that denies inequality and agency: "Identity and representation are not mere performances but rather relations of power with real and differential material consequences for variously located bodies." He goes on to add, "anti-racist practice also requires that we identify those moments when even racialized bodies are working with dominant conceptions of difference in making invidious distinctions" (22), a comment that is intended to apply primarily to *Crash* but that is equally relevant to other well-meaning, quasi-political films. *Water*, Deepa Mehta's probing look at the poor treatment of widows in some parts of India, presents as its heroine the light-skinned, light-eyed Lisa Ray, and Gurinder Chadha's *Bride and Prejudice* (2004) is headlined by the equally fair-skinned, grey-eyed Aishwarya Rai. This is hardly unique to Indian productions, or even to Asian cultural productions in general, although the ties to the caste system – where lighter means better – may be specific to certain Indian cultures. In the North American context, the concern with skin colour represents a long-standing problem in African American entertainment, where the performers considered to have the most European looks (i.e., light skin, fine bones, slender physique) have the most industry currency, a phenomenon that seems to be especially noticeable among females. Examples include former Miss America Vanessa Williams, Oscar winner Halle Berry, singer Beyoncé Knowles, and actress Jada Pinkett Smith. This is not to say that these performers succeed only because of their appearance, but it is possible that appearance offers them an advantage in comparison to their darker-skinned counterparts.

However, problems such as the nature of representation may seem like irrelevant quibbles when so many groups struggle for representation of any kind. A 1994 survey of British viewers found that "members of ethnic minorities were considerably less satisfied than the general population with the programme services provided on terrestrial television" (Morley 2000, 122), a finding echoed in a subsequent 1999 report by Annabelle Sreberny and Karen Ross (cited in Morley 2000, 123). If this dissatisfaction was visible in the United Kingdom, where South Asians, at least, have been recognized in programs such as the sitcom *Goodness Gracious Me*, it is quite possible that similar sentiments can be found throughout North America, especially Canada, which so rarely produces successful indigenous programming. North American programming does make more of an effort to acknowledge minorities than was previously the case, but nonetheless criticism of these efforts can be intense if a minority character is brought in as a perceived token, as in the case of Parminder Nagra's British South Asian doctor on *ER*, who lamented her confused identity at nearly every turn in her first season, or even *Little Mosque on the Prairie*, which carefully includes a progressive imam, an educated woman in *hijab* (veiling), a stern traditionalist man, a white convert, and a black Muslim woman (confined to doing her best work behind the kitchen counter, no less). Major hits such as *24* have danced around tokenism, presenting an extraordinary number of South Asians and Muslims who engage in terrorist plots, even if they lead apparently all-American lives, while simultaneously fending off accusations of racism by offering the occasional Muslim and/or South Asian hero, loyal to America and fiercely opposed to terrorism. Although these heroes often die or disappear, their temporary presence is used as a countermeasure against critics who see *24* as fear-mongering and discriminatory.

Television and film produced within North America and Europe are often criticized for their inability to understand not just minorities but also, more specifically, those living in the developing world. Shohat and Stam (1994, 31) note that it is still common to perceive a kind of one-way global media flow, wherein North America exports tremendous amounts of highly influ-ential media but receives very little in return. What exceptions there are, such as Bollywood cinema, telenovelas, or Hong Kong action movies, tend to be produced by transnational corporations. Nonetheless, they argue, prognostications of media imperialism and the eradication of local culture are overly simplistic. Some media industries in the developing world have arrived at a level of significant influence in their own countries and in other regions, creating "reverse currents" in this overall media flow and also dem-onstrating that a strong local culture is entirely capable of thriving alongside a global one.

At the same time, Johnson (2007) points out the degree to which film-makers in multicultural countries such as Canada have become increasingly internationalist in their focus, to the extent that Toronto-based filmmaker Deepa Mehta received an Oscar nomination for her Canadian movie *Water*, filmed in India and in Hindi. Directors such as Mehta have helped pave the way for Canada's film industry to follow a path already adopted by some of the country's most successful novelists; they tell stories with a strong global component while seeing their work as Canadian. The producer and director of *Partition* (2007), a Muslim-Sikh love story set in South Asia, describes the scope and setting of his movie by saying, "It's a totally Canadian film" (cited in Johnson 2007, 55). In light of the earlier discussion on the significance of visual media and appearance, however, it is worth noting that this Can-adian film, which explores Muslim and Sikh history, features an actress of Chinese Dutch descent, Kristin Kreuk, in the lead role of a young South Asian woman, despite the existence of many South Asian actresses who would have presented a more realistic appearance. Although it is possible that Kreuk was believed to be the best actress for the part, trumping the dissonance of a lead South Asian character played by a young woman who appears white, the South Asian viewer, staring back at Kreuk and at the white Neve Campbell, the only other female lead, is left with the uncomfortable sense that "multicultural," "internationalist," and "Canadian" are merely euphemisms for whiteness as usual.

This may call into question Hussain Amarshi's claim that there "is a deep desire, given the cultural makeup we have, for films that are more inter-nationalist" (cited in Johnson 2007, 55). Amarshi, whose Toronto-based Mongrel Media has helped to distribute films such as *Water* and *A Touch of Pink* (2004), says he's "loath to classify the country's South Asian cinema as such," adding that "*Water* could not have been made in any other country" (55). Arguably, then, audiences are now treated to a more diverse offering of films and entertainment than was previously the case, but even so, I suspect that this plurality is far from becoming the norm. If it does manage to become the rule rather than the exception, it may speak to a new mean-ing of what it is to be Canadian and what is meant by national productions.

Although there is plenty of evidence to track production and distribution of these different sorts of media, the reception of such texts is a far more open question and constitutes the basis for this study. Debates over the meaning and themes of media are rendered irrelevant in the absence of proof regarding the way these media are read, and there are far more ways of reading than may be assumed.

In Your Eyes: Audiences Reading Media

> *More persons throughout the world see their lives through the prisms*
> *of the possible lives offered by mass media in all their forms. That is,*
> *fantasy is now a social practice; it enters, in a host of ways, into the*
> *fabrication of social lives for many people in many societies.*
> *(Appadurai 1991, 198)*

Early models of communication flows tended to assume passive and simple acceptance of media messages by the audience, but key studies indicating that media users do not always act as expected led to a gradual shift. Katz (1987), perhaps one of the greatest proponents of an active audience, notes that media effects do exist, but they may be far more limited than previously thought. One key reason for this is selectivity: audiences can in fact be relatively selective about what media they consume and how they interpret the information they receive. In such cases, media may work more to reinforce pre-existing beliefs than to create new ones or to alter them. Many scholars do agree that a model of absolute media effects, in which a passive audience merely absorbs the messages of the all-powerful media, is outdated. However, there is no definite agreement regarding alternative models. Some theories of critical research contend that one must still hesitate to attribute too much power to the audience, given the vast economic resources available to producers. The Frankfurt School, for instance, continued to believe that the media maintained the social order, feeding meaningless entertainment to the masses and distracting them from reality and the possibilities of individual critical thought.

Other theories do take power disparities into account, but they also acknowledge the diversity within audiences. For instance, Ang (2001) notes the influence of David Morley's 1978 and 1980s research regarding reception of the British show *Nationwide*. Discovering that people in different economic and social positions interpreted the same television show in a wide variety of ways, Morley began to question the then-prevailing preoccupation with the messages embedded in texts. Although Morley did not rule out the significance of media messages, he did conclude that analyses of media must recognize that meaning depends to some extent on the context of reception.

The release of *The Nationwide Audience* (Morley 1980) coincided with an overall shift in the social sciences and humanities toward a more audience-centred approach, best exemplified by the 1960s and 1970s rise of British cultural studies and its most famous practitioners, such as Raymond Williams and Stuart Hall. In an often-cited article on encoding and decoding, it is Hall (1980) who suggests a typology for the ways that messages embedded in media may be read. Offering the possibility that readers or viewers may interpret media messages exactly as the producer intended (a dominant reading), in complete opposition, or with a certain amount of selectivity and criticism (negotiated), Hall argues that both sides of the production/consumption equation must be taken into account. Hall's model becomes particularly significant in this study, where participants alluded to all three possible readings, partly confirming Desai's (2004, 114) theory that diasporic "viewers do not eagerly and passively consume ideologies and products exported by the homeland nation but actively produce meanings through translation, negotiation, and adaptation." Ang (2001, 181) suggests that the publication of Morley's book (1980) provided an important acknowledgment within cultural studies that television viewing is a practice involving active production of meaning by viewers. Nonetheless, this does not translate into a concession that all power resides with the audience.

The labels for perspectives vary, but critical researchers have in general gradually allowed for some audience authority while maintaining a belief in the influence and power of producers and of some economic and social structures. As Kellner (1995, 5) notes, even Stuart Hall's article "Encoding/decoding" (1980) with its attention to receivers, maintained cultural studies' original emphasis on "political economy, process of production and distribution, textual products, and reception by the audience." Acknowledging that media can be used in a variety of ways, Morley and Robins (1995, 127) advocate a cautious compromise, suggesting that we "must balance an acceptance that audiences are in certain respects active in their choice, consumption and interpretation of media texts, with a recognition of how that activity is framed and limited, in its different modalities and varieties, by the dynamics of cultural power."

Studies like Morley's (1980) help to indicate the individual factors, such as gender, race, and class, that underlie interpretation, while Radway's (1984) work on romance readers has affirmed the importance of these factors and of the context in which consumption takes place. In Radway's case, her readers recognized the formulaic nature of much of the material they read, yet they felt there was importance and relief in the act of reading itself and saw themselves as active in their ability to reject demeaning narratives. However, Radway's readers did not provide any alternatives to the patriarchal, capitalist machine. They continued to make its existence possible and even valorized it. Studies such as Radway's suggest a split regarding both the possibilities for resistance and the dangers of patronizing media users who may be able to reconcile their behaviour in a way that makes sense to them and adds meaning to their lives.

To a certain extent, what is taking place here is a layering of interpretations; the scholar researching reception relies on the audience's explanation of its readings and then suggests some possible meanings for these. What remains clear is that numerous possible interpretations exist, as demonstrated through Ien Ang's 1985 study of the television show *Dallas* and its reception by Dutch audiences, which suggested individuals actively create their own meanings while still retaining an understanding of the storylines (cited in Lorimer and McNulty 1996, 152). Similarly, Elihu Katz and Tamar Liebes's own study of viewers of *Dallas* produced a smorgasbord of readings, with Israeli audiences of Russian, Arab, Moroccan, or American origin approaching the specifics of the story very differently (cited in Martin 1997, 141-44). These readings appeared to suggest that there is indeed a cultural difference that influences audience interpretation, an interesting finding for this research, which is very much concerned with the overlap between reception and national identity.

Certainly, the connection between national identity and reception is not lost on media producers, some of whom consciously manipulate feelings of patriotism. In the case of media targeted at Muslims and South Asians, national identity may take on a new meaning. Muslims have no unitary state, and South Asians belong to a region that is diverse, fragmented, and may not have a genuine connection to people who have never been there. Indeed, a deepening connection to Bollywood within the diaspora does not necessarily indicate a similar motivation among all audience members: "Whereas for some Bollywood might be a means of reconnecting with a homeland, [Manas] Ray argues that for Fijian Indians (or Tanzanian or Trinidadian Indians) India remains an imagined entity and Indian films function as introduction to a whole way of life about which they know little and have experienced even less" (Larkin 2003, 174). This complicated state of affairs, as well as a new interest in Muslims and South Asians around the world, means that media offerings to these groups are equally complex, providing attention to patriotism but also to a sense of loss, confusion, and displacement.

Bringing It Home: South Asians, Muslims, and Media

Media offerings to minorities in Canada may take a variety of forms, including books, newspapers, magazines, websites, movies, and television. Not all of these can be discussed here, although each is important in its own way. Books by authors of South Asian origin, for instance, have done very well throughout the diaspora, and Canada has some literary stars of its own in this regard, including Anita Rau Badami, Rohinton Mistry, Shyam Selvadurai, and M.G. Vassanji. However, although books may provide an educational, moving, or familiar experience, they may not be able to speak fully to Ice Cube's earlier observation that the inability to see oneself reflected in electronic mass media can have deleterious effects on self-esteem and confidence. Even though mainstream television and film have made improvements in this regard, it is still rare for Canadian Muslims of South Asian origin to see themselves reflected positively in most electronic mass media, and as noted above, this lack can be crucial to the formation of a positive identity and sense of self.

Those young people who do wish to see cinematic representations of South Asians or Muslims work around the lack of mainstream options by seeking out alternative sources of information and entertainment. Advances in technology, such as satellite dishes, DVDs, and the Internet, facilitate ethnic narrowcasting, "a manifestation of the emergence of new media sites that address the experience of hybridity, migration and diaspora, speaking to the disruptive spaces of postcolonialism" (Sinclair et al. 2001, 44). These new media sites may appear marginal at times, such as the websites and satellite programs about religious issues accessed by some of the young Muslims in Mandaville's (2001) research, but their effect can be powerful within specific groups. Moreover, their use does not preclude the consumption of more mainstream forms of information and entertainment. The 2007 premiere of CBC's *Little Mosque on the Prairie* is perhaps the most mainstream example of all, offering a nationally broadcast show that aims to portray Muslims within the context of that idyllic Canadian setting, the Prairies.

Like Muslims, South Asians have access to a wide variety of specialized media. Most commonly, South Asians living in Canada have drawn on a global system of circulating videos or DVDs to view entertainment that would not be widely available in theatres or on television, such as Bollywood films or other movies with reference to South Asian culture. However, as the South Asian population has grown, it has become more common – although not widespread – to see Bollywood films in theatres, as well as alternative films that tackle issues of identity in a relatively less traditional way, such as *East Is East* (1999), *American Desi* (2001), and *Bend It Like Beckham* (2003), which have been equally popular among youth. Both genres command a loyal following and offer commentary, however implicit, on cultural values, national ideologies, and belonging.

Although some of the participants in this study indicated that they did not see any particular difference between Bollywood films and these alternative movies, Desai (2004) offers a clear division, one that I consider justified given the consistent distinguishing marks of most Bollywood films in terms of production, distribution, and content. Bollywood is not the only form of

Indian cinema, but it is the best-known form, based on its enormous commercial success, its widespread distribution, its carefully fostered star system, and the song-and-dance formula that can draw in viewers as easily as it can alienate them. In contrast, movies like *Mississippi Masala* (1991), *American Desi* (2001), and *Monsoon Wedding* (2001) can be identified, using Desai's (2004, 40) terminology, as South Asian diasporic films, which "are located in relation to the expanding (dominant but not hegemonic) power of Bollywood, which has sought to challenge the global domination of Hollywood cinema by positioning itself as a global cinema." Their storylines do not necessarily conform to a particular formula, nor do they have the constant emphasis on romance or the musical sequences found in many Bollywood films. Desai's use of the term "diasporic film" is not intended to suggest that Bollywood films are not also diasporic to some degree or that there are no spaces of overlap; indeed, she acknowledges that "South Asian diasporas are one of the largest sites of consumption of Bollywood films and are considered a distribution territory by the Indian film industry" (40).

However, diasporic films do not follow the same patterns of production as Bollywood, sometimes emerging due to the persistence of a single filmmaker's efforts, without significant financial backing or the lure of a well-known Indian star. As some of these independent filmmakers have become successful, they have tended to demonstrate their own moves toward hybridity, with *Salaam Bombay* (1988) and *Mississippi Masala* (1991) director Mira Nair plunging into a remake of *Vanity Fair* (2004), starring Reese Witherspoon, and *Bhaji on the Beach* (1993) and *Bend It Like Beckham* (2003) director Gurinder Chadha attempting to merge past and present, Britain and India in *Bride and Prejudice* (2004), featuring Indian, British, and American stars. Significantly, the latter film starred one of Bollywood's most popular actresses, Aishwarya Rai, a former Miss Universe and current L'Oréal model, who has spoken openly about her desire to attain broader appeal in order to provide the world with a sophisticated, educated image of India that may counteract ignorance and stereotypes. Given Rai's undoubted success as a Bollywood star, it is interesting that she apparently feels compelled to branch out into other fields to truly promote contextualized depictions of India and Indian culture.

Diasporic films are labelled as such because they speak, or attempt to speak, to the issues that are relevant to audiences living in diasporas. The filmmakers themselves may occupy a place in a diaspora, and production may span a number of regions. However, as the diasporic audience has become a more important source of Bollywood revenue, popular Indian cinema has itself assumed some of the characteristics of diasporic film. Unlike many diasporic films, however, Bollywood films have a strong national base and, accordingly, much of their content valorizes India – in ways discussed more specifically in subsequent chapters. Desai (2004, 113) suggests that these recurring, dominant themes around nationalism in Bollywood film provide that cinema's "only mode in which diasporic spectatorship is currently imagined and discussed. However, audience members, building on Stuart Hall's propositions, may construct differing relationships with these national narratives, adopting dominant, negotiated, or resistant modes of decoding in relation to (dis)identification processes." Interestingly, Pakistan's Lahore-based film industry, nicknamed Lollywood, was rarely mentioned by participants in this study, due partly to a lack of availability and middling production values, but generally there seemed to be an overall consensus that Bollywood is perhaps one of the most influential venues for the promotion of a mainstream South Asian culture.

Longevity, effective financing, and a well-established distribution infrastructure may be some of the reasons for this influence. Content, however, is another. Although there are many criticisms of popular Indian films, including the vast disparities in quality within the numerous films produced every year, there are also some consistencies. Bollywood film provides detailed, pictorial information about South Asian rituals and culture, information that is then put to extensive use by many individuals in the diaspora who replicate these rituals in their own weddings and celebrations. It is fairly common, although certainly not universal, for South Asian weddings in the diaspora to be at least partly modelled on the themes, songs, or fashions of a particularly popular film, something that is enabled chiefly through Bollywood's visual nature and emphasis on aesthetics. Although some rituals and practices can be observed in everyday life, the visual portrayal of these in film may reinforce the appeal and importance.

In diasporas, rituals are not always reprised in exactly the same manner as they might have been two or three generations previously. This is partly a function of time but also one of space. Sometimes exact facilities and resources are not available to maintain such practices, and occasionally families may choose to discard those rituals in an effort to integrate or to evolve. At the same time, there is an equal chance that families who wish to hold on to their memories and their cultural knowledge are at a disadvantage in terms of knowing current practices in South Asia. Occasional visits, e-mail messages, and telephone calls may not offer the same window onto the homeland as that offered by cinema, which can display visual images and explanations of the rites and customs that accompany life events, even if these rites and customs are not necessarily the same for each regional, religious, or ethnic group. Desai (2004, 221) notes this phenomenon in her own audience study of second-generation viewers:

> Several second-generation South Asian-American viewers in my forthcoming study on the consumption of Indian cinema reported that the films function performatively and pedagogically in that they teach rituals, traditions, and

social practices as well as identifications. These films are ethnographic and pedagogical for multiple audiences. In addition to Western viewers, South Asian diasporic viewers also may view these films as documents recording South Asian or Indian cultural practices.

Desai goes on to note the other ways that such films may inform the lives and habits of South Asians living in the diaspora. Bollywood films are the heart of a vast enterprise that includes magazines, live variety shows, television and radio programming, websites, audio recordings, DVDs, and clothing. This last feature, Desai (2004, 221) notes, is especially useful in teaching young South Asians to be consistent consumers, as some viewers regularly seek out the glamorous – and expensive – clothes and jewellery worn by their favourite stars in recent movies. Although the constant weddings and changing trends depicted in popular Bollywood films may promote a high level of consumerism, they also offer a challenge to the fashion trends popular in the West. Adil, a participant from Toronto, spoke at length about the racism he experienced as a youngster growing up in the suburbs and about the way that Bollywood has now helped to educate people about Indian culture and style:

> I think Bollywood has put Indian people on the map. I can remember growing up and people calling me Paki, where's your turban, where's your dot on your head, and you were made to feel really crappy about being Indian, but when people started to appreciate Indian culture, became more open-minded ... people admire our food now, the way our women dress, the way the guys dress, so it's obviously a kind of positive thing.

The intense interest some young South Asians invest in Indian fashions may demonstrate an identity-affirming embrace of alternative cultural norms, although this is somewhat undermined by the ambivalent response of Gillespie's (1995) and Handa's (2003) subjects when asked about appropriate times and spaces for wearing South Asian clothes. Ambivalence, in fact, may be the one factor that consistently recurs in studies of Bollywood and popular Indian culture.

Bollywood itself, despite its self-assumed role as the cinematic bastion of Indian community, is a hybrid entity, and second-generation migrants are the same, demonstrating "dynamic hybridising tendencies easily sufficient to withstand the community's displacement into a Western culture" (Ray 2001, 182). Ray describes multiple migrants, people who may be especially inclined toward the fusion of numerous cultures and cultural products as they sew together an identity out of the fabrics they encounter. Music offers an obvious example of this, with digital technology providing a method for individuals living in diasporas to create their own creolized forms of song.

It is not only Bollywood films that can attain the status of classics but also their songs. The soundtrack of a film may cause people to return for multiple viewings or may serve as the background music for events such as weddings and birthdays.

Kumar (2002, 198) suggests that South Asian musical forms transmute into something different in the diaspora, with digital sampling and remixes transforming songs of the past: "Remembered songs of the parents, in Hindi or Punjabi or Bengali, are altered through repetition, scratching, and mixing, so that nostalgia is turned into an affect that is wholly different and new." Ray (2001, 173), writing mainly of Fiji Indians, also notes the tendency of their youth to rely on remixes:

> Fiji Indian young people use a wholly hybridised genre like the remixes to fashion a discourse of authenticity. On the one hand, they will deploy the remixes as part of syncretic metropolitan culture and thus break out of the cartography that views their culture as *ethnic*. On the other hand, they perceive these remixes (for them, an essentially diasporic phenomenon) as part of their attempt to promote Indian popular music by making it contemporary. (Original emphasis)

There are, then, competing imperatives at work here: unlike those migrants who may believe that authenticity is best captured by leaving cultural products untouched and unaltered, these young people try to create a form that can retain popularity in modern times and across ethnic groups. At the same time, a diaspora can sometimes offer a space in which the old becomes new again and gains widespread acceptance. Ray (2001, 174), for example, points out that bhangra, a rural and masculine music phenomenon in the Punjab, took on a radically new cast in places such as London and then spread to other countries such as Australia; mixed with pop, reggae, and rap, bhangra took on a new life, providing one significant instance of what Ray calls "the diaspora reworking the homeland." Although it would certainly be overstating the case to suggest that the South Asian diaspora reworks Bollywood, it is hardly surprising that Bollywood is at least aware of its diasporic audience and makes some adjustments accordingly.

Responses, Reactions, Resistance: Reading Media

Frequently criticized for its lavish borrowing from the Western musical oeuvre, Bollywood has responded to the dispersal of some of its audience by incorporating even more sounds: "From being mostly a combination of Indian folk music, light classical Indian music and the standard Western popular music, Bollywood now freely mixes rap, Latin American and Black music with traditional Indian music" (Ray 2001, 172-73). This is simply a musical example, but in Bollywood cinema, music and narrative content are closely linked, and both can be incorporated into the diasporic lifestyle. They do, as Ray and Kumar note, function in part to evoke nostalgia, but they also evolve and transform to meet the competing demands of various audience members, and these demands may indeed be markedly different. India produces roughly 700 to 1,000 films a year (Shohat and Stam 1994, 29), and although the Indian film industry is far more heterogeneous than one might guess, in commercial terms Bollywood continues to lead the pack. As a way of maintaining this status, Bollywood has acknowledged the challenges of the diaspora and the demands of hybridity, yet it has also, as the following chapter discusses, found its own methods for ensuring that those demands are met only if they enforce a commitment to Indian culture as envisioned by that industry. The simultaneous and intersecting tendencies of Bollywood and its viewers or listeners to work toward the creation of popular hybrid forms make it difficult to assess whether the efforts of youth in diasporas to create their own cultural capital will always be commodified.

Some directors and producers do make a sincere effort to address the meaning of migration and hybridity, functioning as the filmic version of what Pico Iyer has described as a seasoned translator, one "who commutes between cultures and writes from a space of 'in-betweenness.' As hybrid souls, these writers give voice to hyphenated identities" (cited in Kumar 2002, 178). However, in many cases, Bollywood uses its position as a way to call members of the diaspora home, to remind them of what it perceives as an essential Indian identity. As Karim (2003, 10) notes, despite the best efforts of diasporas to use media in the re-creation of a new, more fluid understanding of home, electronic media can be used equally frequently in the attempt to reterritorialize diasporas, their tentacles reaching those populations that might otherwise be outside of a country's orbit. There are many possible examples to be examined here, but the focus is on Bollywood because of its consistent emphasis on nationalism, its attempts to promote a certain kind of culture, and its long-standing global appeal, even as times change and people disperse. As the following chapter notes, Bollywood has experienced mixed success in addressing change and dispersal while presenting clear messages about the ultimate consequences of wandering too far away from a purportedly authentic culture. Although much of the emphasis in this study remains on the interpretation of these messages, it is worth examining the content of Bollywood at greater length to assess why it has the myriad effects that it does and why, in a hypermediated landscape, it manages to adapt continuously to a hybrid existence without surrendering its insistence that identity need not be constructed. For young South Asians, wherever they may live or however removed they may be from the subcontinent, an identity already exists, waiting to be claimed, affirmed, and reproduced.

6

"My Heart's Indian for All That": Themes of Nationalism and Migration in Bollywood

I've been doing a lot of travelling. I just came back from South Africa.
I was in the motherland. Not my motherland, obviously, you know
what I mean, it's black people's motherland. You know, I'm Indian,
we have our own motherland: England. (Comedy Network Presents
Russell Peters 2007)

This quip from comedian Russell Peters, while intended to provoke laughter, does speak to a widely accepted understanding that India still has a complicated relationship with its colonial masters and, indeed, that members of the South Asian diaspora have an even more complex tie to host societies and homelands. Blockbuster films such as *Hum Aapke Hain Koun* (1994) and *Kuch Kuch Hota Hai* (1998), for all of their popularity with diasporic audiences, do not offer any significant room to explore these complexities, in sharp contrast to those movies that Desai (2004, 43) identifies explicitly as diasporic: "Diasporic films are not always oppositional, however, they employ repetition with a difference and are focused on the politics of displacement, alienation, or loss." Admittedly, this distinction is difficult to make in the context of the current study. Bollywood films also represent a form of diasporic cinema in terms of their target audience, their distribution, and some of their content, but they rarely explore difference or displacement in ways that are oppositional or even necessarily alternative. However, this can occur, so it is not possible to make a distinction strictly on the basis of content.

When making any distinction regarding Indian cinema, it is important to note that there can be considerable overlap in categories, where even some regional or highbrow films may demonstrate elements of Bollywood stylings. For the sake of simplicity, I also adopt the category of diasporic films, but I do recognize the complexity of such a term. In this book, the term "diasporic films" can be seen as separate from Bollywood films and would apply to movies such as *Mississippi Masala* (1991), *East Is East* (1999), *A Touch of Pink* (2004), *Bend It Like Beckham* (2003), and *Monsoon Wedding*

(2001), which do feature oppositional content but, more important, are not produced by the Bollywood system. Filmmaking is rarely an entirely linear process, so co-productions do occur; Bollywood screenwriters or actors may lend their talents to a diasporic film, as is often seen in the work of filmmaker Deepa Mehta. All the same, I maintain that a diasporic film is one primarily made outside of the Mumbai-based Bollywood industry and often made by producers or directors who are themselves diasporic.

These filmmakers work hard to convince audiences that change in South Asian communities is not only possible but already happening. The heroine of *Mississippi Masala* leaves her family to be with her African American lover, the entire family revolts in *East Is East* against their father's authoritarian rule, and the strict Punjabi father in *Bend It Like Beckham* suddenly withdraws his previously staunch opposition to his daughter's decision to play soccer and to move to California. Some of the young adults interviewed here expressed more ability to relate to these stories on the basis of language, if nothing else – diasporic films are usually filmed mainly in English – but several criticized them for being as unrealistic and simplistic as Bollywood films. Some suggested that stereotypes were equally at work in these films, pointing to the extremist and hypocritical Muslim father in *East Is East* or to the overbearing mother in *Bend It Like Beckham*. Others critiqued the easy solutions to problems posited by some of these films. The taboo issue of homosexuality is a source of never-ending tension in *East Is East*, but in *A Touch of Pink* it is played up within an environment of such caricatured characters that the resolution has a rather false ring, only marginally more realistic than Bollywood's pretence that homosexuality is nothing more than the source of the humour implied by the presence of drag queens and transvestites, who merit no real stories of their own. Similarly, although *Monsoon Wedding* does wink at stereotypes by offering viewers a young Indian woman whose romantic aggressiveness takes a diasporic relative by surprise, its treatment of pedophilia is handled rather neatly by a family willing to discuss and address it. Even *Slumdog Millionaire,* a film that garnered mainstream attention despite its minimalist budget and its setting in Mumbai, undermines its hard-hitting messages of poverty, inequity, and despair by offering an improbable happy ending, allowing the down-on-his-luck hero to win a game show with an enormous cash prize before he is reunited with his one true love.

Regardless of the assumed merits or failings of such movies, they do resonate within the South Asian diaspora to a certain degree, and this popularity is not something that Bollywood has ignored. Fiercely proud of its Indian identity, Bollywood has worked hard to keep nationalism and migration in the forefront of its films, mirroring some of Indian cinema's previous reflections on the transition from rural to urban life. In *Shri 420* (Mr. 420, 1955), the rural boy who attempts to survive in the cold, corrupt city expresses his love for the nation, as well as his awareness of foreign influence, in a song whose lyrics continue to be well known today:

Meera jota hai japani, ye patloon englishstani,
Sar pe lal topi rusi, phir bhi dil hai Hindustani ...
(My shoes are Japanese, these pants are British,
A red Russian cap on the head, but still, my heart is Indian).
(Cited in Virdi 2003, 99)

The hero's sentimental patriotism, maintained in the face of deprivation and disappointment, remains the model for many a main character to follow as "India, imagined in films over the decades through binary oppositions – the feudal vs. the modern, country vs. city, east vs. west, rural vs. urban – now pits the national against the transnational" (Virdi 2003, 202-3). Popular films within the past fifteen years have spoken more to the encroachment of perceived Western ways and ideals on traditional Indian life, even as they valorize an ethos of economic achievement and consumerism that seems drawn particularly from the United States. More protagonists engage with the world outside India, and several succeed there, although in the end nearly all return to the motherland – and India, in this case, is positioned heavily as the national incorporation of a mother figure. The goal is not to ignore life outside South Asia but to overcome its lures; to return from overseas, a place of much temptation, and apply one's knowledge to the betterment of India is a laudable goal. Globalization is a behemoth that cannot be put aside, yet in the end its alienating tendencies cannot overcome India's traditions and deep sense of self.

Along with a number of other critics, Pendakur (2003) points out a growing tendency in Indian film to address "this duality of living in two cultures and longing for a past that just does not exist anymore" (43). Suggesting that policies of economic liberalization may have inspired some of the major producers, he notes that 1990s films began increasingly to look at people living abroad (110). He names some of the better-known examples of the form, such as *Dilwale Dulhania Le Jayenge* (*DDLJ;* The Lover Takes the Bride, 1995) and Subhash Ghai's *Pardes* (Foreign Land, 1997), yet there are forerunners in films stretching as far back as *Purab aur Pachhim* (East and West, 1970), whose protagonist, Bharat, studies in England and falls in love with his host family's daughter, Preeti, whose smoking and leather miniskirts distinguish her from a typically demure Indian woman. Convinced by Bharat to visit India once before their marriage, Preeti "slowly becomes enamored of the country and transformed by the 'spirit' and 'essence' of the land, kicks her smoking and drinking habits, and chooses to live like a 'traditional Indian woman.' The family never returns to England" (Virdi 2003, 63). Although economic liberalization, then, may have accelerated the production of movies addressing the diaspora, it is not the only explanation for Bollywood's long-standing fascination with foreign lands and their perceived inadequacies.

Films such as *Pardes* revisited many of the themes found in a film such as *Purab aur Pachhim*, valorizing India's purity when compared to the jungle of "the West," a catch-all term that encompasses England, the United States, and other countries: "The west – specifically England, once the colonial master – is an emotional wasteland of derelicts without 'family life': alienated individuals seeking refuge in sex, alcohol, and promiscuity" (Virdi 2003, 64). In *Pardes,* as in the earlier film, it is also inevitable that the female character must be the one to rediscover her Indianness, as she is the one responsible for preserving and transmitting culture. Interestingly, however, in films such as *Kuch Kuch Hota Hai,* the miniskirt-wearing young woman from abroad is wrongly accused by her eventual husband of not being Indian enough. When he mocks her, she replies by revealing her fluent knowledge of Hindi, a response that wins his heart and indicates that, no matter how Westernized she may appear, she is culturally pure. Once this perceived barrier has been overcome, the two can fall in love and marry.

The question of diaspora, then, is not new in Bollywood, but both Desai (2004) and Dwyer (2000) suggest that the way diaspora is treated had changed by the 1990s. As opposed to "earlier films where foreign locations were used only for spectacle" (Dwyer 2000, 141), a rash of films began to appear in the 1990s that explore diasporic themes, such as Yash Chopra's *Lamhe* (Moments, 1991), part of which takes place in London but indicates its lack in comparison "to Panjab's extended family and traditional hospitality" as well as the belief that Indianness is not simply about citizenship but also about "family values" (Dwyer 2000, 141). These themes resonate in other films, such as *Pardes* and *Kabhi Khushi Kabhie Gham* (Sometimes Happy, Sometimes Sad, 2001), but both Desai (2004) and Mishra (2002, 250) assign a singular importance to the very popular *Dilwale Dulhania Le Jayenge,* described by Mishra as "an indispensable archival material for a sociology of diasporic formations."

From its first frames, as Desai notes, *DDLJ* is a song of nostalgia for the motherland, yet it also grapples with the reality that the motherland is by no means the space of purity and reliability imagined from the disconnected shores of the South Asian diaspora. Although the father in this film longs for home and Indian grooms for his daughters as a way of fending off Western corruption, the "real" Indian son-in-law he has chosen turns out to be a schemer who hopes to advance himself through settling abroad. In contrast, Raj, a young man living in the diaspora, proves to be sincere in his love for the heroine, as well as in his respect for her family: "The true son of Hindustan proves to be the British Asian Raj who is honorable and loyal; Raj is shown to be more than capable of maintaining his 'Indian values and culture' though residing abroad" (Desai 2004, 134; see also Mishra 2002, 253-56).

Unusual in a film of this nature, Raj and Simran, blessed with her father's consent, return to England, while her family remains in the Punjab. It is interesting, too, that the character of Raj is played by Shahrukh Khan, who appears in other films with diasporic themes (*Pardes* and *Kabhi Khushi Kabhie Gham*) and has become, argues Mishra (2002, xv), "the first Indian star to play some of his best roles in Bombay's own version of films about the Indian diaspora."

DDLJ's importance as a film, says Desai (2004, 133), lies in the fact that "it is one of the first to signify the diasporic subjects as Indian national subjects rather than as corrupted Westerners. The 'Indian and his family' can and have remained intact despite its transplantation abroad." The unusual ending clearly resonated in the diaspora, where the film was an enormous success, yet it did not herald the beginning of a new era in Bollywood cinema. Films continue to grapple with the question of movement and living abroad, but for the most part the nostalgia experienced by the characters is appropriate and justified.

Most movies have departed, however, from the heavy-handed condemnation found in works such as *Pardes,* where a daughter of India is exported to the United States as a potential bride for a young man whose American upbringing has left him spoiled, selfish, and violent. The heroine is the archetype of all that is good about India and Indian values: she is respectful, demure, virginal, and extremely patriotic. Yanked from her simple village life and thrust into the world of wealthy non-resident Indians in Los Angeles, she is overwhelmed by the superficiality and coldness she espies, contrasting it to the warmth and love of her home. It is this film that provides a modern-day counterpart to Raj Kapoor's earlier pro-India anthem:

London dekha, Paris dekha, aur dekha Japan
Michael dekha, Elvis dekha, sab dekha meri jaan
Saare jag mein kahin nahin hai doosra Hindustan
(I saw London, I saw Paris, and I saw Japan
I saw Michael, I saw Elvis, I saw it all, my dear
But there is nothing in the world that is like India).
(Cited in Kumar 2002, 217)

Although the opposition between East and West is not always bifurcated quite so clearly, one aspect does remain very common: the woman in these movies remains the standard-bearer for Indian culture (Kumar 2002, 218), a burden seen clearly in *Kabhi Khushi Kabhie Gham.*

Kabhi Khushi Kabhie Gham serves as an interesting example because of its layering of identities, its strong bias toward Indian culture, and its suggestion of the sense of exile that can afflict diasporic communities. In this case, the exile is almost literal since the main characters have left India in reaction to the strong disapproval of their marriage displayed by the husband's parents. Having relocated to London with the heroine's younger sister, the family enjoys an affluent lifestyle, complete with wealthy non-Indian neighbours and friends, expensive cars, and extravagant Western clothes, especially those worn by the younger sister. In the midst of plenty, however, the heroine is perpetually dissatisfied, longing for return and for the reconciliation of her currently fractured family, which she equates with restoration to India. Significantly, despite the differences between the younger woman's revealing Western clothing and flirtatiousness and the heroine's constant wearing of saris and her status as a devoted homemaker, both sisters are eventually united in their desire to return to India and to be accepted into the family home, a desire that is fulfilled by the end of the movie. In describing films such as *Kabhi Khushi Kabhie Gham* and *Yaadein* (Memories, 2001), in which a father upset with his London-bred daughters' excesses packs up and takes them to India for maturity and marriage, Desai (2004, 194) suggests that "the trope of the family is employed to reproduce national narratives of belonging to satisfy diasporic desires."

There are subtle differences in these films: whereas the daughters in *Yaadein* and the American-raised son in *Pardes* may risk losing their identity in the face of Western corruption, the son and daughter-in-law in *Kabhi Khushi Kabhie Gham* and the son in *DDLJ* are all capable of maintaining their patriotism and Indian identity while in the diaspora. However, separation from the mother/land in *Kabhi Khushi Kabhie Gham* leaves the heroine unable to learn all of the rituals she needs from her mother-in-law. At the same time, it is worth noting that her English neighbours, whom she ridicules constantly, eventually make an effort to learn about India and to show respect for it. Although it is clear that the family cannot stay in England if they wish to remain wholly Indian, it is also clear that London need not be a space of complete alienation, representing a departure from *Purab aur Pachhim*. The latter film serves to validate Virdi's (2003, 197) assertion that "the figure of the diasporic Indian is metonymic of this anxiety of the invasion of the west and disappearance of an 'Indian identity,' which it cleverly manipulates to reimagine the nation in response to changing conditions," as well as Kumar's (2002, 216) comment that films such as *Pardes* and its companion feature *Taal* (Rhythm, 1999) indicate a willingness on the part of diasporic viewers to "see the West as urban, and as tainted with modernity, while India continued to be fixed in the imaginary as rural, bound to fixed locations of home and heart" (see also Nayar 2003, 78).

In most of these films, the return to India and to a united family is inevitable, as Nayar (2003, 78) remarks, as is the condemnation of diasporic life as a permanent solution to globalization. At the same time, Bollywood is unable to dismiss the fact of diasporic life, and it continues to address this in ways large and small, such as using North American and European settings that diasporic viewers are most likely to recognize (Mishra 2002, 260). Additionally, although few movies have validated a diasporic existence quite as significantly as has *DDLJ,* some films do exist that present characters living outside of South Asia with very little reference to a politics of return. For instance, *Kal Ho Naa Ho* (Tomorrow May Not Come, 2003), another very popular film, depicts characters settled in the United States. Although the pivotal character does visit from India, there is minimal emphasis on the superiority of India or the possibility of moving there. In fact, in one unusual sequence, the hero performs a dance where his backdrop is a prominent American flag. The insertion of this flag may affirm the characters' American identity, or it may speak to the alliances being built at that time between the United States and India. Whatever the reason, the central characters of *Kal Ho Naa Ho* do not appear to experience any kind of crisis over national identity.

Similarly, the characters in *Kabhi Alvida Naa Kehna* (Never Say Goodbye, 2006) are quite clearly settled in the diaspora, with most of the action occurring in the United States. Admittedly, they engage in behaviours that may well be linked to their settings – placing career demands, individualism, and New York's social scene before their spouses – but if their corruption is linked to the environment, this is not explicitly stated, so it is possible to suggest that this is another case where characters are seen living in the diaspora with no weighty nationalist implications attached. Notwithstanding examples such as these, many films do exhibit a frequent inability to address the realities of diasporic life, equated most often with materialism, loss of values, and engagement in immoral activities (Mishra 2002, 267; Virdi 2003, 202). When promiscuous, disrespectful, or otherwise immodest behaviour is perceived, it is criticized as Western, or inauthentic, non-Indian conduct, a binary construction that discredits both cultures by suggesting that they can even be categorized in terms of such an opposition. Curiously, these films still value certain aspects of Western culture at the same time as they portray it as threatening.

In South Asia, colonialism has left a more complex legacy than some would admit. An English-style education can be seen as a passport to economic success. Speaking English may denote a higher class. In popular Indian cinema, characters may speak English to attract diasporic viewers or to indicate high levels of education and attainment, yet truly heroic or good characters are ultimately expected to embrace Indian culture and to exhibit proof that this culture is what really represents them. A character who can fit easily into the West – most often presented as the United States or England – is accomplished and admirable, whereas a character who cannot fit into India is lost. The West is seen as a place where people can lose their values and morality and where they are often cast adrift in a sea of individualism, a state of affairs to be avoided at all cost. Exceptions do exist, such as *Kal Ho Naa Ho,* but they appear to be rare.

As some of these films demonstrate, in the same way that colonizers once feared the contagious disease and dirty habits of the natives, the natives fear an entirely different disease – that of Westernness. The implied anxiety expressed in Indian movies, especially Bollywood ones, suggests that the perceived amorality of Westernness may be infectious, turning otherwise demure and obedient Indian youth toward an empty and meaningless life. Yet even as Indian cinema rejects the values it assumes to be consonant with Western culture, it is increasingly likely to feature light-skinned, sometimes light-eyed, young men and women as its stars and as the archetypes for attractive Indians, and is also capable of simultaneously promoting and critiquing modes of dress, language, and behaviour that are perceived as socially liberal and hence Western. The contradictions that underpin this indicate the extent to which even the West, and whites, can be exoticized. In the same way that travellers from the Occident once – and to a certain extent still – ventured into the heart of darkness to find evidence that they were superior to the primitive cultures of the East, the Orient is now reversing that gaze, alternately curious and cautious.

The result is a caricaturized version of diasporic life that young viewers outside of India may find inaccurate and offensive, yet at the same time they may recognize some of their parents' and grandparents' ideas in these films, ideas that perhaps speak more to the experience of first-generation immigrants who are battling a sense of loss and alienation. These films are most likely to address the poignancy of leaving, or of never having experienced life in, a homeland and to suggest a facility of return, even after an absence of many years. In Indian films, at least those of the Bollywood genre, one *can* go home again, and whenever possible one certainly should. Until that idyllic moment arrives, one should nurture memories of traditions and cultural values, protecting them against loss and preserving them for transmission to potential offspring. Bollywood cinema may well be consumed for the reasons that some critics have suggested, such as its ability to remind the departed of, or to educate those who have never been to India about, Indian values, traditions, music, clothing, and culture. However, it may also participate in a mythical structure that suggests there is such a thing as Indian culture and an Indian homeland, to which members of the diaspora certainly belong and which they should reclaim in some form.

In the United States diasporic audiences, especially South Asian youth, can be courted by organized political groups – such as the right-wing nationalist parties the Bharatiya Janata Party (BJP) and Shiv Sena, an influence discussed further in a later chapter – and the significance of these parties' global reach may have some connection to the fervent nationalism seen in a number of Bollywood films. After all, audiences may be differently affected by the spilling of the political process into the diaspora, but they receive largely the same cinematic content if they are viewers of Bollywood film. Alessandrini (2001, 336) posits the question of whether the film industry intentionally plays into the hands of nationalist groups such as Shiv Sena since the industry has done well under Shiv Sena's rule in Mumbai.

Given the long history of promoting nationalism in popular Indian cinema, and the complexity of South Asian history, it is difficult to say whether groups such as Shiv Sena bear any significant responsibility for the heavy patriotism, especially the Hindu-inflected Indian nationalism, in many Bollywood films. It is possible to say that these pro-Indian elements are unlikely to disappear, but they may, as in the case of *DDLJ*, present themselves in ways that are more sympathetic to diasporic characters. Certainly, these films do accommodate, in their own ways, the pressures of modernity. For critics such as Bhabha (1994), modernity allows local and/or minority populations to resist the pressures of a dominant culture and simultaneously to avoid marginalization by creating an entirely new entity, a hybrid culture that differentiates itself from the other traditions pulling at it while still fulfilling the needs of the alienated (see Karim 1998, 6; Kraidy 1999; Araeen 2000, 9-17; Khan 2000).

In terms of Indian cinema, these alienated individuals can be easily found in an age that has scattered members of the South Asian diaspora around the globe, attempting to reconcile the values embedded in Indian culture with the practices seen in their new homes. The rigidity of these values varies from one film to the next; the unyielding father in *Kabhi Khushi Kabhie Gham* is eventually convinced to soften his position and accept his son back into the family following the intervention of his wife and his younger son, both of whom challenge his position as patriarch if he cannot recognize his own injustice. However, once he has been induced to look more forgivingly on his son, the family is reunited within the same order they once occupied, and no essential change occurs.

Interestingly, in *Veer-Zaara* (2004), a substantial change can be said to take place, given that the Pakistani Muslim Zaara's father eventually withdraws his sustained insistence that she marry a pre-selected Pakistani despite her love for an Indian man, Veer. Eventually, Veer and Zaara find their way back to one another and to happiness, a rare onscreen occurrence for an interfaith couple. All the same, the collapse of the father's opposition occurs offscreen and is only described to the audience by a peripheral character. Oppositional discourses are often smoothed over in such ways, offering mild alternatives that can satisfy viewers of different generations, ethnicities, and beliefs. In a sense, then, the individuals who watch these films come to inhabit an entirely new space constructed to meet their layered needs, and as part of that process the film can be seen as creating a "new space of signification" (Dhareshwar and Niranjana 2000, 195), one that recognizes the importance of the local but also acknowledges that the "MTV culture, as well as more generally the global televisual culture, is here and we have to negotiate it" (193).

In this formulation, the notion of displaying spirited resistance to the imperialist culture by encouraging the development of untainted local practices becomes an outdated paradigm. Although resistance to cultural imperialism is still widely discussed and promoted by some scholars, advocates of hybridity seem to suggest that it is almost naive, and restricting, to attempt to avoid altogether the dictates of a dominant culture. Rather, it is more realistic to acknowledge that those who feel threatened will find a need both for their (perceived) cultures of origin and for the culture that saturates every aspect of their present-day lives. As Nayar (1997, 77) points out when speaking of present-day Indian practices, "modern life, 'western' life, is very much a part of Indian culture, of urban Indianness, and with it comes numerous 'universal cultural trends.'" She argues that selective borrowing from the West can palliate the problems caused by the many competing cultures within India:

> Since Hindi popular cinema's intention was always to appeal broadly across the subcontinent – a nation ceaselessly struggling to keep its commercial, regional and linguistic factions from splintering – Bollywood came to rely, ironically, on the uniformity of the West (or rather, what it *chose* from the West) to provide its films with a generic coat of all-Indianness. (75, original emphasis)

An argument can be made, then, that Indian cinema demonstrates its cultural roots by melding, however opportunistically, a time-honoured marketing formula with ideas extracted from more traditional forms of drama (Dickey 1993; Booth 1995; Vasudevan 2000). Under this argument, it is possible to view the popularity of films such as *Hum Aapke Hain Koun* through the glocalized lens (Kraidy 1999), where global and local forces combine to create a strong pull for audiences: "Western culture and glitter are very attractive. So *Maine Pyar Kiya* and *Hum Aapke Hain Koun* offer the solution: a happy marriage between the two worlds. I can have everything offered by modernisation, and still hold on to family values and tradition at the same time" (Kabir 1999, 95; see also Gokulsing and Dissanayake 1998, 11). Nandy (1995, 235) seems to see Bollywood as a venue for more clearly defined resistance than can be found elsewhere: "However much we may bemoan the encroachment of mass culture through the commercial cinema, the fact remains that it is commercial cinema which, if only by default, has been more responsive to such demands and more protective towards nonmodern categories."

At the same time, Bollywood's struggle to reconcile India and the diaspora, tradition and modernity, does produce a form of nationalist pride that may be oppressive in itself to groups whose history and positionality are not acknowledged within these films. Undoubtedly, Bollywood has done well in transmitting nationalist themes and highlighting tradition and ritual. In the same way that Bollywood does not always speak to its diasporic viewers with absolute success, it also does not speak with equal weight to other members of its audience. For the most part, the traditions and rituals promoted so heavily in Bollywood films tend to be derived from Hindu mythology and symbolism, and this presents an interesting paradox given that its audience is not composed exclusively of Hindu viewers. The focus of this study, of course, is on a Canadian audience, particularly a Muslim one, and members of this group did indicate their awareness of Bollywood's shortcomings when portraying Islam.

Popular Indian Cinema: Froth, Friction, and Faith

This tension may seem odd given that Bollywood's production and content are touched by the influences of other cultures and religions, including Islam, and that Muslims may constitute a significant part of the Bollywood audience. This section focuses specifically on the role of Islam in Indian films, analyzing central themes and production practices and assessing whether these have changed substantially over time. Given India's complicated political, cultural, and religious history and the more global concern with Islam's meaning and significance, Islam inevitably plays an important – and somewhat transformed – role in popular Indian cinema. However, in the films discussed here, it also carries familiar associations with terrorism, violence, and intercultural misunderstanding, in contrast to Hindu symbolism and mythology, which carry considerable dominance and authority. Danger to Hindu – or Indian, as the two are often elided – values can come from many sources in Indian cinema. The most innocuous threats may come from frivolous youth who dismiss the importance of culture and history, while greater danger may lie with outright colonizers, such as the British, or anyone who embodies difference, such as people of other religions or cultures who would challenge Hindu primacy. Islam, already the focus of stereotyping and misrepresentation in various forms of media, is presented in some Bollywood films as one such threat to the Hindu nation.

Like North American and European media, Bollywood does reference some of the usual stereotypes, such as terrorism and extremism, but the complicated history of India and its peoples means that Indian films may provide a different context for producing and viewing stories about Muslim characters. Thoraval (2000, 90) suggests that to address the sizable Muslim minority still living in India following Partition, Indian cinema worked hard to provide positive Muslim characters, even if there were only one or two per film. Prior to Independence, there were films depicting Muslim stories and themes, such as *Noorjehan* (1923) and the big-budget *Phool* (Flower, 1944), made by Karimuddin Asif, who would also go on to create the major hit *Mughal-e-Azam* (1960), described as an attempt to emphasize the common history of Hindus and Muslims while depicting the glamorous, lost empire of the Mughals. *Mughal-e-Azam* remains one of the best-known Indian movies and has been reissued over the years, and other films, such as *Umrao Jaan* (1981), about a nineteenth-century cultured courtesan in Lucknow, have gone on to be remade (Thoraval 2000, 91, 103-4).

At the same time, these attempts at representing diversity are not wholly positive. Not surprisingly, given the overarching importance of Partition in the lives of so many Indians and Pakistanis, this event and its aftermath underscore a number of themes related to Islam and to Muslims (Mishra 2002, 210). Although 11 September 2001 may have raised global awareness regarding Islam and Muslim practices, India has long struggled with its relationship with Pakistan and with the Muslim minority within its own borders, and the shadows of this struggle fall over a number of Bollywood films. Where Muslims are given important roles, which is hardly common, they are frequently presented as threats of some kind: terrorists, sexual predators, traitors, or nonconformists who in some way have departed from the cherished values of the nation. As Rai (2003) points out, the danger that the Muslim represents to the nation in Indian cinema is sometimes so pronounced that the state must adopt its own violent techniques to put down such a threat. If not for aberrations such as Muslims and other minorities who refuse to respect Indian practices and boundaries, India could easily maintain its status as a pluralist, united family.

Western films, novels, and news reports have been accused of fetishizing Muslim men and women, treating the former as lustful predators and the latter as mysterious figures who veer between innocent damsel in distress and exotic seductress, a kind of Madonna/whore complex revisited and tweaked for the Orient (Ahmed 1982, 1999; Kabbani 1986; Karim 1997, 2000). The topoi of hypersexualized Muslim men are even more powerfully charged when placed in an Indian setting, where the honour of women is often equated with that of the country. In the controversy over the filming of Deepa Mehta's *Fire* (1996), where the two female leads, neglected by their husbands, become romantically involved, one group of protestors indicated their distaste for seeing Hindu women's sexuality portrayed in such a way by suggesting that they would withdraw their objections if the main characters were given Muslim names instead (Desai 2004, 180).

The symbolism of Indian female purity is invoked, Mishra (2002, 214) points out, in the Inter Dominion Treaty, which was in effect between 1947 and 1957 and aimed to recover those Hindu and Sikh women who had apparently been abducted by Pakistan during the chaos of Partition. The exact number of women who were lost to each side – Muslim women were of course also abused, abducted, and displaced – is difficult to ascertain, and there are hints that some women voluntarily chose their new location. However, the recovery of those women was framed as a matter of honour and principle. The film *Chhalia* (The Trickster, 1960) discussed this very issue, featuring a woman from each side who was lost during the struggles that erupted and who took a number of years to reach home or family. That film also manages to invoke the dark spectre of consequence for Indian women who may have been sexually assaulted during or after Partition – in the movie, the main character eventually finds her way back to her family only to be rejected by her husband, who is unable to believe that she was not assaulted on the other side and who thus considers her tainted.

Given the emphasis on female chastity and female honour, it follows that an implied fear of intermarriage or cross-cultural romance seems to run through a number of Indian films, as it once – and some might argue, still – formed a constant undercurrent in so many American films. This may seem contradictory since there are a number of pronounced similarities between Muslims and Hindus on the subcontinent, whereas the themes of miscegenation that anchor so much early American film consistently emphasize difference. The threat of the Muslim may appear greater because of the fact that he or she can "pass" for Hindu so much more easily than an African American can pass for white.

In fact, in the 1940s, 1950s, and part of the 1960s, when Muslims were explicitly singled out as potential threats to the film industry, many Muslim actors did make the choice to pass themselves off as Hindus, at least at the most superficial level. Facing the All India League of Censorship, which hunted down Muslims and Parsis who might destroy the Indian film industry with their "decidedly anti-Hindu agendas," Muslim actors took the path of least resistance by adopting Hindu names (Mishra 2002, 217). Examples include Dilip Kumar (an alias employed by Yusuf Khan), Meena Kumari (Mahjabeen Bano), Madhubala (Mumtaz Jehan Begum Dehlavi), and Ajit (Hamid Ali Khan) (217). An atmosphere that would persuade actors to suppress markers of their Muslimness, then, may explain why, when Muslims were not lustful, threatening, or terrorists, they were sometimes invisible in stories that could have reasonably included them (Chakravarty 1993).

An alternative point of view, however, is provided by Thoraval, who waxes enthusiastic about the fusion of cultures in Indian cinema, seen in the linguistic combination of Hindi and Urdu into Hindustani, a language that came to be understood by many despite its mixed origins. Noting the number of Hindus and Muslims working together in the Indian film industry from the 1940s to the 1960s, Thoraval (2000, 69) suggests that "directors or artistes, whether they are working in commercial or art cinema, and whether they belong to any of the faiths, Hindu, Muslim, Sikh, Parsi, Christian, etc., almost always portray the 'other' culture in a fair and impartial way with all its wonders and grandeur." Similarly, Mohammad (2001, 299), claiming that Bollywood is one of those rare artistic forms that has managed to overcome differences within the audience, displays similar admiration for the cultural crossover that defines Bollywood operations: "In the subcontinent itself, the Bollywood cinema is hailed as one of the most efficient instruments for the promotion of communal harmony: this harmony can be observed in the industry itself (actors, directors, play-back singers, and so on, working together whatever their ethno-religious background) as well as in the popularity of this cinema which largely crosses boundaries."

Although this positivity may be somewhat overstated, there is a case to be made for Indian cinema as a place where certain aspects of Muslim culture do thrive. There are Muslim influences to be found throughout, such as the use of Urdu and the continued popularity of musical forms such as the *ghazal* and the *qawwali*. Indeed, Virdi (2003, 19) cites Mukul Kesavan's belief "that popular Hindi film is the last 'stronghold' of Urdu in India." Unlike Hindi, the language of instruction and administration, Urdu could have disappeared from widespread use; indeed, it is no longer as common in Hindi films as it was in the 1950s, although some words live on through that medium (20).

Many Muslim producers, writers, lyricists, and actors have made and continue to make significant contributions to popular Indian cinema. As Mishra (2002, 63) remarks,

> The discourse of Hindi cinema remains to this day markedly Urdu and many of its key personalities have been Muslim – Mehboob Khan and Nazir Hussain (producers/directors), Javed Akhtar and Majrooh Sultanpuri (scriptwriters and lyricists), Naushad and A.R. Rahman (music directors), Dilip Kumar, Madhubala, Aamir Khan, Shah Rukh Khan, and, of course, Nargis (actors). Add to this financiers and the largest single group of Hindu/Urdu speakers (some 120 million), and we begin to get some sense of the importance of Muslims to the industry.

Thoraval (2000, 71) also names actors Waheeda Rehman, Shabana Azmi, and Naseeruddin Shah, music directors Ghulam Haider and Ghulam Mohammed, singers Talat Mahmood, Shamshad Begum, Ghulam Ali, and Mohammed Rafi, and lyricists Sahir Ludhianvi, Kaifi Azmi, and Shakeel Badayuni.

Since there is clearly no question of underrepresentation within the industry, inaccurate portrayals may instead arise from how Muslim producers and actors have been schooled to present themselves and from the limitations posed by working within a form of cinema that has so forcefully come to equate Hinduism with a unified India, fortified against any and all threats. If performers came to limit Muslim signifiers behind the scenes, the same was true on the screen, where Muslim traditions and history often fell by the wayside. When Muslims did make an appearance, they often appeared as token characters or as ones whose roles served to emphasize the impossibility of a real relationship with Hindus, who are generally the principal characters in popular Bollywood films.

Moving Forward: Admitting Muslims into the Nation?

> *This story is set on the bank of the Jhelum river, which begins in India and flows through Pakistan. On one side, Hindus worship it, praying to the rising sun, and on the other side Muslims offer prayers to their Allah at sunset. The water doesn't make distinctions between different human beings. Then why do people observe difference in their hearts?* (Virdi 2003, 35; her translation of the voiceover that opens the film Henna)

Of course, examples of Indian films that explore Muslim themes do exist. Ghuman (2006, para. 2) notes that in the past *Mughal-e-Azam* (1960), *Mere Huzoor* (My Lord, 1968), *Pakeezah* (Pure of Heart, 1972), and *Nikaah* (Marriage, 1982) ensured a "distinct Muslim presence. The Muslim political film also carved a niche for itself." He goes on to cite the treatment of poverty and despair in *Salim Langde Pe Mat Ro* (Don't Cry for Salim, the Lame, 1989) as well as the depiction of the personal tragedies created by Partition in *Garam Hawa* (Hot Wind, 1973). So politically charged was *Garam Hawa* felt to be, with its pioneering depiction of a Muslim family's experience during Partition, that censors prevented its release for almost a year (Pendakur 2003, 77). After such films as this, however, Ghuman believes that the Muslim presence in Indian cinema actually took a turn for the worse, moving toward marginalization and extremism.

Ghuman (2006) cites a rather broad range of films, moving between the 1960s and the early 1990s. Mishra (2002) agrees that the portrayal of Muslims did change markedly during this period, but he identifies a more specific moment when this occurred. Discussing the film *Amar Akbar Anthony* (1977), the Amitabh Bachchan hit that featured three brothers separated and then raised under three different religious traditions, including Islam, Mishra suggests that this film represented a liberal and inclusive politics of India that would eventually dissipate as, following the late 1970s, India began to experience intensified regionalism and political fragmentation. The Iranian Revolution, in which the Western-supported shah was ousted from power in a revolution led by religious leader Ayatollah Khomeini, and later the fatwa, or death sentence, issued against writer Salman Rushdie by Khomeini are among events that "confirmed old Hindu phobias about Islam's essential inflexibility. Two factors define the post–*Amar Akbar Anthony* world: the rise of Hindu fundamentalism and cultural globalization" (Mishra 2002, 203).

Bollywood cinema, in turn, began to reflect a protectionist tendency found elsewhere in Indian society. I have suggested in this study that the events of 11 September 2001 have affected the way Muslims are perceived in North America and Europe, as well as the way they have come to view their own position. Bollywood producers are unlikely to be unaware of the increased debate over the role of Muslims since 11 September, but they are also in a rather different position than writers, producers, politicians, and other commentators in North America and Europe. The notion of Muslims as a threat is not new to those living in India, who have grown up with stories of recurring interfaith conflict and may have even witnessed the results of such tensions. Although Muslim viewers of Indian cinema may be more acutely aware than ever before of negative portrayals, Bollywood's insularity and its refusal to privilege Islam, Sikhism, or Christianity in its texts are hardly new. Seeking to protect Hindu values in the midst of a cultural onslaught coming from different corners of the globe, popular Indian cinema restored Hinduism to its primary, authoritative place at the centre of most films. Muslims did appear in films and could contribute to the salvation of India, as in *Karma* (Action, 1986), when three convicts of different religions worked with a police chief on behalf of the nation. However, in *Karma* it is perhaps no coincidence that the Muslim character is the one who must die for the cause, whereas the other convicts are permitted to survive.

Similarly, in *Henna* (1991), a Pakistani female character falls in love with the Indian hero, only to be killed while attempting to help him return to India and to his true love there. Although *Henna* does seem to send a message of peace and unity, it also concludes with a reminder of the impossibility of cross-border or cross-cultural love. Virdi (2003, 36) suggests that even though this film attempts to deconstruct notions of essential difference, it also offers a tale of Hindu-Muslim love that can only be realized during a temporary, unusual event – the hero's experience of amnesia. As soon as the Hindu hero, accidentally stranded in Pakistan, has been nursed back to health by the title character, he embarks on a journey home, one that kills Henna even as it returns him to his true (Hindu) love. The tragic Henna, however, does offer a rare entity: "In *Henna*, perhaps for the first time ever, the 'enemy,' Pakistan, is given a face – even a humane one" (Virdi 2003, 42). As Virdi points out, whereas the state is associated with manipulative and unsympathetic characters, the ordinary people of Pakistan are shown to be simply that, ordinary people, rather than sworn enemies of India, a trend that would be echoed more than a decade later in *Veer-Zaara*.

Mani Ratnam's *Bombay* (1995) takes the Hindu-Muslim romance further, allowing the Hindu hero and Muslim heroine to marry and have children, but it also depicts the brutal consequences for those children when rioting breaks out and anyone who cannot claim to be strictly Hindu or Muslim, rather than a mix of both, is at risk. *Bombay*, like *Garam Hawa*, attracted negative attention from censors who continually requested that the political content be diluted (Pendakur 2003, 79). Viewers also had mixed reactions to *Bombay*, which appears relatively neutral in its portrayal of Muslim and Hindu political parties as equally complicit in stoking interreligious tension yet also "shows angry Muslims taking to the streets with weapons after the Babri mosque is destroyed by Hindu fundamentalists" (Pendakur 2003, 79). Moreover, even a show of apparent neutrality may indicate bias in this case, ignoring suggestions from groups such as Human Rights Watch that Muslims were primarily victims in the 1993 riots. In cities with large Muslim populations, such as Hyderabad and Secunderabad, reaction was sometimes negative, and some Muslim fundamentalist politicians were displeased, especially by a scene that depicts the Muslim protagonist discarding her veil (Pendakur 2003, 81). It may be significant that *Bombay* was itself a kind of hybrid cinematic form: initially made in Tamil, it walks a fine line between Bollywood and art film (Virdi 2003, 73), a rare approach that might be said to align comfortably with Ratnam's willingness to tackle the previously taboo.

Prior to *Bombay*, Ratnam also courted some controversy by making *Roja* (1992), a film set against a Kashmiri backdrop and featuring Muslim militants. Drawing on ongoing issues such as tensions with Pakistan, Bollywood films provide a depiction of Muslim enemies that holds some familiarity for an Indian audience. Unlike later films such as Khalid Mohammed's *Fiza* (Air, 2000) or even, to a lesser extent, Ratnam's own *Dil Se* (From the Heart, 1998), *Roja* does not explore the issue of how such extremism is fostered; Ghuman (2006, para. 4) suggests that it instead paves the way for "a number of slash-and-burn movies that target Pakistan and the Indian Muslim (not explicitly stated but implicitly implied) without making any attempt to delve into the several complex processes that breed or sustain terrorism." As examples, he cites movies such as *Sarfarosh* (Self-Sacrifice, 1999), *Gadar* (Revolt, 2001), and *Maa Tujhe Salaam* (I Salute You Mother, 2002), the first of which bears particular scrutiny.

Among many insidious messages, *Sarfarosh* features a *ghazal* singer who publicly preaches cultural unity and understanding while privately working as an arms smuggler and insurrectionist. Even those who pretend to be friends of the Indian nation, and who appear to fit in, may in fact pose a serious danger (Rai 2003). *Sarfarosh* does attempt to offer counterposing narratives, portraying a hardworking Muslim inspector, Salim, whose actions all fall under suspicion due to his religion. Removed from a major case because of his failure to detain a Muslim suspect, Salim is brought back into the fold following the alternating entreaties and rebukes of his former student, Ajay. Ajay, now leading the investigation, implies that Salim should swallow his pride and provide assistance to prove his Indian patriotism. Despite the fact that Salim taught Ajay much of what he knows, the resulting scenario presents Ajay, the Hindu protagonist, as the natural authority between the two.

Salim, however, at least bears the distinction of bravery. Two of the other prominent Muslim characters, Sultan and Gulfam, are depicted as cowards who exhibit other Orientalist tropes. Sultan is sensual and hedonistic, indulging in massages from his mistress and sunbathing when he should be attending to business. His failure to accomplish the tasks assigned to him is punished by death, meted out by Gulfam's minions in a way that evokes even more stereotypes – a terrified Sultan, forced to flee the country, is decapitated by a turban-wearing, camel-riding companion using a sword as they cross the desert. If Sultan is incapable of handling his own work and pays the ultimate price, Gulfam takes this to another level. Enjoying the luxury of being a musical star, Gulfam spares no one who fails to live up to his expectations, yet he does not directly involve himself in the arms trade or in murder. At the end of the movie, prodded by Ajay, Gulfam loses his composure out of fear, and he shoots another suspect. Although he is struck by the realization that he has committed a sin, Ajay argues that Gulfam is guilty of much worse: he has rewarded India's hospitality with treachery.

Gulfam's counterargument that Muslims have been damaged by Partition is easily dismissed, partly because Gulfam has already been revealed as evil and duplicitous but also because this argument is framed by Ajay as simply a refusal on the part of Muslims to let go of the past and to accept that people of all faiths on both sides of the border paid the price for Partition. In this part of the movie, which finally touches on a period in Hindus' and Muslims' shared history that could be valuable and enlightening, Ajay offers facile, simplistic conclusions on all points involving Indian-Pakistani, Hindu-Muslim conflict. Indeed, when the character of Gulfam faces obvious racism, condemned as a "mohajir," or refugee, because he is an Indian by birth but a Pakistani following Partition, this bigotry stems from his fellow Pakistanis. Indian characters are seen as friendly and open, representatives of a pluralist and welcoming India, whereas the representatives of Pakistan, including military and diplomatic personnel, are sly, manipulative, and corrupt.

The only trustworthy Muslims in *Sarfarosh* and in other movies are those who place India first and who do so in an overt manner. Muslims may be allowed to pray and to assert pride in their religion, but they must do so in a way that also proclaims profound loyalty to the nation. As Rai (2003) notes, the title character in *Fiza*, *Sarfarosh*'s Salim, and *Mission Kashmir*'s (2000) Inayat Khan are all religiously devout, but they are also devoted to India. A more recent film, *Fanaa* (Annihilation, 2006), raises the stakes with a Kashmiri heroine, Zooni, who opens the film with patriotic song, continues it with a dance dedicated to the unity of her country India, and closes it by murdering her husband and the father of her child, a man whose terrorist activities place the entire nation at risk (see Khan 2009a, 2009b). Zooni's loyalty to India is well established throughout *Fanaa,* but Salim has to indicate his clearly, especially in a scene where he remonstrates with a fellow Muslim who attempts to solicit his co-operation. In one of the few moments when the film actually delves into the question of religion, Salim denies that the arms smugglers' brand of Islam has any authenticity or relevance to him and goes on to assert his loyalty to his country and compatriots. Similarly, in *Fiza* the heroine is constantly forced to defend her own patriotism, in one case rebuking a cynical and bigoted politician who implies that Pakistanis and Muslims are always causing trouble. Despite learning of, and experiencing, much discrimination and hostility, Fiza continually expresses love for India.

Fiza, in fact, serves as the character who must protect India from any potential threat, including that posed by her brother, in the movie that speaks perhaps most poignantly to issues of Muslim alienation. The movie stars Hrithik Roshan in a role similar to the one he later played in *Mission Kashmir,* where the main character turns toward terrorist activity after a traumatic event. In this case, the event is the 1993 Bombay riots, in which Roshan's Amaan flees for his life, coming across acts of brutality and even a policeman who refuses him aid, advising him to go back to Pakistan. Backed into a corner, Amaan joins a terrorist group so that he will be able to defend Muslims, only to discover, as does Altaaf in *Mission Kashmir,* that he has been manipulated. Having carried out a high-profile political assassination, Amaan is targeted by his own comrades. Fleeing for his life and his freedom, Amaan is found by Fiza.

After discovering what her brother has done, Fiza kills him at his own request, ensuring that the dissident Muslim meets the only possible fate in store for him. As a reminder that the problematic character is Muslim, Amaan offers a last expression of faith as he dies, uttering the Shahadah ("There is no God but Allah and Muhammad is his final prophet"), the recitation of which is considered by many Muslims to be a pillar of Islam. Having removed this threat to the nation, Fiza confirms her own worthiness as a heroine who can preserve the correct state of affairs despite her personal feelings, an echo and simultaneously a perversion of the most symbolically weighted film in Indian cinema, *Mother India,* in which the mother shoots her rebellious son in order to protect female honour – and, in effect, India herself.

Mission Kashmir, similarly, requires a female figure to act as nation and as unifier. The mother in *Mission Kashmir,* Neelima or Nilu, is the Hindu wife of Kashmir's inspector general, Inayat Khan, and for a brief time the adoptive mother of Altaaf, a youngster whose biological family is accidentally killed by Khan during a terrorist raid. Khan and Nilu adopt Altaaf, but when the boy discovers Khan's role in the death of his parents and sister, he runs away and devotes his future days to seeking revenge. Embittered and isolated, Altaaf is exactly the type of youth preyed on by terrorist groups seeking new members. Although *Mission Kashmir* explores the familiar territory of Muslim men as people inevitably linked to violence, terrorism, and destruction, it does successfully depict the confusion and despair of youth such as Altaaf, portrayed as a man who genuinely loves both Nilu and his childhood sweetheart, Sufi, but whose torment is used to advantage by mercenaries such as the villain Hilal. Mouthing religious platitudes, Hilal convinces his young charges that he is leading them on a path of righteousness, even as he lies to them about their real mission – to create interreligious chaos by bombing a mosque and a temple – and even as he extracts large fees for himself. Hilal is not a man motivated by Islam, but he uses religiosity to drive his charges while discouraging them from maintaining any contact with their loved ones.

It is the appearance of loved ones that offers a counterpart to the angry Muslim men, Altaaf and Inspector Khan. In a dreamed exchange with Sufi, who has found out that Altaaf is a terrorist and refuses contact with him, Altaaf tries to win her over by explaining that he is carrying out a religious mission. Sufi, depicted as an honest and patriotic young woman in the same mode as Fiza, rejects this explanation, responding: "I'm a Muslim, too. Islam doesn't permit the murder of innocents." She points out the truth to him – that his real motive is revenge. Trite as this scene may appear, it does offer one of the few positive commentaries on Islam, which is mainly used elsewhere as the backdrop to discussions about jihad and war. It is another woman who finally, although belatedly, effects a resolution to this film. In this case, as in so many other Indian films, the Hindu mother becomes a thinly veiled metaphor for the nation, and the war between Altaaf and Khan ultimately results in her destruction when a bomb intended for Khan kills Nilu. Khan seeks Altaaf to enact revenge, but in the end his love for the nation overcomes all else. Khan finds Altaaf and secures his assistance by invoking Nilu's memory and Altaaf's own childhood ties to the temple that would be destroyed by Hilal's missile. Ultimately, Altaaf's willingness to sacrifice himself helps to save the mother country and ensure his redemption.

A very different film from these previous ones is the 2004 blockbuster *Veer-Zaara*. The Zaara of the title is a young woman whose fate becomes determined, in part, by her connections on both sides of the India-Pakistan border. The Muslim daughter of a prominent Pakistani politician, Zaara travels to India in order to fulfill her surrogate grandmother's last wish – that her ashes be scattered in the place where she resided prior to the division of India. While there, Zaara encounters Veer, with whom she falls in love despite her engagement to a Pakistani man. Her fiancé successfully conspires to separate the two for many long years, during which Veer languishes in a Pakistani prison and Zaara, unaware that Veer is alive, moves to the Punjab to continue his adoptive parents' work in the community. Eventually, a

Pakistani lawyer assigned to Veer's case serves as the instrument of his release and the couple's reunion, and Veer and Zaara are free to live together at last. The emphasis is on romance, and political tensions are merely alluded to, not fully explored.

The clash of religions, however, does come into play at more than one point, as when a Muslim prison guard who had sneered at the Hindu Veer is answered sharply by Veer's lawyer, Saamiya, who asks him to consider why Veer has been assigned a prisoner number of 786, the number many Muslims treat as spiritually significant. Taken aback, the guard eventually accepts Saamiya's proposition that Veer may in fact be under the protection of Allah. Most religious and cultural differences are resolved with equal ease, if acknowledged at all. For instance, Veer's adoptive father suggests that Zaara is the perfect match for his son and dismisses Veer's instinctive protest that Zaara is Pakistani. Rather than dwelling on the differences between India and Pakistan, the film constantly establishes universalities and cultural melding. The Sikh priest asked to assist Zaara in immersing her surrogate grandmother's ashes does so gladly, praising her devotion. Zaara fits easily into Veer's home and family and embraces Punjabi tradition.

However, Pakistani and Muslim traditions are also highlighted, with at least two major climactic moments set against the backdrop of stirring *qawwalis,* while others are set against soaring Islamic architecture, an ode to Muslim culture and Indian diversity also found in *Fanaa's* poetry and song. As in *Fanaa,* where the heroine emphasizes her belief that all elements in the country are one, people and places are shown to be the same no matter where they are. Zaara's mother shows herself to be the same kind of loving parental figure for Veer that his Maati and Bauji were for Zaara. When Veer assents to the tearful request of Zaara's mother that he allow Zaara's marriage to go forward without interfering, she asks whether every son from his country is like him. He responds that every mother from India is just like her. Later, Saamiya responds to a comment from Veer by agreeing on the universality of maternal habit. Again, maternal figures serve to provide a sense of uniformity and similarity.

In contrast to religion's treatment in *Bombay,* by the end of *Veer-Zaara* religion becomes highly unproblematic and is not really the chief obstacle to this romance. Even the hostile prison guard opines eventually that "this Hindu here [Veer] is Allah's noble servant," and a freed Veer comments on how alike Pakistan and India really are. In a dramatic speech, he remarks on the features of Pakistan that brought his own home to mind, asking, "they say that this is not your country, then why does it feel like mine?" Political tensions vanish in this epic love story where personal relationships transcend borders. The difference between Pakistan and India is treated as minimal – although it may be significant that Veer and Zaara leave to make their new life in India – and indeed, early in the movie, the two leads offer a kind of "this land is my land" song-and-dance number set in the Punjab during which they conclude that their countries are truly far more similar than different. Saamiya's legal opponent, not unlike Ajay in *Sarfarosh*, acknowledges her victory and suggests that the future belongs to those who can ignore religious difference and who are not compelled to continually invoke India and Pakistan's troubled past. Positive as this message is, it does seem a bit of a truism, ignoring the fact that Partition is rooted in a tangled and complicated history and has left a legacy that some feel must be addressed.

Conclusion: On Melding and Masalas

Bollywood cinema is both more and less than it seems, offering films that appear designed for easy consumption and that avoid some hard questions yet still manage to encode social and nationalist commentary into their storylines. Although a relatively new wave of films that are not Bollywood productions, such as *American Desi* (2001), *Monsoon Wedding* (2001), and *East Is East* (1999), undertake a more detailed and daring exploration of the type of issues that diasporic South Asians struggle with, such as the inability to reconcile long-standing conservative values surrounding love, religion, and behavioural norms with so-called modern standards (see Desai 2004), these films do not necessarily displace the crucial role played by Bollywood cinema. Ultimately, Nandy (1983, 108) sees Bollywood as exhibiting not India's faults but its overall strength: "The uniqueness of Indian culture," he hypothesizes, "lies not so much in a unique ideology as in the society's traditional ability to live with cultural ambiguities and to use them to build psychological and even metaphysical defences against cultural invasions."

These cultural invasions can be seen as approaching from a variety of sides; the idea of an all-Hindu, middle-class, united India can exist without complication only in film, and even in this area some fissures are being addressed. Indian cinema is not blind to changing trends, although it does employ its own methods in an attempt to control them. Increasingly, it chooses to speak to South Asians living in the diaspora, and it does, at times, try to offer commentary relevant to those who are not Hindu. In both attempts, it experiences its failures and its successes, although members of the diaspora, especially Muslims, may be more likely to remember the first. *Veer-Zaara*, rather than marking a wholly triumphant and pluralist new era in Bollywood cinema, merely serves as a reminder that themes of religion have not become significantly more nuanced. It may, however, reflect a more global emphasis in Indian cinema. Observers of the film industry have suggested that Indian films are increasingly marketed to the affluent diaspora, a shift in focus that may explain why "a Punjabi ethos (Sikh and Hindu) is displacing the old North Indian Hindi ethos of Bombay Cinema" (Mishra 2002, 260; see also Desai 2004).

This focus does not necessarily open the door to more Muslim themes or to a clear interpretation of diasporic experience, but it may indicate some loosening of the previous guidelines that privileged one particular culture as that of all India. Ideally, the current political and media focus on Muslims in the diaspora would prompt Bollywood to treat issues around Islam seriously. Certainly, there has been a concerted attempt to talk about Islam more directly than before, and it is interesting to note the ambivalence underpinning two of the films that do address cross-border themes – *Veer-Zaara* and *Fanaa* – and that were produced after 11 September 2001. Both reproduce familiar tropes about Indian patriotism, but *Veer-Zaara* makes a concerted effort to avoid the political and to emphasize Indian-Pakistani unity at the expense of treating Indian and Pakistani history seriously, whereas *Fanaa* raises the issue of politics and even allows one character to explain the position of Kashmiri nationalists but ultimately ensures death for those nationalists, who prove themselves to be corrupt and ruthless (Khan 2009a, 2009b). Despite the superficial departures from the norm in these films, most of the evidence to date ultimately suggests that expanded consideration of other cultures and other religions continues to rely largely on many of the same stereotypes, misrepresentations, and lack of contextualization. In the words of Simran, a young Sikh participant in Toronto describing how she came to view Bollywood more critically:

> My professor is really focused on subaltern studies and the whole construction of nationalism, and I would say, looking at Bollywood now, yeah, they really focus on nationalism, and actually encourage this idea of a homogeneous nation that is dominated by Hindu elitists.

This focus on nationalism comes through even in the relatively serious *Mission Kashmir,* which attempts to speak to a critical political and social moment in history – one that is larger than Kashmir itself. The film encompasses current global realities while raising the possibility that Muslims can be viewed only in relation to violence and crime. Films that try to offer a rounded portrayal of Muslims through the lens of recent fears regarding global terrorism and Islamist radicalism both hurt and help Muslims everywhere. There are films that manage to break through the stereotypes, and some make a praiseworthy attempt to promote cross-border or cross-cultural harmony, but for the most part ideology either seeps into many recent films or is replaced instead by an apolitical, dehistoricized depiction that ignores crucial facts. The same can be said of films with diasporic themes such as *Pardes* and *Taal,* which refuse to fully acknowledge what it means to live outside of South Asia and to still nurture a sense of cultural identity. Neither approach serves Bollywood viewers well.

Ultimately, as films such as *DDLJ* and *Fiza* indicate, there is some recognition that diasporic and Muslim characters, respectively, can be multi-faceted, interesting, and relevant, but the very different ways these films handle the challenge of Islam and diaspora also implies that it is still not possible to view Bollywood cinema as a venue in which people belonging to either or both are completely understood or appropriately portrayed. Nonetheless, there is much to be said for a trend in filmmaking that seeks to address difference and to acknowledge the reality of Islam and diasporic South Asians, and as directors and writers continue to tackle these topics, it can only be hoped that they will do so with sensitivity and balance. This study, however, seeks to address the present implications of such work as much as it tracks recent change in the industry. This chapter treats some of the most relevant themes and characteristics in popular Indian cinema, especially in works addressing nationalism and religion. The following chapters examine whether selected audience members living in the diaspora read such themes in a particular way and what meaning this holds for them.

7
Up Close and Personal: Methodology for Obtaining Audience Opinion

Extensive research already exists in terms of analyzing Bollywood films and their content, and speculation often takes place regarding the role of the audience in interpreting this material. For the most part, however, firsthand audience accounts continue to be rare. Dwyer (2000, 169) claims, with some justification, that one "of the most important gaps in the study of Hindi cinema is the absence of any ethnographic study of the cinema audience." Indeed, although some of the major films have been discussed at length, the audience's reactions are often assumed rather than investigated. The audience in India is still neglected as an object of study – ethnographic or otherwise – whereas viewers in the South Asian diaspora are acquiring a definite allure for researchers. In particular, recent studies on second-generation viewers by Khan (2009b), Desai (2005), and Durham (2004), as well as Jiwani's (1989) unpublished research on young Canadians of South Asian origin in the late 1980s, indicate that there are a number of approaches and areas of interest worth investigating in terms of the diasporic audience's reception.

Regarding the interests that drove this particular study, I have already noted that I brought a specific perspective to researching Bollywood as well as its possible effects on identity construction. Raised in a household in Vancouver where national identification tended to be almost entirely Canadian, with occasional nostalgic references to Tanzania, I felt no connection to South Asia as a child, a sentiment that is also found among some of Jiwani's (1989) respondents. This feeling did not alter significantly even in my early twenties, when increasing pluralism, changing fashions, and cinematic evolution made it more socially acceptable to claim Indian origins, to wear Indian clothing, or to watch Indian films. However, at this point I did start to notice that some of my peers identified enthusiastically with aspects of South Asian culture that were literally foreign to me. Of those individuals, several seemed to have derived at least part of their understanding of South Asian culture from Bollywood films, which contained fashions they copied, songs they sang at parties, and a version of

Hindi that they taught themselves in order to enjoy the movies. I was particularly surprised to realize how popular Bollywood films were among these youth, having been a very occasional viewer myself, and I was even more fascinated by the lure these movies held for Muslim viewers, whose own religious traditions were not likely to be depicted in these films in great depth.

I became interested in further investigating this connection, particularly when I realized how many people in this age bracket were grappling with questions of ethnic and religious identity. A kind of unintended melding of South Asian cultural and religious influences seemed to come together in the lives of many families, leaving some young people with an unclear impression of what it means to be Indian or Pakistani, for example, or Hindu or Muslim. The hybrid nature of the identity forged here under the pressure of parental or other influences is not in itself a matter of concern for me; rather, I began to consider what some of these common influences might be, such as Indian films, and whether they might contribute to the determination some individuals felt to maintain a truly South Asian identity, even though in many cases they were not direct migrants from South Asia. Moreover, I questioned what role these influences might play in helping young adults to articulate a clear sense of self, and since I was aware that much of the literature on Bollywood suggests that it is infused with a strong sense of pro-Indian, Hindu nationalism (see, for example, Dickey 1993; Mitra 1999; Vasudevan 2000), I began to construct research questions that examined how such themes might be interpreted by viewers who were both inside and outside the group being depicted in such movies. My overarching research question asks what role Bollywood films play, if any, in the process of constructing a sense of identity and belonging for young Canadians of South Asian origin, particularly Muslims.

With this in mind, I decided to maintain the focus on the diaspora found in other studies but with specific emphasis on young people living in major Canadian cities. Although young Canadian Muslims of South Asian origin are the primary focus of this research, young people of other religious backgrounds were included for the purposes of comparison. The initial research plan consisted of focus groups and follow-up interviews in Toronto and Vancouver, two cities with significant Muslim South Asian populations in relatively different settings, although Ottawa was later added as a third site due to the accessibility of participants. In total, I conducted focus groups and interviews with twenty-eight young people, including Muslims, Hindus, Sikhs, and Christians, from 2006 to 2008 in Toronto, Vancouver, and Ottawa, seeking to obtain firsthand evidence of the strategies employed by young Canadians of South Asian origin, especially Muslims, and the shortcomings they perceive, if any, in the existence they lead. I also tried to determine whether young Muslims of South Asian origin really do occupy a unique position within the larger Canadian community and whether their readings significantly differ from those of other young South Asians.

Early Stages: Establishing Participant Criteria

When you talk to young people who came from Islamic-majority countries (or whose parents did), you increasingly hear them describe themselves as "Muslims" and identify themselves with a broader worldwide community of believers. Their religion has become their primary identity. (Saunders 2007, F3)

The reports of hostility toward South Asians and/or Muslims following 11 September 2001 demonstrate that some of the North American public may consider these groups to share the same ethnicity and religion. In actual practice, however, Islam is home to many different sects that hold, on selected points, very distinct and sometimes conflicting viewpoints; in fact, certain branches, such as Ismaili Muslims and Ahmaddiyas, are sometimes not recognized by others as Muslim. I anticipated some possibilities for disagreement, but instead participants treated difference more as a point of interest than as a source of friction.

However, the real problem in terms of sampling arose in relation to the question of selecting participants of South Asian origin: I had to determine whether I wanted to conduct a comparative study of first-, second-, and third-generation immigrants and ultimately decided to examine whether young adults from these communities, who have resided in Canada and operated in Canadian socializing institutions for enough years to understand Canadian socio-cultural norms, consider themselves fully integrated Canadians. In keeping with this, as well as Schensul's (1999, 63-65) advice that focus groups should include sufficiently diverse representation but should also bear in mind the population the researcher truly wishes to address, I placed less emphasis on recruiting specific generations of immigrants than on recruiting participants, regardless of place of birth, who had lived in Canada from at least the age of five years.

This provided participants who have undergone the bulk of their schooling in Canada, even if the actual institutions vary. Many of the participants were born in Canada following their parents' immigration in the 1970s, whereas other participants were born outside of Canada but immigrated to Canada at such a young age that they remember nothing of their homeland (for related discussions, see Gillespie 1995; Handa 2003). As Maira (2002, 17) explains in her own decision to apply the term "second-generation" to children of immigrants or to those immigrants who arrived in the United States before age seven or eight, "the rationale ... is that second-generation

Americans 'come of age' in the United States, that is, share in the rites of passage of American high school and have socialization experiences very different from those who come here as young adults."

As Handa (2003) notes, a number of young immigrants, regardless of generation, share the experience of double migration since it is not uncommon for them or their parents to have lived in colonies in East Africa, the Caribbean, or Fiji, for instance, prior to coming to Canada, which adds another layer to their experience as South Asians whose notion of homeland is already complex. It is clear, however, from Handa's (2003) and Khan's (2000) studies that such double migrants nonetheless identify themselves as South Asian based on their ancestry while alluding to East Africa – or other countries – as steps within the migratory experience. Thus participants may identify as South Asian for reasons other than their place of birth. Since this is a study largely about identity construction, it encompasses participants who can explain in what way they are descended from one of the South Asian countries under investigation. For the sake of convenience and consistency, I have followed Desai's (2004) categorization here by including Pakistan, Nepal, India, Sri Lanka, Bangladesh, Bhutan, the Maldives, and Tibet under the banner of South Asia.

I chose to solicit participants from relatively large and multicultural cities, Toronto, Vancouver, and Ottawa, which meant that my sample population was urban and had lived in a diverse setting. Toronto, which is especially diverse and has a high South Asian population, provides an environment in which South Asians and Muslims may theoretically integrate but may also attempt to mark out space that is distinctly their own. Vancouver is equally diverse but with a different ethnic composition and with a high proportion of South Asians, including some who wield considerable political influence. In their study of immigration in Toronto and Vancouver, Hiebert and Ley (2006, 71) illustrate the significance and pluralism of these cities:

In Canada, Toronto and Vancouver have emerged as the nation's two primary windows on the world, and both, if not yet global cities, are in the process of gaining this stature. In 2001 these cities had some of the highest proportions of foreign-born residents among advanced societies: 43 percent in the Toronto Census metropolitan area (CMA) and 37 percent in the Vancouver CMA. These ratios are much higher than those found in Los Angeles, New York, London, and Tokyo, the quintessential global cities of our era.

The main aspects of this research plan were carried out in Toronto and Vancouver, but the differing availability of participants meant that many of the discussions were conducted in small groups or even individually, which provided data of greater depth but also reduced the planned number of participants. Accessibility to participants in Ottawa then led to the inclusion of that city as a third research venue.

In regard to the selection of participants between the ages of nineteen and thirty years, the initial justification for this criterion rested on the import- ance of citizenship for Canadians in this age range. It may be argued that these are still formative years in terms of identity, and indeed Mahtani's (2004) study indicates that identity is always in flux for visible minorities living in a host society that is not wholly welcoming. All the same, as I had observed informally, these years also represent a period in which young adults start to think about or are already thinking about what kind of life they would like to lead, what kind of city and country they want to live in, how they perceive themselves, and their sense of belonging. The key rela- tionships in the major Bollywood films often take place between characters within this age range, so it is possible that participants in their twenties may constitute one primary target audience. Such respondents may have already pondered some of the issues so frequently discussed in Bollywood films, like marriage, children, where to settle down, what values to embrace, and so forth, and they may be wrestling with intergenerational or cultural conflicts and may also be aware of competing cultural values and possibilities.

Preceding studies of South Asians, Muslims, and diasporic communities have produced interesting findings, but few have specifically targeted the intersection of media use and identity construction for young Muslims of South Asian origin. The most relevant and recent, in the Canadian context, investigate the experiences of female subjects only. Both Handa's (2003) and Khan's (2000) works investigate the issue of identity among Canadian women who are also South Asian and/or Muslim. Likewise, Alvi, Hoodfar, and Mc- Donough's (2003) anthology is devoted to Muslim women's experiences and use of veiling in North America and, in combination with Handa's and Khan's works, has helped to lend more specificity to the type of research questions employed in this study. In particular, Khan (2000), Moghissi (2006), and Alvi, Hoodfar, and McDonough (2003) identify key reactions demonstrated by minorities when their ethnic identity represents an obstacle in the process of integration, such as denial/rejection of ethnicity, the aggressive defence of identity, or alternately, a more ambivalent, hybrid standpoint.

Similar strategies can be seen in Jiwani's (1989) interviews with young Ismaili Muslims of South Asian origin. Although a considerable amount of time has passed since these interviews were conducted, they are relevant here, especially because of the related focus on Muslims and South Asians. Despite the years and attitudes that separate them, Jiwani's participants gave answers that form a bridge to the interviewees in the current research. Al- though they had lived in Vancouver for some time, alongside other South Asians, Jiwani's respondents were less likely than the young people in this study to claim South Asian ancestry, differentiating themselves by drawing on their African heritage and their religious identity, which they framed as specifically Ismaili more than Muslim. They described a Vancouver characterized by racism and lack of acceptance, a place where some of them felt compelled to position themselves as separate from Hindus and Sikhs, who were more subject to discrimination. Indeed, both the vertical and horizontal racism described in Tamale (1996) are present in the accounts of Jiwani's respondents. As Tamale explains, vertical racism is the kind most easily recognized since it originates with a person in a dominant position and is directed at the oppressed. Horizontal racism, however, occurs within oppressed groups, some of whom may believe in a hierarchy between races or even within each race. In such a case, physical attributes such as skin colour or socio-cultural differences can still determine one's status, even among people who experience varying levels of oppression and marginalization.

Speaking in the late 1980s, when South Asians and Muslims were integrating in different ways, some of Jiwani's (1989) participants commented on the ways that they had assimilated while critiquing other South Asians who had retained traditional dress or who had not learned English (for similar findings, see Pyke and Dang 2003). In one case, an interviewee condoned the racist discourse that whites used toward such immigrants and even employed some of it himself. My own study produces somewhat different findings, but Jiwani's provides important context, particularly since my participants do identify racism from their childhood. Moreover, few of my participants deny that racism still exists, although the form that it takes may have changed, just as their own coping mechanisms have become more established. The confusion regarding identity and belonging experienced by some of the youth Jiwani interviewed may also help to shed some light on the determined search for cultural and religious information cited by several individuals in this book.

Gillespie's (1995) work on South Asian teenagers in the United Kingdom focuses on slightly different questions but is highly applicable here, particularly given that she was one of the first researchers to explicitly address the educational and socializing role of Indian and non-Indian cinema for South Asian families. Although her work addresses only certain aspects of nationalism and identity, the pedagogical role she identifies for Indian cinema is pertinent because questions of identity, tradition, and nationalism are so strong in these films. Like Kraidy (1999) and Maira (2002), Gillespie employs ethnography in her study, an appropriate choice in her case considering that, as a teacher of numerous Punjabi youth, she already had command of the language and access to subjects who felt at ease in her presence. Based on the foundational questions underpinning my research, I chose not to pursue this route due to a conviction that ethnography would not necessarily allow me to gain insight into the kind of perceptions and beliefs under examination.

I hoped to elicit further information regarding issues such as the way participants view themselves in terms of national identity, the degree of belonging they experience in different communities, and what role Bollywood films play in affecting their notions of identity and nationalism. These personal questions regarding individual perceptions and beliefs were unlikely to be answered in an entirely cohesive way through ethnography. In a group of young people who juggle different behaviours, social circles, and expectations, it was not entirely clear which setting would be most appropriate for evaluating a sense of identity or readings of Bollywood film.

My original intention was to conduct focus groups and then follow up, where necessary, on an individual basis. I developed a relatively structured process, in which I distributed a questionnaire and also provided myself with some basic questions to direct the areas of conversation. Each participant completed the questionnaire and answered these questions, but I tried to leave the questions open-ended, and in several cases this helped to facilitate a free-flowing, wide-ranging discussion. Unless the conversation moved notably off topic, I allowed participants to raise their own points on this topic and also asked them at the end whether they had additional comments they wanted to make.

All of the eventual participants were recruited through direct advertising or through a form of snowball sampling, where friends, early participants, and other contacts passed on the information to others in their own social networks. The drawback of this approach is that it can lead to participants who are acquainted with one another (Schensul 1999, 72; Seale 1999, 116), but this did not seem to be a major factor in most cases, especially since the contacts recruited were not necessarily interviewed at the same time or in the same city. Invitations to participate were also extended to specific community organizations, such as South Asian dance troupes, community centres, and region-specific associations, but these rarely received a response.

Those contacts who did participate often demonstrated a high level of interest in the subject at hand, particularly questions of nationalism and identity. Perhaps not surprisingly, given the intense media and political focus on Islam and integration, several of the Muslim participants had clearly devoted considerable thought to the subject of personhood and belonging in Canada. Many of their observations offered interesting twists on my initial theoretical framework around ethnicity, hybridity, diaspora, and transnationalism, which was helpful given that I was cautious about the use of theory as a beginning point in qualitative research (Bryman 1988, 97-98, 120). I anticipated the possibility, discussed in Orona's (1997) use of grounded theory, that in conducting and transcribing interview proceedings, I would discover that the theoretical frameworks I had chosen were not as relevant as I had supposed and that other possibilities would arise. Ultimately, I found that they were applicable and provided an ideal lens through which to interpret respondents' comments.

Insertion of the Self: Issues of Reflexivity

> *As qualitative researchers engaged in contemporary practice, we accept that the researcher is a central figure who influences, if not actively constructs, the collection, selection and interpretation of data. We recognize that research is co-constituted, a joint product of the participants, researcher and their relationship. We understand that meanings are negotiated within particular social contexts so that another researcher will unfold a different story. We no longer seek to eradicate the researcher's presence – instead subjectivity in research is transformed from a problem to an opportunity. (Finlay 2002, 212)*

In addition to determining which theoretical frameworks might be applicable, I also kept in mind some of the precepts of critical discourse analysis and conversational analysis techniques (van Dijk 1988, 1991, 1993, 1996, 1998; Stillar 1998), which allow the reader or listener to deconstruct words or phrases typically employed in the subjugation of the Other or in the denial of racism. The experiences of Jiwani (1989), Gillespie (1995), and Handa (2003) had already indicated that racism might reside within my participant groups rather than remaining an external issue. Expressions of possible racism or bigotry were very rare, but there were a few moments when I detected a negative subtext in discussions of a particular religion, usually occurring in the absence of people who actually practised the religion in question. Although it was tempting at that time and other moments to address such comments directly, I felt this would result in even more blurring of the lines between participant and observer. As it was, I did occupy a bit of a participant-observer role whether or not I had intended to; some of the discussions unfolded more like comfortable conversations than interviews in the strictest sense, and I sensed that the group of young women I interviewed in Vancouver might have been especially forthcoming with opinions because they saw me as part of the group. Another contributing factor is that some of these young people appear to view the opportunity to participate in one of two ways: they may be eager to share experiences that they cannot discuss freely in other venues (as seems to be the case in Khan 2000; Handa 2003), or they may be wary to do so because there are such strong cultural taboos around some subjects. The first case seemed to be more common, and this is where the less-structured approach yielded both irrelevant detail and interesting revelations that might not otherwise have surfaced. The open-ended interview was helpful in this sense, allowing for a "fairly close relationship between researcher and subject" rather than the impersonal distance sometimes created by rigid structures (Bryman 1988, 96, 115-16).

There is, as I have already noted, some overlap between my roles as a researcher and as a member of the group I am studying: I am the Canadian-born daughter of immigrants whose ancestry is South Asian, although they themselves were born and raised in East Africa. I am also Shia Muslim and was in my late twenties when conducting the research. This commonality was beneficial in the sense that it seemed to provide a feeling of ease for participants when discussing cultural questions, and it also allowed conversations to flow more naturally than they might have within a rigid question-and-answer format. As Tamale (1996, 489-90) suggests, a conversational, relaxed style may elicit more truthful responses and is more likely to be found in interviews where researcher and subject share commonalities, such as ethnicity. For the most part, it did appear that participants in this study felt comfortable and seemed to expect that others, including the investigator, might have a sense of identification with some of the experiences they described.

Despite this familiarity, I tried to listen to the experiences of others rather than interjecting too many of my own thoughts. If any curiosity about my subject position and identity had been expressed by my participants, it is possible that my approach would have needed adjustment since attempts on my part at self-concealment could have been viewed as facilitating a mode of non-reflexive research that reinforces unequal power relations (McCorkel and Myers 2003, 208; see also Bryman 1988, 111). However, reflexivity, defined loosely by Finlay (2002, 210) as "the project of examining how the researcher and intersubjective elements impinge on, and even transform, research," was not as great an issue as I had thought it might be. This potential difficulty might have been alleviated because, unlike McCorkel and Myers (2003) and Tamale (1996), I was not called on to interview subjects whose position in society was very different from my own; similarly, the potential problems posed by "going native" described in Bryman (1988, 96-97) are minimal when the researcher is already affiliated with the subjects.

For this reason, however, I discovered that I had some preconceptions about the factors that might influence viewers to immerse themselves in Bollywood. Despite attempting to ensure, like Tamale (1996), Ahmed (1999), and Handa (2003), that my biases and beliefs were clearly articulated in my research plan from the beginning, I still came to realize the ways my standpoint may have affected my initial approach to interviews. As I conducted these interviews, I was reminded that preconceptions must be left behind and that my impressions might well have been grounded in the fact that my participants and I did not all come from the exact same cultural background. What struck me as traditional and highly immersed may have been regarded in different ways by others.

I approached this research, then, as someone who was, in essence, both inside and outside the group under study. I was of approximately the same ethnicity and age as my participants; in some cases, we shared a religion. Many of us had some level of postsecondary education; a few of the participants had graduate-level education. Although many of us had been raised as members of the working class or remembered an initial period of settlement and financial restraint, most of us were now either edging into the middle class or had aspirations to do so. In terms of their connection to the subject matter, some interviewees, like me, were infrequent viewers of Bollywood, whereas others ranged from avid to utterly indifferent. The individuals being interviewed at any given time, then, helped to determine the extent to which I was an insider or an outsider, although I tried to conduct myself relatively consistently in each instance. To a certain extent, both interviewer and interviewee contribute to a state of affairs where the investigator must contend with "the knots of place and biography and ... deconstruct the dualities of power and antipower, hegemony and resistance, and insider and outsider to reveal and describe how our representations of the world and those who live there are indeed positionally organized" (Macbeth 2001, 38).

Overall, I conducted five group interviews. The remaining interviews were all individual, due to scheduling difficulties or the failure of some participants to arrive at the group meetings. In cases where participants could not make themselves available in person, I conducted some interviews by telephone and two others through e-mail/mail, with the latter providing contact information in case further discussion was required. Regardless of the setting or number of people, I started with the same basic questions, but where necessary I added questions for the purposes of clarification or to elicit further information. In some cases, participants spontaneously raised and expanded on points of their own while answering a particular question. For instance, in discussing a selected film, a respondent in one Vancouver group mentioned the portrayal of gender, sparking an animated discussion of gender relations in South Asian culture that occupied at least ten minutes and then recurred throughout the remaining questions and answers. In terms of time and breadth, then, these interviews all varied considerably.

In total, the twenty-eight people to whom I spoke included sixteen Muslims, six Hindus, four Sikhs, and two Christians (see Table 7.1 at the end of this chapter). Their ages ranged from twenty-two to thirty and most were born in Canada, with two or three exceptions. Five traced their ancestry back to Pakistan, although one of these also noted a familial history of migration that involved Burma, Pakistan, and Canada. Twelve identified

Indian origins only, and another eleven noted Indian ancestry combined with a history of African migration. There were more young women than men, with only eight males in the total group. As Gillespie (1995, 71-72) notes with some regret in her own study, male participation can be more difficult to secure. Even with the best of intentions, my own study, like hers, is informed more strongly by young women than by young men.

Additionally, even with attempts to diversify, there were some distinct commonalities within the group in terms of class and education, which limits the applicability of findings to other South Asian youth. Not all of the participants had obtained postsecondary education, but most had, and for some this clearly influenced their answers and their ability to be critical. This education and their other experiences may also have been linked to the fact that most participants were either middle class or at least upwardly mobile, although some remembered a childhood that was far from affluent and marked by struggles to integrate. In anticipation of this kind of fluctuation in socio-economic status, I did not attempt to categorize my participants by class, nor did I collect data on annual income. Class is certainly an important factor in determining identity and belonging, as additional economic capital can at times be equated with increased cultural capital. However, in this case, I felt that it was difficult to accurately categorize the class of the participants, even if I requested financial data or asked them to self-categorize. Self-categorizing would likely lead to some confusion, as perspectives on what constitutes working class, middle class, and so on are bound to vary. Annual income statistics might not be particularly representative given that some of the participants were students or recent graduates, resulting in low salaries even if their families were affluent. Also, individuals who have been touched by migration may well experience periodic changes in socio-economic status. A wealthy, respected family in Pakistan or Kenya might have become relatively poor on settling in Canada, only to regain some of its status at a later date. Such a family might slip into the working class for a time while retaining a desire and a plan to return to the ranks of the middle classes.

For these reasons, I did not use class as a category. My impressions, based on the level of education and the occupations of those who participated, are that the majority of respondents were middle class or belonged to families whose aspirations aligned with those of the middle classes. Some may have been poor at a point or points in their lives, but most had some form of postsecondary education as well as steady employment. This rather nebulous understanding of class further illustrates the myriad factors that contribute to identity for these young people. It also serves as a reminder that the findings here are not applicable to all young Canadians of South Asian origin, nor can the data be used to draw conclusions about the smaller groups within the overall body of participants.

The representation by city was similar, with nine participants in Vancouver, twelve in Toronto, and seven in Ottawa, although not surprisingly some individuals identified with more than one place of residence, especially if they were students or had recently moved to assume a new job. The sample per city was too small to allow for geographical comparison, although some participants offered anecdotal observations about the differences. The use of the different sites tended to confirm some general conclusions rather than to provide a means of comparison. Key findings around national identification, beliefs about gender, and views about stereotyping or lack of realism in Indian cinema tended to repeat themselves across cities, suggesting that these were relatively consistent.

Within the group, there remained sufficient difference to render it almost impossible to offer generalizations about religious groups. However, one factor appeared to be unifying and certainly offered possibilities for future research: the Sikh and Muslim respondents were often more critical about the media they viewed, including Bollywood, a trend that appeared attributable to a pervasive consciousness about outsider status. Although these young people were able to consume many different media and enjoy them, they seemed more sensitive to inadequacies of representation, and they indicated that these shortcomings were not new but long-standing and pervasive.

I sought to ascertain whether factors related to the viewing of these films are as important as the films themselves. For example, Gillespie (1995) suggests that viewing Indian films is an important family activity for some Punjabi youth living in the South Asian diaspora and may provide a gateway for discussion of other cultural and religious matters. Similarly, Pendakur (2003, 97) notes that in India, movie-going "is still very much a family affair," while many of the participants here highlighted such viewing as a domestic, familial activity. Accordingly, questions related to the context of viewing were asked, and some of the interviewees elaborated further on this of their own accord. The experiences were different for many of the participants, but family and cross-generational bridge building were clearly key in a number of cases, and it was also apparent that film watching was linked to other discussions or activities, as discussed further in the next chapter. Although few of the participants cited a level of engagement quite as pronounced as that described by Pendakur (2003, 97) in his discussion of cinema-going in India, where viewers may dance, use musical instruments, or recite dialogue while watching, it appears that viewing was far from a passive activity for many of the families, affirming the belief that "the cinematic experience and meaning-making by the audience is not idle, analytic activity but real engagement with the film."

At times, such real engagement is neither achieved nor desired, and in some cases participants attempted to offer examples of alternative media that would satisfy their needs or to explain why Bollywood fell so far short of accomplishing this. Others gave answers that corresponded extremely strongly with Desai's (2004, 221) findings following her own study of second-generation immigrant youth in the United States:

> Several second-generation South Asian-American viewers in my forthcoming study on the consumption of Indian cinema reported that the films function performatively and pedagogically in that they teach rituals, traditions, and social practices as well as identifications. These films are ethnographic and pedagogical for multiple audiences. In addition to Western viewers, South Asian diasporic viewers also may view these films as documents recording South Asian or Indian cultural practices. Watching films is identified as pedagogical in these viewers' method of learning about India and Indian culture, what it means to be Indian; it is also a lesson in how to be good consumers, as some commented on how they watch films to get ideas about the latest fashions in India. In this manner, visual media, especially cinema, functions as a significant site in constructing and disseminating discourses on weddings and marriage, family, and culture.

These same themes came through strongly in my own investigation, although they were also juxtaposed against the cynicism and wariness of some viewers who felt that these practices were depicted against an unrealistic cultural backdrop that fed misconceptions about India.

For the most part, answers were thoughtful and revealing, but there were few predictors for what the responses would be, as interviewees of the same religious background, gender, or age could still vary widely in many of their observations. Even heavy viewing did not indicate the eventual answers, as some heavy viewers were entirely uncritical and others were highly analytical. Some of the salient points that emerged, such as discomfort with increasing sexuality and revealing clothing, came up much more persistently than I had anticipated.

Participants whose approach vis-à-vis Bollywood was entirely oppositional also offered revealing commentary when explaining the source of their disaffection; and light viewers, despite referring to their input rather deprecatingly, sometimes raised highly pertinent issues around identity construction and nationalism. One such viewer spoke with definite feeling about his commitment to a Canadian identity and noted the way that differing linguistic ability separated him from his parents when considering attachment to South Asian culture. One young woman who denied being influenced by media in any way at all, and who rarely watched Bollywood, began the discussion by insisting that she had little to contribute but then made comments on her struggle to achieve a true Indian identity, on the way she used some media and cultural forms (books, dance, language) to return to her roots, and on her desire to transmit some sense of ethnic identity to her children.

Radha: But I find that, well, I'm going out with a white guy, and I found that the minute I started going out with him, I started desperately clinging on to anything Indian –

Musnah: Really!

Radha: And I didn't have this sort of – explicit's the wrong word, but I never made an outward effort to grab onto it as much as I did, so now I find that Indian authors and stuff, that's how I try to relate to the culture. I mean, movies are okay, but I don't watch a lot of movies ...

Table 7.1

Participant demographic information

Participant pseudonym	Age	Gender	City	Ethnicity	Religion
Adil	30	M	Toronto	Indian*	Muslim
Adit	28	M	Vancouver	Indian	Hindu
Alia	29	F	Vancouver	Indian*	Muslim
Alma	26	F	Toronto	Pakistani	Muslim
Asha	29	F	Toronto	Indian	Sikh
Chandra	26	F	Toronto	Indian	Hindu
Farah	27	F	Toronto	Indian*	Muslim
Iram	24	F	Vancouver	Indian*	Muslim
Iyla	26	F	Vancouver	Indian	Christian
Jaya	29	F	Toronto	Indian	Hindu
Kahil	27	M	Ottawa	Indian*	Muslim
Khatija	27	F	Vancouver	Indian*	Muslim
Lalita	29	F	Toronto	Indian	Hindu
Maida	22	F	Vancouver	Indian*	Muslim
Musnah	22	F	Ottawa	Pakistani	Muslim
Nadim	28	M	Ottawa	Indian*	Muslim
Nalini	26	F	Toronto	Indian	Hindu
Nazia	29	F	Toronto	Pakistani	Muslim
Nimrit	24	F	Vancouver	Indian	Sikh
Radha	29	F	Ottawa	Indian	Hindu
Raveena	25	F	Toronto	Indian	Sikh
Rehman	26	M	Ottawa	Indian*	Muslim
Sheila	22	F	Vancouver	Indian*	Muslim
Simran	26	F	Toronto	Indian	Sikh
Steve	27	M	Vancouver	Indian	Christian
Suhil	29	M	Ottawa	Indian*	Muslim
Tariq	23	M	Ottawa	Pakistani/ Burmese	Muslim
Zara	27	F	Toronto	Pakistani	Muslim

* Via East Africa

In turn, Radha's observations prompted her fellow interviewees to raise questions around class and migration, a framing that seemed to inspire her to interpret her thoughts and situation in ways that she had not done previously. In fact, in a later conversation, she suggested to me that she had never thought of many of these points before and found herself engaging with them following the interview, a comment that other participants made as well. This echoed some of what I glimpsed in Jiwani's (1989) interview transcripts, where her line of questioning prompted respondents to view ethnicity and race in different ways, with some of them modifying their understanding of ethnic origin and cultural practices following her inquiries.

The interviewing in this case was not such a pronounced two-way process, but it did seem to provide some positive outcomes for the individuals concerned. The interviews offered a framework for conversation that benefited some participants who were able to articulate thoughts about identity and media for the first time and to meet others who grappled with the same issues. The interviews did not provide definite, closed answers for me or, most likely, for them, but they did offer lucid commentary on issues such as being Canadian, holding insider/outsider status in the home/host societies, juggling competing societal pressures, and the significance and/or shortcomings of a number of media. These views are detailed more extensively in the following chapters, indicating not only the percipience of these individuals but also the promise encapsulated in their clear-sighted ability to detect problems and their resolution to overcome them.

8

"But, I dream in Canadian": Constructing and Maintaining Plural Identities

When I say that my mother dreamed in Canadian, it is part of an
expression of hope in the potential of the Canadian Charter of Rights
and Freedoms, and in the individual human rights and obligations that
this document entails. The Charter does not express the society that
we have, in my opinion, but the society we glimpse, and that we each
create in our day-to-day choices, and in the actions we take within our
communities. Where a true multicultural society exists in Canada,
it exists in the choices and consciousness of the people to see minor
difference for what it is, and to know that the rights we hold are
equal. (Thien 2003, A13)

The construction of identity for minorities in Canada is a question that has
attracted attention for some time, and although some argue that integration
and belonging come with increasing ease to immigrants and more particularly to their children, others suggest that there are some individuals who
are resistant to all attempts to fold them into the fabric of society. This study
does not seek to explore every possible angle of identity construction, but
it does have a consistent focus on the way media may contribute to the
formation of a national identity and on the role that ethnicity and religion
may play in this process.

The discussion that follows recounts twenty-eight young Canadians of
South Asian origin speaking on these topics for themselves, articulating their
thoughts on being Canadian, on having South Asian ethnicity, on the influences that shaped them, and on their reading of media that attempt to
capture their attention and even, at times, their reality. Their answers varied
in some respects, especially in their interpretation of the content and cultural
relevance of media, including but not limited to popular Indian cinema,
which some young adults considered an essential part of their upbringing

and which others dismissed as unrealistic and distorted. Some of these divisions are explained below in the participants' terms, which were often perceptive and insightful. Aside from this, there were also points of almost universal agreement, particularly concerning their sense of nationalism and nationality. Their thoughts in this regard seem to turn aside concerns about young people who refuse to fit into Canadian society; indeed, although they admitted to making routine compromises in order to accommodate competing community demands and walk, to paraphrase Handa (2003), a cultural tightrope, they rejected attempts to exclude them from Canadian society on the basis of their ethnicity or religion. Some have felt the sting of racism and, accordingly, have given much thought to the way they want to position themselves in terms of identity; others noted that their quest for a clearer sense of identity had more to do with what is missing than with an awareness of racism. Seeking answers from their parents or relatives regarding their culture, history, and faith, some participants discovered that these were often unavailable or inadequate, and they explored new avenues to come to terms with their identity.

Staunchly Canadian and clear-eyed about the cultural challenges they must face, these young people are indeed exemplars of "the Canada we are becoming. It is fashioned by the now-grown children of immigrants from 210 countries, who are blending the roots of their past with the nation of their future" (Anderssen and Valpy 2003, A10). They were not blind to the challenges of coming from one cultural tradition and having been raised in another, yet they would likely have echoed Thien's contention above that this existential quandary did not in any way diminish their Canadianness or their right to assert cultural authenticity within their respective ethnic and religious communities. Answering a number of questions on ethnicity, nationality, and media, they indicated clearly that they know what difference is, both as they saw it depicted onscreen and as they viewed it within their overlapping communities, and like Thien, they understood this layered sense of difference as part of their selves and part of their country. The participants in this study speak to a specific segment of society and are not wholly representative of all immigrants or descendants of immigrants, yet their explanations of how they were arriving at a sense of self and their accounts of the strategies they employed in crafting their future, including the use of various media such as Bollywood cinema, contain lessons and insights whose significance transfers well beyond themselves or this moment in time. They speak, in fact, to all those who, like Canadian-born writer Madeleine Thien and her immigrant mother, might answer individuals who question their sense of belonging by responding simply, "But, I dream in Canadian" (Thien 2003).

"Canada is home": Articulating National Identity

> Tariq:[1] *I don't typically use the hyphenated term [Pakistani-Canadian],*
> *I don't have any problems with anyone using the hyphenated term,*
> *I think that's one of the perks of being Canadian, you can use the*
> *hyphenated term and that's cool. But I guess my rationale behind not*
> *using it is just that being Canadian is the ultimate unifier, so once*
> *you're here – and also, given the fact that I was born here, you know,*
> *I ... regardless of me not knowing necessarily what Canadian identity*
> *is, Canada is home and I'm Canadian. I've always felt really strongly*
> *about it. And almost, I guess, if you are going to nitpick about it, then,*
> *you know, I'd much rather refer to myself as a Canadian Pakistani or*
> *Canadian Burmese rather than a Pakistani-Canadian type deal,*
> *because I feel the Canadian part should trump anything else.*

The questionnaires and the interviews in this study commenced with inquiries regarding the identification of nationality, inquiries that were simple for some to answer but more complicated for others. Most of the participants described themselves as Canadian and considered themselves Canadian but also commented that they sometimes employed different answers depending on the context. When travelling outside of Canada, nearly all identified as Canadian first if asked. Some interviewees pointed out that they had no choice to identify as anything else when in South Asia, for instance, because the difference in their accents, dress, or demeanour seemed to function as markers that they were not residents of a South Asian society. However, a number of participants noted, often with humour, that they were forced to elaborate on the identifier Canadian when speaking to others within the country itself. Despite their own belief that they were Canadian, they were asked frequently by others of South Asian origin or by non–South Asians about their real nationality. In the first case, those of South Asian origin seemed to be curious about whether they possessed similar backgrounds; in the second case, the query carried an embedded assumption that to be a minority in Canada disqualifies one from being simply Canadian. Some addressed such inquiries with hostility, whereas others merely expanded by commenting on their birthplace or that of their parents or grandparents, but their assertion that they were Canadian, no matter the skepticism they encountered, appears to validate Anderssen and Valpy's

---

1 To protect anonymity, each participant has been assigned a pseudonym. The letter "F" is used to identify the interviewer where applicable.

(2003, A11) conclusion about integration and nationalism: "With each generation, Canadians in general become more comfortable calling themselves Canadians. The youngest are most likely to do so, with 40 per cent of 20s listing at least part of their ethnic origin as Canadian in the 2001 census, compared with 32 per cent of those over 65."

Not only were these young Canadians increasingly comfortable describing themselves as such, but they had also developed strategies to combat those who disagree. There were situations in which participants recognized a legitimate route of inquiry when questions about nationality arose, but for the most part they viewed such requests for information as a way of denying their identity, a process in which they would not engage.

Khatija, who is Canadian-born and whose parents migrated from East Africa, said, "I make a point of saying that I'm a Canadian, and if they seem to imply well, you're brown, you can't be Canadian, then, if pushed and depending on who it is, I'll go into the whole history of India and East Africa. But most of the time I keep repeating that I'm Canadian." Likewise, Kahil said firmly, "I always identify myself as Canadian," and he went on to explain that he never changed this answer, even in a different context, because "the inquiry is usually asking me, 'no, but what are you really?'" and hence "my response doesn't change until they ask me the right question, which is, what's your ethnic background?"

Alma, whose appearance and name are not obviously South Asian, used this to her advantage, refusing to answer the question under most circumstances. She would occasionally relent for other South Asians, explaining she felt they were less likely to judge her than non–South Asians, who she thought carried pre-existing biases about her ancestry (Pakistani) and religion (Islam). Nimrit, whose entire interview indicated a similar degree of resistance to others' desire to categorize her, nonetheless conceded that at times she found it necessary to answer questions about nationality with "Indo-Canadian," in part because the question was rarely phrased directly as a formal inquiry about nationalism. Like many respondents, she commented that the question was often – sometimes naggingly – posed as, "What are you?" and she felt that "Canadian" clearly did not satisfy those who would ask the question in such a way. She expressed this with a mixture of exasperation and resignation, whereas Iram, who was equally aware of these tendencies, seemed to take a rather playful, inconsistent approach. Canadian-born and of Indian ancestry, the daughter of African-born immigrants, she said that her typical answer was, "Indian," followed by further explanation if pressed. She was the only respondent to give this answer, which she explained by saying that she felt close to this lineage. However, at times, she would even use African, which she employed mainly to puzzle her interlocutors, not because she felt a particularly resonant connection to East Africa.

Musnah, who was born outside of Canada and whose parents, as migrants who moved from India to Pakistan to Canada, had their own complicated relationship with national identity, also took a more relaxed approach to the question, but unlike Iram, she seemed to feel that a certain amount of effort – sometimes too much – went into answering it:

> Sometimes, I find that with South Asians who are first-generation, who have just immigrated, when they're talking to me, they'll do that, they'll say, well, where are you really from? They don't understand that I'm Canadian because they want to befriend me or something like that [laughs] ... I find that people who are like me, who are second-generation, they don't do that as much. If I want to just leave it that I'm Canadian, or that I'm from Toronto, they'll leave it at that.

Musnah's comments are significant on several levels. On the one hand, she indicated a kind of sympathetic current of thought among second-generation Canadians, who are more able than their elders to leave aside the question of ethnic difference, and this impression was echoed throughout the study by a number of individuals. She also suggested that older Canadians of South Asian origin may experience difficulty in understanding Canada as her primary residence or national identifier, and in her conclusion, as well as in comments not excerpted here, she mentioned that she experienced weariness at times with the repeated discussions of her national and ethnic origins.

Tariq's insistence that he is Canadian above all does not speak of this weariness, merely of his determination to be accepted for who he is and to have Canada fulfill the promise of its vision of itself. This theme was implied on a number of occasions: although the state appears to accept plurality, the individuals within it must fight repeatedly to enforce this right. Young people such as Tariq were prepared to mount this struggle, but they were also aware that it could be a continuous one. Tariq dismissed the possibility of hyphenation, although he did not display criticism or hostility of those who embrace that choice, but like Suhil, quoted below, he saw himself as a product of not simply a place but also a moment in time, the era of Pierre Elliott Trudeau, when Canada sought to define itself as an inclusive, multicultural nation: "The reason I identify so strongly as Canadian is that Canada allows you, by law, to identify with any culture and the country must accept it; if anything, the ability to do this makes me embrace my Canadian identity even more strongly. I never need to hyphenate; I can always say, 'I'm Canadian.'" Others separated nationality from ethnicity and religion but saw the last two as intertwined, with at least two Sikh participants explaining that, in their lives, religion and culture demonstrated considerable overlap.

Indeed, following some rumination by Musnah regarding her sense that she does not fully belong to either Pakistan or Canada, her fellow interviewee

Radha interjected that her own references to belonging had more to do with culture than with nationalism, a distinction that Musnah seemed to think was arbitrary at times since she had been taught to regard these as interwoven. Musnah was one of very few interviewees who had been raised to be fervently nationalistic about her parents' home country, Pakistan, a place where she was taken for visits and one that was evoked frequently in her Toronto home. Over time, she had become self-conscious regarding this process and spoke of the results in a way that indicated a greater degree of confusion and analysis than many others expressed:

> Musnah: I still don't feel like I belong there [in Pakistan]. Because the culture I've created for myself is a combination of the culture here and like ... it's just totally different. It just can't be that culture and then this culture, because they're just sort of combined, like this big ball.

> Radha: Agreed. I think for all of us.

Clearly, then, nationalism was still complicated for some respondents, despite the fact that they were fully integrated into Canadian society in a number of ways and identified themselves as Canadian with little hesitation or, as Musnah suggested when describing her travels in Pakistan, were of necessity identified as such due to obvious markers of difference. Speaking in the Canadian context, Nalini also indicated her childhood awareness that she was different in significant ways, and she was one of the few to say that her answer about nationality had changed over the years, linking her sense of being an outsider in Canada to her belief that she was more Indian:

> I think growing up, because of reasons like racism and xenophobia, I think I definitely would have identified as being Indian more than Canadian. I never felt white, I never had blonde hair, blue eyes. But as I was growing up, and perhaps more interested in the reasons I would have felt that way, I started feeling more comfortable saying, "Canadian."

This comment serves as a useful reminder of the evolution that takes place among young people who are sorting out questions of identity, and it further supports Moghissi's (2006) claim that retreat into ethnic enclaves or communities may be a response to alienation from the mainstream community. A few participants indicated their confusion or discomfort during childhood, as they grappled with the question of how they could remain Canadian when they were also different in noticeable ways from their classmates or playmates. For most, this discomfort eventually diminished, even if it did not disappear, but Nalini, who had clearly grown into a confident and articulate young woman, had evidently internalized beliefs over what constituted a true Canadian. In fact, although most participants were generally quick to assert a Canadian identity, one that they saw as chiefly national, not ethnic, there was some evidence that they had been affected by implied arguments that Canadian nationalism is the purview of white Canadians. Articles such as Howard-Hassman's (1999), with her suggestion that an ethnic Canadian identity exists, skirt around this particular question of race, instead offering the possibility that ethnic Canadians are bound together by their common language – in her commentary, this is simply English – and by the dominance of Christianity, which provides some commonalities even for those who do not actively practice. This argument may sound delimiting, but Howard-Hassman (1999, 524) claims that her goals are strictly integrative; most people raised largely or exclusively in Canada, she says – not unlike the young people participating in the current study – become ethnic Canadians. They do this, she seems to say, against all odds: "Both public policy and much academic analysis conspire to prevent Canadians from recognizing this by insisting that their 'ethnic' identity must be that of their ancestors." The danger of encouraging Canadians to identify their ethnicity in this way, she persists, is that it may "render it difficult to instill a sense of Canadian identity in the population at large," a suggestion that is repeated in a different form by Reitz and Banerjee's (2007) conclusion that second-generation immigrant youth fail to identify as Canadians, an observation based on their inquiries into the ethnic origins of these young people. In making this claim, Reitz and Banerjee seem to align with Howard-Hassman's belief that nationality and ethnicity can be collapsed into a single category.

Interestingly, most of the young adults questioned here did not appear to agree, providing thoughtful answers on their ancestry, their difficulties arriving at a clear explanation of ethnicity, and the challenges of explaining their nationality to others. Several commented on Canada as a place defined by difference, a country whose identity is diverse, plural, and tolerant. They may not have found it simple to identify as Canadian, South Asian, and Muslim/Hindu/Sikh/Christian all at once, but they found it entirely possible and even laudable that their country supports such multi-layered definitions. Speaking of this group of second-generation Canadians, Abu-Laban and Stasiulis (2000, 482) observe that "they have developed a hybrid sense of identity. While they are of Canadian *nationality,* their complex ethnicity is not simply that of being of English-Canadian *ethnic* identity" (original emphasis).

In keeping with this, most participants here seemed to indicate their own belief that their national identity could be Canadian while their ethnic identity was different and reflected factors such as ancestry as well as parental migration. At the same time, they were aware of the existence of Canadians who, like Howard-Hassman (1999), seem to have suggested that some people are more Canadian than others and that this identification may be grounded in a conflation of national and ethnic identity. Acknowledging such an argument, Simran also noted that the way she articulated her national identity had changed over the years, and she too echoed the sentiment expressed by most of the participants that a question about nationality was in essence a question about one's "real" origins. Her experience within Canada was one of the more varied, as she had been raised in a small town that was not particularly diverse, before moving to Vancouver for a brief time and then Toronto, whereas most participants had been raised primarily in major Canadian cities – indeed, Nadim and Farah, both raised in the suburb of Brampton, Ontario, commented on the overwhelming South Asian presence there and on the way this had shaped their upbringing and understanding of identity. Pluralism may not have been seen so extensively in Simran's small town, yet she had still found ways to forge a sense of belonging.

A number of participants made a point of attributing their sense of acceptance to their generational position, ushered into a Canada that had become officially multicultural under Trudeau but had truly begun to realize this policy during these interviewees' formative years. Tariq, speaking of the effects of multiculturalism and its significance in recent years, had this to say: "If you were to have Indians coming in now or within the past fifteen years or twenty years ago, there's a big difference between the multiculturalism – or yeah, just the multiculturalism in Canada and what existed back then [sounds of general agreement] and the whole assimilation process versus integration process." None of the written or verbal questions asked the participants to compare this process to that found in other countries, but the interviewees brought their own experiences to bear when explaining how Canada was unique in its acceptance of immigrants. Suhil was firm in his belief that he should feel no dissonance in identifying himself as a Canadian whose religion is Islam and whose ancestry is Indian because, as he pointed out, the only Canadians who did not come from elsewhere are Aboriginals. Hence he had the same right to live in Canada and call himself Canadian as any other settler on that land, a point also made by Nazia, who did complicate this relationship somewhat more by suggesting that notions of nationalism can be problematized considerably by colonialism, a fact of life that is more relevant in Canada than many allow.

However, for the most part, those who commented on Canada's shortcomings were not necessarily critical of life there. Nalini was one of the few to speak explicitly about racism in Canada, although the attendant struggle she faced for self-acceptance is noteworthy and perhaps not unique. Most saw their existence there as entirely natural and preferable to the alternatives they had glimpsed elsewhere. One remarked on London, England, as a place that had integrated South Asians with extraordinary thoroughness, but at least two – both Muslim – observed that they considered the immigrant experience in the United States to be notably different from what it was in Canada, and generally they saw this disparity as reflecting poorly on the former. The reasons for this may be manifold, including policy, but Maira (2002) also points out the external pressures brought to bear on American immigrants, ones from which Canadians are perhaps exempt.

Explaining the influence of right-wing nationalist Indian groups on the South Asian diaspora, Maira (2002, 137-40) notes the extent to which these parties have succeeded in herding American South Asian youth into religious camps that reinforce their sense of Hinduism and nationalism without necessarily explaining the political activities to which these parties are linked in India. In Canada young adults are perhaps less susceptible to these influences; although a few identified campaigns on the part of elders and community groups to strengthen their sense of South Asian identity or their religious identity, none referred directly to Indian politics or Indian organizations. It may be that the smaller number of South Asians attracts less attention from political parties abroad; it may be that these parties focus their efforts on American youth in the hopes of forging stronger ties to a country distinguished for its economic and political might.

It may also be that the supposedly multicultural politics of a country such as Canada provide less fodder for right-wing nationalists than can be found in the United States. At least two individuals in this study noted the difference between being a Muslim in the United States and being one in Canada, suggesting that the pressures of American nationalism combine with a distinct marginalizing process to create young Americans who feel less at ease with their identity and who may react to this discomfort in more extreme ways. Of course, it is far too simplistic to posit that Canadian immigrants of any generation are all well integrated and comfortable in their skin. The young people in this study appeared to be integrated, were often well educated, and took pride in their country and their origins. However, few considered their identity to be entirely unproblematic. Several described a process of coming to terms with their ethnicity and religion as much as their nationality, and others offered that this process was still ongoing.

Can You Go Home Again? Diasporic Youth Speak Out

Maida: You realize what your culture is when you start articulating it to other people.

As much as the participants expressed their firm belief that they were truly Canadian, many were also conscious of expectations and pressures regarding their cultural authenticity as individuals of South Asian origin. Some described these pressures as familial, others as mainly external – coming from South Asian acquaintances, for instance – and several commented on this as an internal dialogue, one in which they sought constantly to reconcile their own beliefs regarding their heritage and nationality. Although these young people may not have been courted by nationalist groups in the manner described by Maira (2002), a type of confusion does seem to exist in South Asian culture, where individuals, especially those living in the diaspora, are warned ominously to lose neither their cultural values nor the rituals and markers that identify their heritage. As one journalist notes, "To be brown in a white world post-9/11 is fraught with complexity. Do you become a coconut (brown outside, white inside) to survive or do you reinvent yourself, complete with a cool new brand – desi?" (Yelaja 2006, A1). The coconut accusation echoes ones commonly heard among people of other races (e.g., Oreos for blacks, bananas for people of Chinese ancestry), but the sting within is the same each time: it suggests a binary way of being in which the ethnically loyal consistently pledge their allegiance to their true race while denying that they have been corrupted by the West, by whiteness, and by Canadian culture.

For Musnah, this emphasis on loyalty was tripartite: her parents' decision to relocate from India to Pakistan to Canada created a strong sense of nationalism and identification with Pakistan, which they attempted to transmit to her. They taught her to embrace Pakistan as a nation, as the source of her culture, and as a place identified with her religion. They succeeded in engendering an interest in some aspects of South Asian culture, but they could not engender a sense of belonging when they took her to Pakistan, despite promoting it as a place where she could be comfortable and could eventually live if she so chose:

> The more I thought about it, the more I realized, oh God, I could never, ever live here. I just can't. I just can't. I wouldn't be able to fit in here. And yeah, just coming back here, my parents were saying, "How does it feel to be in Pakistan, where you're in the majority?" Well, first of all, we aren't really the majority because we're Shia Muslims, so we're a minority there even, but I said to them, you know, it really doesn't feel very different to me, it just feels like we're in Little India or Little Pakistan but expanded, like as a whole country of Little Indias. It just didn't feel different, like, I just didn't feel any more of a sense of belonging there than I do here. I still felt like somewhat of an outsider. So at the end of the day, I think even though I can't just fully say I'm Canadian, I'm Pakistani-Canadian, I still can't say that my heart belongs there. I just don't know the life there. It's too different for me.

Having stated earlier that she had created a culture for herself out of disparate elements, Musnah indicated here that she acknowledged her Pakistani origins and respected them but did not feel essentially bound to Pakistan.

Although this sense of being in-between, of having no notion of full belonging anywhere, may seem marginalizing and even discouraging, it may be the best option available for some migrants and their children. Mitra (1999, 18) advises these individuals to "find an identity for themselves that maintains the connections with their places of origin as well as [to] develop a particular niche for themselves in the West."

Simplistic resistance, after all, is clearly futile, at least for these young people, who have moved substantially past the possibility of refusing to integrate into Canadian culture. As Musnah made clear, there was no option of going home to the place of origin, at least not permanently, and virtually none of the participants addressed this possibility, even if their parents had taken them for frequent trips and they enjoyed their time there. Neither complete assimilation nor complete resistance appeared desirable for these interviewees, and hence several co-existed with the question of how to fuse disparate identities, a conundrum that Mitra (1999, 204) considers the modern dilemma of the diasporic South Asian: "It is finding that critical mix that becomes the crusade of many Indians as they increasingly feel marginalized in the Western public sphere precisely because they still retain many of the Indian attributes which they find very difficult to jettison."

Some interviewees defied their traditional upbringing, rejecting what they saw as outdated or absurd customs, whereas others took comfort in it. The most common strategy for handling the conflicting demands of South Asian and Canadian cultures, however, seemed to be a kind of attempt at hybridization. More than one interviewee suggested that they dealt with culture clashes by adopting the aspects they enjoyed most and creating a shifting mélange that worked for them, although this did not mean that they could escape the inevitable ambivalences that accompany living in a constant state of flux.

Perhaps the least ambivalent sentiment expressed by most participants was a belief that they were Canadian first but that they could not dismiss their ancestry and the influence of traditions transmitted from South Asia. As Radha put it, explaining her reaction to those who prefer to identify themselves using a hyphenated label, "If you're going to label me as something, label me as Canadian and be done with it. And if you want to add extenuating circumstances, then absolutely, I am absolutely Indian. But – pick one or the other." Radha's description of her ethnicity as an extenuating circumstance was apt in some ways. She recounted a childhood experience that seemed to lean toward the highly integrated side, commenting that she had not been required to learn Hindi or to attend religious classes as her peers did, although she had travelled to India and described it on one occasion as a kind of safety net, a place that she could go to if, for example, she could not find a suitable spouse in Canada and needed to seek one elsewhere.

Neither she nor any other participants expressed any real desire to "return" to India or Pakistan permanently, eschewing the idea that these places could be real points of return for them after so many years spent in Canada. However, those who had visited either place voiced their pleasure at being able to do so and the belief that such travels contributed to their sense of self. Those travels also led to expanded insights regarding societal change, difference, and their place within a diasporic patchwork of traditions and beliefs. Not surprisingly, many of the participants explained their construction of ethnic identity by making some reference to their parents or to other members of the family, although they outlined some instances where their parents' views differed starkly from theirs.

Having said that, there was a certain amount of sympathy expressed for the opinions of parents or grandparents who were raised with different societal norms and who found it difficult to believe that those norms could change in any significant way. There was some agreement that part of the culture clash experienced with immigrant parents arose, to a certain degree, from the fact that their parents and grandparents believed that Indian society remained almost the same as it was at the point of their initial departure. Radha and Musnah concurred that there is some truth in this viewpoint, but Radha's reaction was slightly more positive than that of Musnah, who seemed inclined to comment on ways that this refusal to change may enact itself in proscriptions on her behaviour:

Radha: I think that what most people think is that when our parents immigrated, their idea of India froze while India itself progressed. And so they're still clinging on to that idea. But to be honest, I like that idea. Obviously, I'm biased because I grew up with it. So when I do go to India, I do see things that I think are ridiculously risqué, but they're things that Indian Indians think are American and are normal, whereas I think they're way too, too much.

Musnah: My parents, oh my gosh, are so conservative. Even when we go to Pakistan, like, we just went, and it's just so different there now. Even like the clothes, I was looking at the display windows and stuff, they have sleeveless, and they show their belly, and whatnot, which we never, ever do. My parents certainly don't let me dress provocatively at all. When I'm at home, I just can't show – I can't wear a short skirt or anything, and there they don't care, like, I mean, still, you would get stared at, but like in Karachi and everything, apparently people do this, they wear miniskirts.

Opinions differed among the informants regarding the exact degree of difference between culture in South Asia and South Asian culture as it had unfolded in the diaspora, but most tended to believe that it was impossible to overlook the dialectical interplay between these, a finding that echoes Raj's (2003, 48) comments about the shock experienced by British youth of South Asian origin when they discovered that the India their parents described to them was an imagined place anchored in the past. Whether or not they agreed with their parents' envisioning of home and culture – and it is worth noting that several participants described parents who were highly integrated and who considered Canada home – nearly all suggested that it was very difficult to dismiss the role of ethnicity in their lives, and they also offered a scenario where Indians or Pakistanis on the subcontinent were influenced to some degree by the globalization of popular culture. Radha, whose own ancestry is Indian, commented on the desire that some Indians might feel to assimilate into American culture, a desire that she saw as being tempered for Canadians of South Asian origin: "Now that we're in Canada, we don't feel the need to try to assimilate. We already realize we're different. We know what we can and can't do."

This comment implies a high level of confidence and comfort with identity, feelings that were echoed by several others, but Musnah was certainly not alone when she returned again to the notion that nationalism is not cleanly delineated when one's ethnic origins are on frequent display:

> I also think that it made a big difference that my grandparents grew up with us in our house and my grandma didn't, doesn't speak English at all, so that was like a big thing. Like here is my grandma, so Pakistani and, so like, just cannot integrate or whatever, so that always reminded me as well, we'd get home or she picks up the phone, and she'd be speaking Urdu, saying hello, hello, and they're like I just want to speak to someone and she can't answer back. There's no way you could just say Canadian when you have that whole other aspect, that cultural aspect in your home, reminding you of that.

Although Musnah – who does speak Urdu – identified language as important in the sense that her grandmother could not speak English, which served as a constant reminder of her ethnic background, other interviewees saw loss or limitation contained in their inability to speak the language of their parents. This loss is described in a different context by Wayson Choy, whose autobiographical work touches on the way that language and identity are closely linked. Learning English and losing his mother tongue, the young Wayson fears that he has become, as his grandfather says, a *"mo-no,"* "Chinese and not-Chinese at the same time ... doomed to be brainless" (cited in Costantino 2008, 137). The participants here did not describe themselves in such stark terms, but they did signal that their sense of identity had been substantially affected by their use of English.

One participant, who remarked early in his interview on his inability to relate to Hindi, felt that he had lost a great deal culturally throughout his life, and he had some misgivings about the fact that his children were likely to lose even more. Suhil, a Toronto-born resident of Ottawa, made the following observation in the questionnaire when explaining how he perceived his culture: "I've seen my heritage as being Indian but heavily influenced by my parents' East African roots. However, without fully speaking the language (Gujarati), these cultural influences have been limited." His observations are particularly pertinent, as they seem to validate those made by another Ottawa interviewee, Kahil, whose ethnic background is almost identical to that of Suhil.

Also Canadian-born, Kahil was raised in an environment where his grandparents refused to speak English with him, ensuring that he became fluent in Gujarati and conversant in other Indian languages, a legacy that he cherished and identified as central to his understanding of ethnicity. Whereas Suhil seemed to feel a sense of distance from his Indian ancestry, acknowledging it but hardly immersing himself in it, Kahil was far more invested in South Asian culture and norms, conducting himself with no difficulty on trips to India or neighbouring countries, for instance, and having an obvious familiarity with and enjoyment of Indian songs, films, and fashions. Although Suhil and Kahil differed in some ways regarding their cultural activities and their level of affiliation with South Asian cultural norms, both said that they would identify themselves as Canadian, and both were adamant about refusing to accept other characterizations.

Alma was similarly resistant to those who would deny her nationality, but her comments on the link between ethnicity and nationality were interesting because she incorporated a rather different perspective. In fact, although many of the participants tended to address only the link between ethnicity and nationality or between religion and nationality, Alma's response indicated how much thought she had given to what she saw as a kind of sea change in the way the three co-existed:

> They [ethnicity, religion, and nationality] are intertwined just because originally, I would say my religion is very culturally interpreted. I'm going to be a little specific here, Islam is a very Arabic culture in its interpretation but I find that real Islam is not so much Arabic interpretation; it's more, it's supposed to be universal. Pakistani culture and Islamic religious values, they can intertwine, but it won't be in the more widespread or traditional way. Most countries now, including Pakistan and India, tend to redefine Islam in a very Arabic way, and the way they use the religion to define the culture has changed a lot, so the religion itself is actually redefining the culture instead of the other way around.

Alma's reasons for blending the three here were clearly articulated and implied a fairly broad concern with the interpretation of her own religion, Islam, a concern that was echoed by other young Muslims, several of whom felt that it was difficult to speak of their identity without commenting on the role of faith in their lives.

Keeping the Faith: Religion and Identity

One group in particular interested me because at least two of the members moved quickly toward the topic of religion when discussing how they articulated their nationality. Although one said that she would identify as Indian and another noted her parents' African birth, both said that in expanding further they would explain that they were Ismaili Muslim. This was the only group where such an interplay occurred, and it took place with some consistency. There could be any number of reasons why this was the case, including the possibility that these individuals – who were among the youngest in the study – had not given as much thought to the parsing of these identities as had the other participants, but their later comments on religion and culture suggested to me that in fact they had pondered these issues before and simply saw their faith as essential to every aspect of their identity.

Their willingness to identify as specifically Ismaili Muslim in speaking to others could also be read through the lens of their geographical placement – as Nimrit noted, Ismailis are relatively prominent in Vancouver, especially in the suburb of Burnaby, so to describe oneself as Ismaili may frequently evoke recognition from knowledgeable listeners who understand their history of migration. Ismailis are present in larger numbers in Toronto and have a small community in Ottawa, but they do not appear to be as well known in those cities as they are in Vancouver, an impression remarked on by Nimrit, a Vancouver Sikh with many Ismaili friends in Vancouver. She lamented that she was unable to see any Ismailis on a visit to Toronto. Rather, she stated, she saw large numbers of Pakistani Sunni Muslims, people to whom she felt unable to relate: "I don't relate to their thinking at all, because I find there's a lot of difference between Ismaili Muslims and other Muslims in terms of how you approach a lot of social issues."

Clearly, there is considerable diversity among Muslims in Canada, a diversity that is perhaps not reflected entirely in this study. Whether there is, as Nimrit apparently suggested, a pronounced conservatism among some Canadian Muslims, particularly Sunnis, it did not come out here, as few Sunnis responded to invitations to participate. There were, however, Muslims of Pakistani origin, and they did describe seeing such conservatism without necessarily endorsing it. Alma, a Shia Ithnashri, spoke of the considerable pressures she experienced from community members when she began to explore her religion and culture more deeply and hence made decisions with which they did not agree, such as ceasing to wear a headscarf. Although her parents supported her choice, other family members and friends made it clear that they saw her decision as a repudiation of her faith, something she denied. She pointed out that her attire remained modest and that she was a practising Muslim, but she no longer saw the headscarf as a crucial element of her faith. She was certainly not the only woman in the study to describe pressure to conform to communal norms around gender, but she was one of the few who experienced pressures explicitly linked to differing interpretations of religion.

In fact, the scenario Alma outlined is one that perhaps aligns most clearly with popular renderings of the Muslim woman in Canada as a potential victim of masculine and communal domination, renderings that Bhimani (2003, 6) suggests are deeply rooted in history and that reflect "the fact that Muslims and Muslim societies have not been the storytellers of their lives." This study cannot in itself reverse that trend, but there is an attempt here to allow young Muslims to speak in their own words about the role of faith in their lives. Several spoke of a resistance to negative depictions of Islam and indicated both a sense of reservation about indicating their faith to others, who might form mistaken impressions of them on that basis, and an increased sense of identity and awareness about being Muslim. Very few mentioned the events of 11 September 2001, but there seemed to be an implicit undertone to their comments that suggested their awareness of an increased marginalization and pronounced scrutiny of Muslims and Islam. There seemed to be an accepted understanding that Muslims had to explain themselves to others quite frequently, and in one or two interviews, there was an acknowledgment that this requirement was more pronounced for some Muslims than for others. Although the participants in one group seemed to comment in passing on the conservatism of Sunni Pakistani Muslims, they also indicated a certain amount of solidarity when critiquing non-Muslims and non–South Asians who asked uninformed questions about headscarfs, arranged marriages, and terrorism.

Saunders (2007), writing for the *Globe and Mail*, indicates something similar following an interview with several young Europeans who identify as Muslim first, a viewpoint that he admits to disliking. However, probing more deeply, he uncovers signs that these young Muslims have no desire to renounce their national identity or to work toward creating a Muslim state. Rather, with the spotlight frequently turned on their religious identity and on other Muslims around the world, they tend to be constantly aware of their faith. In fact, Saunders (2007, F3) concludes, it is not necessarily the Muslim youth who attempt to marginalize themselves; instead, they are simply reacting to those who consistently refuse to overlook their difference: "Once we get past the hysteria and look at the facts, something becomes apparent about the Muslims: They're just like any group of immigrants, except for the stories we tell about them."

None of the participants here went so far as to identify themselves as Muslim first, but it was clear that several of them had given considerable thought to their positioning as Muslims in a time when such identification might evoke preconceptions on the part of others. These feelings came out even more strongly in discussions of Bollywood depictions of Muslims, but Tariq's more general rendering of his religious identity seemed to summarize what many of the Muslim participants felt:

> I do feel the need to identify the fact that I'm Muslim, I wouldn't write it down necessarily because I wouldn't want anybody to characterize me as such, but I think it is an integral part of who I am today, and how I continue to essentially choose how I proceed in my everyday ongoings as a Muslim. Now, that may be very different in terms of how a person would perceive me to be acting as a Muslim, but I feel that everything that I do on a given day is guided by the fact that yes, I am a Muslim, and I am a Canadian Muslim.

The emphasis in this study is on Islam, so it is perhaps no surprise that the Muslim participants were the ones who occasionally expressed a sense that they and their co-practitioners were under siege, to a certain extent. However, one interesting aspect that emerged was the willingness of the participants here to acknowledge the hybrid and pluralist legacies that many people deny when discussing the history of the subcontinent.

Nimrit, a Sikh, commented on the fact that different religious groups had co-existed harmoniously in South Asia, a fact that she believed should be more commonly known, while Simran noted that as she had grown older, she had realized the influence of Hinduism on her everyday life in her Sikh parents' home. She attributed part of this to their place of birth, which was in an area adjacent to Punjab but not in it. The closeness to other Hindus may have made her parents more aware of Hindu customs and rituals, some of which they adopted. As a child, she did not understand that any distinction might exist, but as she became more aware, especially during visits to India, she realized that she had experienced a kind of dual Hindu-Sikh legacy. Several of the Muslim participants also indicated their awareness that Hindu rituals inflected their lives, although they commented that this was something their parents participated in without fully acknowledging this influence. Indeed, a desire to understand religion more completely was expressed on several occasions, with many of the young people explaining that they had to seek knowledge outside of their households. This desire was not limited to religious education, but religion did seem to be a powerful motivating factor for the Muslims and the Sikhs involved in the study, many of whom found their answers in formal education but a number of whom supplemented this in other ways.

Looking for Answers: Family, Education, and Media

Perhaps inevitably, most of the young adults interviewed here pointed to family as one of the primary influences in their understanding of culture and religion. Nationality was occasionally tied into this but most often seemed to be filtered through the world outside their homes. Inside their homes, individuals were acculturated in a number of ways, and even those living separately from their parents sometimes indicated that they participated in cultural or religious rituals more often when they visited home. Whether they were raised in small towns or big cities, the influence of family was undeniable and appeared to operate in similar ways. Although the options for participating in community events had become widespread in Vancouver and Toronto, Alma pointed out that this was not the case when she was growing up and immigrants were still establishing themselves, so families often had to assume considerable responsibility for educating children about religion and culture. Tariq also noted the importance of family, and again the importance of language was raised, although other factors evidently played a role:

> Family plays an integral part, especially given the fact that you're born here, that's pretty much the first touch that you have, and given the fact that, you know, at home we did speak Urdu or Hindi or whatever. That plays a role. It definitely plays a role. In terms of other stimulus? Everything, really. You're looking at stuff like mass media, you're looking at people you come in contact with, you're looking at restaurants that you go to.

Musnah agreed with this, although in her case she described a scenario where her father's insistence on maintaining national and religious pride was far more pronounced than that of other participants' parents. Radha, for instance, responding to Musnah's comments, said that her own growing interest in culture, or at least language, was not parentally dictated in any way, whereas Musnah spoke later in the interview about the fact that as she had grown older she had developed some notions that differed from those of her parents and that she no longer felt a strict obligation to envelop herself in Pakistani Muslim culture at all times.

> Musnah: I think definitely my parents – or my family. This is the biggest factor, because my parents, or my dad, has always constantly stressed the idea that we're not from here. He would go on huge rants, like, we're not Canadian, we're Pakistani Muslim, everything, just from that kind of thinking, everything else that has also reminded me of what my nationality and

culture is, it's because of them. So you know, we all went as a family to see our first Bollywood film because my dad wants us to know what our culture is, and I went to Sunday school so I could know what my religion is, I was told to speak in Urdu at home because, you know, this is our culture, it's maintaining that sense of pride, so everything just goes back to them, like any other factor is related to their need to remind me of who I am.

F: All right. So a very conscious kind of process then, in your family?

Musnah: Yeah, for sure, like propaganda [laughs].

Radha: I'm getting a drive now to learn the language, my mom speaks fourteen languages, my dad speaks three languages, no one ever spoke anything but English at home, so I never learned anything. And now the reason I'm starting to learn is not actually if I go to India, at least I'll be able to talk to people, for some reason, that probably should be a priority but it's not particularly. The reason I'm starting is so that at least my kids can learn something.

The number of times that family and community recurred as factors seemed quite natural, and these extended into related issues around language, visits to temples/mosques/gurdwaras, travel, and media. However, one other major factor arose throughout the conversations I conducted with these informants, and that was education in a variety of forms. Perhaps naively, I was surprised by the number of times school or education was raised as a factor that influenced understanding of nationality and culture, although interviewees elaborated on this answer in manifold ways. Some identified school as a means of assimilation or integration, a place where new immigrants or second-generation immigrants were taught about mainstream cultural norms. Others, however, pointed to the fact that they sought answers about their ethnic roots through their education, especially at the higher levels, at least in part because their communities or families could not always supply the information they sought. A few noted that their parents or religious leaders simply did not know the history of their cultures, countries, or religions well enough to educate their children outside of a limited point of view, and formal education sometimes led to those children cultivating perspectives significantly different from those of their parents. At the same time, Kahil also suggested that school taught him that being Canadian meant adopting a pluralist philosophy and that it was important to embrace one's own origins but also to respect the views and beliefs of others.

The young adults in this study had a broad range of educational and occupational backgrounds, and their approaches differed accordingly. Simran, whose interview was filled with thoughtful insights regarding religion, culture, and media, commented on the influence that school had on her critical viewing ability. Nimrit expressed a belief that there was significant religious knowledge and cultural or nationalist history that she would benefit from learning, and since there were few avenues for her to attain this through her community, she had chosen to pursue such education independently. As with the young woman described in Maira's (2002, 119) study whose desire to know such answers resulted in frustration from religious leaders or family, several individuals here, especially women, indicated their refusal to accept passively a state of ignorance about religion or culture. Iram's group agreed that parents' understanding of religious and cultural issues is not always the same as that of their children, a gap that Iram attributed to different educational training:

> I also think education is a huge part of it. If you're – I'm not saying that if you're not educated you're not going to understand, but ... I've also taken Indian courses too, at school, it actually opens your eyes up into a different sort of area ... I was watching *Mughal-e-Azam* [1960] and it was right after we finished the Mughal Empire period at school in my Southeast Asian class. And I watched it, and I had already watched it previously and I was getting bored, like I don't understand why they're doing this, this is crap. I watched *Mughal-e-Azam* after my project, and I watched the whole thing without fast-forwarding it. And I understood so much more. I could relate to so many of the themes ... They're just not depicting things in fantasy, this actually happened. And there are books out there with material that can be referenced to the movie, so if I was to do a paper on it, I could definitely use that movie [laughs].

She went on to explain, with agreement from Nimrit, that without the kind of classes she had described, she would have been at a loss to understand all of her history, as the community resources in place emphasized only a few aspects of this:

> Iram: In my class, I had a lot of people that were Punjabi and that were Hindu, and there were only two of us that were Muslim, and it was like, the both of us are sitting there going, I don't really know what's happening, because with our culture, with Muslims, you don't learn about – we learn about the Mughal Empire, but we don't learn about the Muslim-Hindu-Sikh friction or anything like that. The only source of knowledge that we can get besides postsecondary education in that field would be our BUI [referring to religious education at the primary and secondary levels for Ismaili Muslim youth], and they don't even teach that.

> Nimrit: Same with Sikhism. They don't teach you what happened.

Nimrit was one of the participants who referred to her travels in South Asia as a way of alleviating this lack of knowledge, and travel to India and Pakistan did appear highly formative for some, strengthening their ties to what they saw as the culture of origin. Simran spoke clearly of the influence these trips had on her, and she also articulated this influence by speaking with reference to the kind of nostalgia and connectedness that might be attributed more often to a first-generation immigrant:

> I was taken to India quite a few times in my life, when I was growing up. The first time was when I was about seven years old, and it was actually – I think it impacted my sense of identity, and where I belong, and when I was there, the majority of my extended family was there, so I felt very connected to the community and to the country. And for years afterward, we would talk about it as though it was this nostalgic piece in our lives, and then I went back when I was twelve, and that was just as impacting.

Simran's answer indicated the strongest level of emotion and impact, which could possibly be linked to her upbringing in a small town with very few other South Asians. In contrast, Musnah's reference to Pakistan as evoking an expanded Little India, rather than a new and exciting site of belonging, may signify that her previous exposure to Little Pakistan or Little India in Toronto blunted the significance of this in terms of her sense of belonging. However, it is also possible that Musnah's frame of reference and expectations were vastly removed from Simran's because of her parents' emphasis on Pakistan as another home or place of settlement, whereas Simran was apparently subject to no such outlook.

Alma also commented on the importance of visits to Pakistan, where she had family, but she described a shift in attitude that disturbed her and perhaps contributed to her interest in the future of Islam. Although she enjoyed being in Pakistan as a child and then again as an adult, she saw an increasingly conservative form of Islam settling in there, which she interpreted as a distinct response to the events of 11 September 2001 and the subsequent attention to Islam and Islamic practice. Interestingly, although Alma, Musnah, and Tariq all talked about trips to Pakistan, each noted different specifics. Tariq did not necessarily agree with Musnah's contention that Karachi was less culturally conservative than her parents believed, but he echoed her sentiment that there was no stronger sense of belonging in Pakistan than in Canada.

Kahil did not describe his trips to India – most or all of which were business-related rather than familial journeys – as having a strong formative influence, but he did seem to feel a high level of comfort, and one factor in this was his familiarity with Indian film. Not all of the participants identified Bollywood as a major influence in shaping their sense of nationality, culture, or religion, but some did, and a large number did point to media influences in general. One group in Vancouver agreed that film in general was a major media influence, regardless of the category of film being viewed. Other participants suggested that film was not particularly significant, although it was interesting to note that most were able to indicate some familiarity with English-language movies that addressed Indian subject matter, such as *Water* (2005), *Earth* (1998), *Bend It Like Beckham* (2003), and *Monsoon Wedding* (2001). This did not translate into appreciating all of these films, but it was clear that the genre had considerable reach among diasporic young South Asians.

Outside of this major source of commonality, there was variation in the forms of media used, including academic and literary books, news, and lectures organized by various community groups on religious or cultural topics. Books were raised frequently, with even Radha, who refused to concede that media were influential in any way in her life, stating at one point that she had sought out Indian-authored novels as a way of retaining her culture. Like Radha, Nalini said that she did not watch a lot of movies and favoured books, especially those by women of colour, which may call into question the actual popularity and effectiveness of visual media. Radio was not mentioned in questionnaires, but Simran did cite it in her interview, explaining that a multicultural station had been a link to cultural practice when her family lived in a less than diverse area. Nimrit also mentioned these radio stations but made this reference in the specific context of relating radio to the movie *Salaam Namaste* (2005), which featured a deejay as the heroine. Although Raveena did not name radio as an influence, she talked about the fact that Punjabi culture had entered the mainstream and that this resonated with her, especially when rapper Jay-Z released a popular song that included remixed segments from South Asian musician Punjabi MC. Throughout the interviews, in fact, respondents revealed ambivalence about the increased acceptability and globalization of South Asian culture, an acceptability that made them feel less self-conscious or embarrassed about publicly embracing this culture yet one that also cheapened it in some ways, diminishing authenticity and causing them to question their own motivations. The following explanation from Alia, which begins by discussing Bollywood and then broadens into a larger discussion of Hollywood and music stars, indicates the difficulty some felt in breaking down cultural influences to their most basic elements in order to judge which influences were acceptable and which were not:

> I think just for example when I was younger, wearing an East Indian outfit in public to me was something I just could not do. I would be too embarrassed to do that, whereas now as Hollywood and Bollywood sort of merged

I'm more willing to do that. You know, you see Gwen Stefani wearing a little tikka on her forehead, you know what I mean? I'm more willing to go out in public dressed like that but I don't know whether that's more due to Hollywood influence or Bollywood influence.

As the following chapter reveals, Bollywood, then, does have a certain amount of influence, but this is hardly universal, even in the group studied here. This influence must be judged in the context of intertwined cultural factors.

There are in fact no simple answers to many of the questions posed here, and the apparent contradictions that arose seem to speak to the complexity of the lives that these young people lead. Alma's response, like several others that were given throughout the study, is one that considers a number of factors. It dismisses no possibilities, but it does not embrace any uncritically. She spoke of Toronto as a cosmopolitan space filled with promise and choice, and in doing so, she observed throughout the ways that Canada has evolved, a point made by many participants. Their lives are not unproblematic, their identities are not simple, they did not agree on everything, but they did indicate how quickly integration may occur and how meaningful it is to minorities when they see themselves being represented in any way, even if this way is not always as rounded or developed as it might be. That elusive and well-nigh impossible element of authenticity reared its head several times, but the group itself seemed to acknowledge the futility of finding media of any kind that were entirely unproblematic. Even the most well-intentioned efforts to disclose South Asian history may leave out important elements, including the plurality and the joint legacy of suffering that many fail to acknowledge. Among my participants, there was no single solution to this gap in knowledge; some filled it through books, others through film, still others through some form of education. Within this, Bollywood was able to play some part, and it occupied a more meaningful role than perhaps some would have envisioned.

9
Bollywood: Films as Meeting Ground

The paradoxes evidently at work in Bollywood films are by no means lost on their diasporic young viewers, whose own lives encompass a network of contradictions that this study's participants found alternately puzzling and satisfying. Bollywood carried comforting familiarity for some but was far too alien for others. A number of participants remembered growing up with Indian films in the background, and several described the rituals and cross-generational conversations that unfolded around these. Language was taught and maintained through watching these films, and some valued them particularly for this reason. As far as the content, opinions diverged wildly, although there was a notable degree of confluence around topics such as the representation of gender, which was interwoven into discussions around inequity in South Asian culture. Depictions of the South Asian diaspora and of certain ethnic or religious groups were also criticized for their exaggerations and stereotypes, which were sometimes seen as direct insults to the viewers, depending on their own origins.

The complicated, tenuous relationship Bollywood has with modernity and with what it understands to be the West elicited equally complicated reactions from viewers, who alternately deplored the consumerism, the hedonism, and the lack of family values seen in films addressing Western themes. At the same time, the consumerism in the films, as well as the mainstream acceptability bestowed on Bollywood-related goods and fashions, carried their own appeal for young people who had previously experienced embarrassment in relation to their ethnic identity. Individual positioning played a distinct role in determining interpretation and outcomes, leaving only one real conclusion: Bollywood was as intensely problematic as it was significant in the lives of these viewers.

One of the Family: Bollywood at Home
Among the people I interviewed, most agreed that viewing Bollywood films, as Gillespie (1995) notes in her landmark study on Punjabi families living

in the United Kingdom, can provide a convenient and enjoyable venue for family activities. This is particularly true because differing linguistic capabilities may play a role in determining which television or film programs may be viewed by the entire family. Older members may be unable to comprehend enough English to understand the mainstream North American programming watched by young members, who may in turn struggle with Hindi or other South Asian languages used in specialty programming watched by grandparents or parents. Bollywood films are now frequently subtitled in a number of languages such as English, Spanish, Dutch, and Arabic, and they also offer action and narratives that can be easily understood even without the benefit of such subtitles.

It is notable that several young adults, even those who rarely watched Bollywood, described the constant playing of these films as a kind of ubiquitous, background media presence in their parents' homes or in the homes of their relatives. Some said laughingly that they ended up viewing some of the films merely because they were so omnipresent that it was hard to avoid seeing the content. In a sense, then, Bollywood managed to become a visible and accepted part of the family setting over the course of an ordinary day. It was clear that for a number of participants, family rituals constructed around Indian films, such as a regularly occurring Hindi film night, had significantly affected their watching levels and enjoyment. Many commented that their viewing habits had decreased as adults, which was sometimes due to a lack of interest but could also be attributed to a change in lifestyle or in critical-viewing ability:

F: Do you watch Bollywood films?

Alma: I do. Not as much as I used to.

F: Okay. Did you used to watch a lot before because of your family?

Alma: Yeah, because actually it was the only way of involving yourself in the culture. You really couldn't go out to a club and see a garba [a form of Indian dance] or something like that. The only way you could see it was on TV and through Indian movies, so it was just ways to remind yourself that this is what we have, and this is fun and this is how they are. Now I'm not so much immersed, I can't spend three hours watching a movie.

Kahil's parents had made a point of setting aside one night a week that became an evening for the family to watch Indian films, and he did continue to watch occasionally, generally with friends or on his own. Like other young people in this study who now lived away from their parents, his level of watching had dropped significantly, but in childhood his parents had treated film viewing as the prime Saturday night activity, and like Iram, Sheila, and

Maida, whose parents or grandparents had created similar habits in their homes, he retained affection for these films and recalled them as part of his childhood experiences.

Nazia was one of the few whose change in viewing habits had affected a parent. Although she was not very likely to watch Bollywood films on her own, she commented that watching them remained a pleasurable way to share time with her mother. Although an avid viewer of popular movies, her mother attempted to accommodate Nazia's interest in political and social issues by selecting films that addressed these topics:

> I really like Bollywood films with a bit of a political slant to them. So I really enjoyed *Lagaan* [Land Tax, 2001], and I liked *Ek Hasina Thi* [There Was a Beautiful Girl, 2004] and *Swades* [Our Country, 2004]. I am not into corny romance so much, so the more complex storylines are good. I am not sure what you mean if they are important to me. I see Bollywood as another form of corporate entertainment, and while it contributes to identity, I don't feel it completely names or contextualizes my identity. I guess in a sense, it is a way for my mother to bond with me, for us to share with a lost culture, and she tries to find the more political and feminist films for me to enjoy. She simply prefers to watch Shah Rukh Khan movies only.

Simran's childhood experiences tended to be rather different from those of most other participants; a student in Toronto at the time of the interview, she had spent her early years in a small town on Vancouver Island, where other South Asians were scarce. However, she commented that she did have a few other friends of South Asian origin, and they would meet regularly to watch Bollywood films and to discuss them in some detail. Although she continued to watch them now, she tended to select films that were more political or that addressed history or social issues.

Interestingly, Musnah, who described the distinct process of socialization on which her father embarked, requiring his children to view Indian films, also recalled not greatly enjoying the movies. She had more familiarity with some of the older films than did other participants and commented on their socio-political value, but for herself, enjoyment came only with the release of the often cited blockbuster *Hum Aapke Hain Koun* (*HAHK;* Who Am I to You?, 1994). Several young people remarked on lush, quasi-modern pictures such as *HAHK, Dilwale Dulhania Le Jayenge* (*DDLJ;* The Lover Takes the Bride, 1995), and *Kuch Kuch Hota Hai* (Something Happens, 1998) as being among the first films to catch their attention and bring them into the Bollywood-viewing fold, but of these films *HAHK* garnered the most mentions:

> Musnah: I mean, I remember, when I was growing up, I never really cared for Indian, or Bollywood movies, or anything. Like, I don't really remember

us watching them so much, but I just remember like distinctly, like, you know, I was in Grade 6, and my friends were like, "Oh, there's this movie *Hum Aapke Hain Koun* coming out, and we should all go see it, everyone's talking about it." And that was like when it made its comeback. When I watched this movie, I was like, whoa, I liked the music, the family. I don't know, I liked it, after that, I was like, this is cool, and I started learning Indian stars' names and stuff.

Simran described her viewing of Bollywood films as being more a hobby than a cultural influence, although I noticed at one point in her interview that she described one movie in personal and moving terms, an effect that seems difficult to dismiss as part of a hobby: "It's played a role ... I guess like any hobby would play a role. I am the type of person who has used books and movies as a way of understanding issues in life, so yeah, I think they probably shaped my perceptions or challenged my ways of looking." Alma, who, like Musnah, cited the significance of *HAHK*, connecting its depictions of weddings and rituals to those she had seen in Pakistan, viewed Bollywood movies less than she used to, but this had more to do with time and with the fact that she felt different, more authentic cultural options were available to her. However, she still felt that these films had influenced her lifestyle and habits in some way:

F: Do you think watching Bollywood has influenced the kind of person you are in any way?

Alma: It's made me a little bit more cultural, for sure. If I didn't have Bollywood, I wouldn't enjoy the music as much, like Indian desi music, I wouldn't enjoy dancing, all those things, without those initially you didn't really have a venue to see that. With the Bollywood films, at least they gave you that. You can recognize yourself. With the songs, you heard them all the time. They're identifiable everywhere you went because of desi functions, because everyone has their favourites and classics. Same thing with the dance, if you never saw it, you would have no idea how it would work.

Alma's observation that "You can recognize yourself" was significant, as she referred often to the challenges of growing up as a young Pakistani Muslim in Toronto when the community was still in its formative stages. She described it as being a sheltered, closed-in existence that she now saw replicated in some places, including Toronto, as Muslims came under increasing scrutiny. In contrast, she herself had come to terms with her identity in many respects and enjoyed many aspects of South Asian culture, including some of those depicted in Bollywood films.

Although Nazia might not have gone so far as to say that she could recognize herself in these films, she did say that she would be willing to screen them for her children one day, provided that she picked the more political ones: "It is a great way to keep the language going. I can say that the only reason I understand Hindi/Urdu is because of Bollywood." Others remarked on this aspect as well, although some, such as Alma or Musnah, had no real need to view Bollywood films in order to develop linguistic ability. Radha commented on the fact that her cousin had specifically chosen Bollywood as a venue to teach her two children Hindi, a choice that Radha considered interesting given the other avenues available. Jaya, a Gujarati speaker, also learned Hindi partly through viewing Bollywood films, and Iram and Maida, raised in Gujarati- or Kutchi-speaking homes, saw Bollywood as the chief reason they could both understand Hindi quite well.

Language, then, was an important part of the films' appeal and continuity, but Iram seemed to encapsulate her feelings and those of another participant in her group when she said:

It's a part of our culture, right? I would have my children watch Indian movies but I wouldn't force it upon them that, oh, you have to sit here and watch it. You know what, yes, you will make it a night. And you know that every Sunday or every Friday night, that's what's going to happen. The other days, you do whatever you want. If you want to watch another Indian movie or go to a music party or go Indian shopping, we'll do it, but I'd love you to have that and if they don't then that's something they don't ... and that's just based all on personal upbringing and whatever. I want them to understand that it is a part that makes you who you are.

"That Movie Touched My Soul": Films as Agents of Socialization

Iram, in fact, was sufficiently affected by the influence of Bollywood in her life that she commented regretfully on the fact that her brother had strayed away from this influence, which she saw as a form of loss. For those young adults who did regularly watch Bollywood films, the family connection often tended to be of great importance, and as Alma noted, this connection then extended to other South Asians who could comment on the songs, movies, and dances. Although linguistic barriers and the desire for cultural continuity were key in the establishment of a family-film connection, participants also noted that the generally chaste nature of the productions was another strong selling point, allowing them to watch family-friendly content with their parents. Several were strongly critical of what they saw as increased sexual content and immodest behaviour in recent popular Indian films, suggesting that the presence of sexually suggestive scenes, in particular, made it increasingly difficult to use such cinema as a point of commonality with older family members. One group of young women in Vancouver quipped that they needed to be warned about these movies and recommended a rating system similar to that of Hollywood's, where PG would be replaced with "Not recommended with parents."

These informants, along with others, felt that Bollywood's inclusion of such aspects was mistakenly intended to indicate that Indian cinema could be as sophisticated as North American films, although there was a certain amount of puzzlement regarding the ultimate reason for the sexual content. The majority of participants expressed discomfort over the idea of watching explicit scenes with their parents or grandparents, noting that they preferred not to watch English films with older family members because they did not wish to jointly view material seen as having a high degree of sexual content and perceived permissiveness. If the increase in such material in Bollywood films is meant to serve as a bridge to young South Asians living in the diaspora, who presumably have become accustomed to similar content in their North American programming, the strategy appears to have backfired. Alia's input seemed to summarize the general trend in opinion:

F: Since you've been watching pretty much all your life, have you noticed a change at all in terms of that?

Alia: Yeah, I think that there's a lot – a *lot* more North American influence.

F: Do you like it better or worse because of that?

Alia: [considers] I like it worse. [laughs]. 'Cause that's not – if I wanted to watch something North American, I'd watch a North American movie, you know, I wouldn't ... but ... it's just my opinion. I like more classical-type movies.

Viewers complained of Bollywood's mistaken assumptions about people living in the West and seemed to suggest that recent films had in fact lost touch with the values that initially attracted their admiration, the same values that Alia felt her mother had wanted to transmit to her when they began watching Indian cinema together.

It is almost a truism in studies of Bollywood cinema, in fact, that the enduring appeal of these movies lies in their ability to convey a sense of authentic Indian values, whether this sense is accurate or not. Despite the apparently irrelevant nature of films whose chief focus is love and family, this subject matter allows for a continued emphasis on key values and traditions that might otherwise be forgotten or dismissed, especially when South Asians living in the diaspora are offered a host of other cultural influences. By highlighting weddings and other family celebrations, Bollywood films affirm the importance of marriage, reproduction, and respect for relatives.

Some of the participants indicated that they were largely indifferent to the depiction of rituals in popular Indian films, noting that these held no relevance for them. This was true for some of the Muslim and Sikh respondents, who felt unable to relate to the mainly Hindu rituals shown, although a few, including Alma, Nadim, and Farah, did suggest that they derived some pleasure from watching these. When this did occur, it was for one or both of the following reasons: they were able to draw a connection to some ritual in their own culture, or they felt that it helped them to learn about other cultures. Nadim pointed out the importance of growing up in Brampton, Ontario, next to many other South Asians of varying backgrounds, where he and Farah, he suggested, had likely picked up familiarity with many rituals and habits: "If we grew up ... in a pretty white city, not really exposed to other Indian cultures, I think I would find their depictions of Hindus and Sikhs quite foreign." Perhaps in keeping with this, several participants felt largely alienated from what they saw, not simply because it was foreign to them but because they saw the Bollywood version of ritual and tradition as simplistic, generic, and occasionally misleading.

Asked whether being Sikh made a difference to her position as a viewer, Simran replied that she did see herself as a kind of underdog when watching Bollywood movies as a younger person, a feeling that may have been emphasized by her sense of being an ethnic outsider in a small town. However, she also noted that her parents educated her about Hinduism as well as Sikhism, to some extent, which had helped to alleviate some of this feeling and may even have been responsible for her dislike of Punjabi-themed films and her preference for Hindu ones when she was young.

Iram also commented on a kind of outsider positioning but not one that she necessarily blamed on Bollywood producers, admitting that the form of Islam she practises is relatively private: "With religion, with the Muslim religion, I don't know, I think because we're Ismaili, our faith is really closed in, we can't expect to see anything in that Shia Islam be portrayed, it's always Muslims in general, that person saying his *namaaz* [prayer]." On the other hand, Nimrit, a Sikh who indicated that she did not necessarily find Bollywood to be inclusive or representative, nonetheless found films that spoke eloquently to her understanding of history, culture, and religion, and in this sense Bollywood opened her eyes to facts that would not otherwise have to come to light:

I don't think people truly understand – 'cause our parents' generation all felt the effects of that Independence, and I do not think you can truly understand what being Indian is until you understand what happened then to all three major groups that were involved. And for me it was an experience to really embrace my grandparents, my great-grandparents, to embrace my parents, and embrace what I've been given today. Because what I have today is a whole night-and-day difference from what a woman had back then [sounds of agreement from all]. As a female and then even in religious aspects, I mean, Sikhs and Muslims lived together like brothers and sisters and used to share turbans and now all of a sudden, it's like you can't even marry a Muslim boy? Well, at one point I was your neighbor, they used to intertwine. My grandmother, I actually found this out after watching the movie [*Pinjar* (Skeleton, 2003)], my grandmother, her side of the family there were Muslims and Sikhs intermixed. Didn't know that. That would never be heard of now. And for me, that's really hard to believe considering almost fifty years ago it was okay. Not even two hundred years ago, fifty years ago. So for me, that movie touched my soul more than anything.

Bollywood films do provide a certain form of socialization for these young people, then, but in a way that is probably not anticipated by filmmakers. Some did feel slightly closer to their culture through viewing these films, but others felt either ambivalent or alienated. Some acknowledged that their parents or other relatives, all first-generation immigrants, might be able to relate to the values taught in these films, but they saw themselves as being differently positioned, unable to accept unquestioningly what was portrayed. Several participants, even ones who genuinely enjoyed watching Indian movies and who felt that this viewing had helped them to learn Hindi and to understand aspects of Hindu culture, expressed discomfiture with por-trayals of gender, religion, and relationships that they saw as outdated and unjust.

"Bollywood Gave Me Unrealistic Expectations": Representations of Self

Many of the respondents expressed disapproval of the stereotypes they found in popular Indian cinema, particularly those that revolved around gender roles, religion, and South Asians living in the diaspora. Even when Bollywood attempted to portray its own version of modernity, they found it to be flawed and simplistic, and they resented the mixed messages this sent both to South Asians and to non–South Asians whose only knowledge of the culture might be derived from watching such films. Empowerment for women was seen as temporary and superficial, lasting only until marriage, which was still deemed to be the ultimate goal for young Indian women, and apparent signifiers of sophistication or sexiness, such as cropped tops and short skirts, were seen as contributing to an overall objectification of women. Zara, Nadim, and Farah all praised the family values in Indian cinema, but Nadim in particular commented that he was troubled by the fact that women were so often expected to bend to the will of parents in these films: "I kind of see that more with women, that they're held to a standard that's almost ridicu-lous. I see that as almost propagandist, that that's not there by accident."

A number of participants noted that they were so disenchanted with the portrayal of women in Bollywood films that they rarely watched them, and one participant commented flatly that she was completely unable to identify with Bollywood films for this reason. There was some ambiguity over the question of whether these films offered an accurate depiction of Indian women's lives. Some interviewees, rather than criticizing the films alone, expressed disgust with a culture that could allow women to be treated as subservient helpers. Others suggested that Bollywood films presented a version of womanhood – obedient to the husband and parents, educated, lovely, preferably fair-skinned – that was so unrealistic and yet so prevalent in cinema that it fostered unreasonable expectations in South Asian families and men seeking potential brides. Asha and Nazia also extended this analysis to a critique of the portrayal of romance in general in Bollywood cinema, with Asha expressing a concern that some young South Asian women develop a belief that love is meant to be tortured and difficult. Similarly, Nadim noted the fact that the pursuit of unrequited love by men was valorized, promoting a form of obsessive behaviour that he thought would be terrifying in reality for most women. Nazia personalized this observation, responding to a question about Bollywood's influence by suggesting that although she had moved beyond any serious effect, she could see the potential for these films to offer skewed portrayals of gender, love, and marriage:

I watch Bollywood as a form of entertainment, and try to turn my friends on to it. But in terms of who I am, no. I did join a group on Facebook, though. It's called "Bollywood Gave me Unrealistic Expectations about Love" – which is a joke – but somewhat true. As a child, I did watch these films and did have clear messages about heteronormativity and beauty. Naturally, these are unrealistic and sexist – but I had them. I think that as a feminist Muslim, fighting these sometimes sexist notions of love, monogamy, and marriage is a challenge in Canada when those values are so entrenched in faith and in diasporic identities.

Asha answered the same question with a similar emphasis on the representation of gender and added that she felt distress when she thought of non-Indian people using Bollywood as a medium to understand the culture:

I think also I feel the need to explain – I have a lot of friends who aren't Indian who watch Bollywood films, who like watching Bollywood, and they'll tell me they saw this movie or that movie ... I remember we were in Ottawa, and we went to see *Devdas* [2002], and during the whole movie I was so angry and I was so embarrassed by the film. I was so embarrassed that I had brought friends who weren't Indian to watch it. I was really upset ... I just thought it was disgusting. If anything I always feel the need to defend Indian people in the face of Bollywood because the way that Bollywood portrays a lot of especially Indian women is very insulting, very derogatory, and I don't want non-Indian people to think that our culture is like that, how it's portrayed.

Nalini, who repudiated these films almost entirely, tried to convey the reason for the depth of her dislike: "And I feel a sense of – it makes me perhaps upset sometimes, because I feel it's so mainstream, that's what people think Indian culture is, Bollywood and it really bothers me, as a woman who's marked in some ways as geographically connected to India, and I really don't identify at all with that."

Gender, then, was an issue of overriding importance, with many of the women – but also at least two men – raising the question of inequitable treatment and social mores to which they could not relate. Several young women said that they used the representation of men and women in these films to initiate a dialogue with parents, who could acknowledge the injustice of preferential treatment for sons or for beautiful daughters when they saw it onscreen but who denied that they were guilty of the same practices in their own homes.

At the same time, however, although much of the discussion around this topic was negative, Nimrit did locate some promise by singling out *Salaam Namaste* (2005), a film that she otherwise disliked, for its attention to the intellectual talents of its heroine, an aspiring doctor. She saw that as one of the first instances where she witnessed respect for a woman's mind, and she theorized that Bollywood was undergoing a very gradual transformation and that the results would eventually trickle down to the audience. She also noted that, although attitudes differed, some young Canadian men of South Asian origin had developed increasing respect for women's intellects and careers. I was also struck by her comment that the depiction of gender in films was one reason that she had become a feminist, a position the other women in her group endorsed. Although their later discussion about the term "feminist" evidenced some confusion over what it meant to be one in the South Asian and/or Western context, they were clear that they had been inspired to seek gender equity.

Zara also spoke about gender inequity in Bollywood and commented on *Salaam Namaste* as an interesting film because it depicted, quite unusually, a couple living together and conceiving a child before marriage. Zara went on to say that she found the portrayals of women to be far too starkly delineated, allowing little possibility for nuance, although she also, however implicitly, appeared to link her vision of female emancipation to life in the diaspora: "A woman who is modern like in *Salaam Namaste* is seen as bad or not a good Muslim, and for instance, here in Canada, it's not like that at all. I am a Pakistani woman but I can be modern at the same time."

Depictions of gender, religion, and the West attracted considerable attention and occasional enmity, but class seemed less problematic for most of
these viewers. They recognized the unreality of cinematic heroines or heroes
who came from extraordinarily wealthy families, but this did not seem to
anger them in the same way that the other issues did. Most interviewees
noted laughingly that such portrayals offer a strangely skewed picture of
what life is like for many South Asians, with Nadim adding more seriously
that he was unsure why Indian films are so unwilling to portray a financial
middle ground. At the same time, a few of the female participants, as well
as one man, noted with a certain amount of guilty pleasure that the implicit
consumerism of these films, where the stars can be lavishly dressed and occasionally participate in numerous costume changes, was literally a selling
point, providing ideas for real-life couture. Both for casual viewers and heavy
ones, music and clothing were among the chief attractions of these films,
contributing to the escapist appeal or, as Nadim argued, adding to the unique
character and melodramatic quality of Indian film. Although the attractions
of clothing and music were sources of embarrassment for some, Kahil drew
a connection between the trends depicted in these movies and his ability
to have some awareness of Indian social norms when he began to travel
there for work. Superficial as that knowledge might appear, he pointed out,
it did give him a form of cultural capital that eased his path on arriving in
India, where he had no other handy source of acculturation, since his family
is four or five generations removed from that country.

However, as some long-time viewers noted astutely, these tendencies are
more recent. The lavish weddings and happy love stories that distinguished
recent blockbusters were not features of many Indian-cinema classics. Those
viewers who were familiar with older films as well as newer ones suggested
that some of the most valuable material was available in those earlier movies
in terms of education about history and intercultural conflict, although
stereotypes were present even then. Nonetheless, watching selected movies
helped to provide insight about Indian or Pakistani history, particularly with
respect to Partition or the reasons for the conflict between different groups
that they saw in the present. Several of the participants commented that
those conflicts had little relevance for them in their Canadian setting, where
they enjoyed friendships with people of many different cultural and religious
backgrounds, but they benefited all the same from the opportunity to understand their parents' and grandparents' feelings on the topic, especially when
discussing issues such as intermarriage.

Related to this, the linked issues of diversity and intermarriage also arose
during group discussions, with participants expressing criticism of a perceived
hypocrisy both within the films and within their families. Diversity, they
claimed, received only lip service, with filmmakers offering up token Muslims

and Sikhs in a landscape otherwise dominated by devout Hindus. When Muslims did make an appearance, several participants suggested, they were frequently portrayed as terrorists or villains, and Sikhs were fanatical or the object of fun or derision:

Nimrit: You either show them as Punjabis, all they do is bhangra. All they do is feed their kids ladhoos and do bhangra, and that's about it.

Sheila and Maida: Such a stereotype.

Iram: It's the ones that are Hindus that are the most pious. The ones that are the most religious, the ones that have the big lavish houses and the, you know, the excellent family. The Muslims are the ones that are just terrorists.

Maida: They beat their kids, they don't let them show their legs ... you know what I mean, it's so –

Iram: So stereotypical.

In fact, the four Sikhs in the study were unanimous in their belief that Sikhs were portrayed in a stereotypical fashion, and they expanded on this, with one person describing three archetypes that the rest seemed to recognize: the clown, the (possibly alcoholic) party animal, and the warrior. Perhaps due to her own sensitivity on this topic, Nimrit also commented on the misrepresentation of Muslims in these films: "And I'm a Sikh, so I can even say it [other girls laugh]. I'm sorry, I don't care, this is ridiculous. Like yeah, they're all Persian Iranian terrorists. Are you kidding me?" Her group, which contained one Sikh and three Muslims, demonstrated an interesting dynamic, as her comments occasionally appeared to imply a critique of Hinduism itself, although they may not have been intended in that way. There is no way of predicting whether her tone might have been altered in the presence of Hindus, but on one or two occasions I wondered whether I was witnessing a reaction to a sense of disempowerment, something Nimrit alluded to when describing her reaction to Bollywood:

Has it influenced me as a person? Yeah, it gave me a lot more understanding into why things are the way they are. Because when you grow up and everything is Hindu-happy – that's what I call it, Hindu-happy – and you don't get a chance to really see, like for example, going to Pakistan, of course it influenced me. I was scared to death crossing that border. Scared to death about going there. You know, it's portrayed as this poor little country that has no education, all they want to do is fight and make their weapons.

Sikhs and most Muslims had little hesitation raising issues about religious and cultural stereotypes, although Kahil was tolerant of perceived discrimination, commenting that there "are a lot of stereotypes that are reinforced, there are some that are broken as well." Nadim also noted that Indian cinema had once treated Muslim characters and culture in a much more rounded and diverse way, a trend that he thought had now dissipated, although he enjoyed *Veer-Zaara*'s highlighting of Islamic/Urdu culture. In assessing such films, the Sikh and Muslim respondents often gave some thought to the depiction of their own groups vis-à-vis Hindu, North Indian culture. In contrast, among the six Hindus in this study, few were able to comment extensively on the portrayal of their own religion or traditions, which may speak again to power relations. Interestingly, however, Lalita, who was raised as a Hindu, simply said that she did not see Bollywood as an accurate reflection of her culture or her traditions, although she acknowledged the strong pro-Hindu elements embedded within the films.

Unlike Sikhs and some Muslims, who felt a need to respond to inaccurate portrayals, the Hindu participants did not necessarily feel spurred in that way, although Nalini, who identified somewhat loosely as having been raised in a Hindu home and whose sense of disconnect was accentuated by the fact that she was not from a Hindi-speaking part of India, expressed anger in regard to the portrayal of Indian women generally, as did Lalita. Jaya, a practising Hindu Gujarati who watched with some regularity, said that she felt her culture and traditions were not portrayed by Bollywood films. Adit suggested that the films were far more entertaining than anything else, although he allowed that they might provide some idea about Hindu Indian culture. Radha felt that she was too infrequent a viewer to comment, and Chandra remarked that her own religion was well represented, but she noted her awareness that Hinduism is only one religion in India. The two Christian participants did not necessarily note any negative characterizations – although one Muslim viewer actually pointed out that immorality or promiscuity is sometimes elided with Christianity in these films – but they also said that they did not feel their religion was well represented and agreed that they might relate more easily if the opposite were true.

The issue of religious representation was not one that viewers saw as being easily resolved, yet it is also worth noting that no participants actually rejected Bollywood films on this basis. Films that they saw as unfair were simply ones that they critiqued and disliked, but they continued to view others. Gender, however, was more of a sticking point, and at least two people (one man, one woman) suggested that they could not reconcile themselves to films that depicted women as victims or objects of abuse. For others, the question of gender in Bollywood at least opened an avenue for discussion and debate with their parents or other relatives, which was also true of issues such as interfaith marriage, where the scenarios that met with applause in the movies were far less feasible in real life. Parents supported diversity and intermarriage on film but expressed definite resistance to the idea of interreligious unions or friendships in their own families, an echo of the attitudes expressed toward gender equality.

Another point that arose on several occasions was tied less to a generational gap than to a geographical one. In the early 1990s, in the wake of renewed discussions around the world about migration, diaspora, and liberalization, Bollywood demonstrated its own awareness of changing social norms. Films became more explicit, more focused on the happy ending, and as some accuse, more Western. In a concurrent trend, some Western media have incorporated aspects of Indian music and clothing, but critical viewers – a category into which most of these participants can be safely slotted – believe that the Western influence in Bollywood is far more profound. However, it is not the spectacle of Westernization itself that bothered these viewers. Rather, it was their sense that the West portrayed in Bollywood films was such a caricature that they could not relate.

The viewers commented that characters denoted Western influence through random uses of English, through wearing provocative clothing that they found unappealing, and through participation in increasingly explicit sexual scenes that left them somewhat shocked and certainly embarrassed. The increasingly sexualized content left young viewers annoyed and insulted because it robbed them of safe entertainment for familial sharing, and it also appeared to be the product of a belief that people living in the diaspora either lived this lifestyle or were drawn to it. Such material, the participants declared, only indicated the depths of Indian cinema's inability to understand all of its viewers. One of the Vancouver groups, which included some of the most constant viewers of Bollywood in this study, expressed frustration with Bollywood's inability to provide accurate depictions of South Asians in the diaspora, a sentiment echoed by a large number of respondents:

Nimrit: I have a huge issue with this. Just watching that movie, *Salaam Namaste* ... The two main characters in the film were both born in India and then they came out to Australia, so now they're depicting Indians in another city and every Indian they depicted was an immigrant. They didn't want to show an Australian-born Indian and portray what an Australian-born Indian looked like. And that was troubling for me because every Indian you showed throughout that movie was immigrated, the taxi driver was immigrated, the little clerk here was immigrated ... and it was just like, you know, I understand that, but you're totally forgetting about probably –

Maida: Like all the people who were born in that country.

Nimrit: Well, look at Vancouver, I think 50 percent, maybe the ratio is higher, what, it's 70 percent? You know, 50, 60, 70 percent are all born here, you know? That's a huge number of individuals who do not relate to just the immigrant viewpoint. My parents might like that, but the kids were twenty-one in the movie so how do my parents relate to that? They don't. And same with Australia, right? So I find that they only like to relate to themselves. They don't really take the time and effort to go in somebody else's shoes.

Several interviewees linked this shortcoming to Bollywood cinema's emphasis on Indian nationalism. Jaya, a Canadian-born woman of Indian ancestry, suggested that the movies always valorized India above all other countries and that they painted Indians living outside of the country as somehow inferior. Asha did not directly address the question of South Asians living in the diaspora, but she did comment on the extreme nationalism found in these films and on how this flourishes through the use of simplistic binaries:

I think when it comes to Bollywood films, they show it in a very, very over-simplified and extreme way. Basically it's all or nothing. You're Indian and you espouse all the values that entails, and usually they show it with respect to how Indian people react to white people, how Indian people react to the British. Either you're Indian or you're not, and there's no in-between. And I think they make it very emotional, as well. You know they always have the Indian national anthem playing in the background when they have those scenes, and things like that.

She also elaborated on a point raised by several others, namely that nationalist tendencies in Indian films had evolved over the years from an early emphasis on India as an independent postcolonial entity to a newer trend, focusing on South Asians who are, in some sense, trying to address a kind of war within:

I watched a lot of really old films, like black-and-white films in the '50s and '60s, and I think at that time they were still trying to establish a national identity because it's still so close to Partition, right, so movies like *Mother India* [1957], they really tried to highlight the prospect that you could be from the lowest economic class in India or from the highest, but when it comes to nationality you all have an understanding that you are all Indian first, you have to work towards that goal of establishing a national identity. But I think since then – I think at that time it was really ... I can see why people's agenda was to have different Indians, people from different backgrounds come together and unite – but I think since then, and maybe also

partly because of the influence of Western culture, they're starting to highlight differences. Maybe not so much in Bollywood films but in films like
Earth by Deepa Mehta, they sort of highlight them. You have the complexities
of being Indian and maybe it's not so united. Movies like *Veer-Zaara* [2004],
where people are trying to say you're Pakistani or Indian, which is a category
that you're put in, but really it's kind of the same thing.

Although Kahil observed, along with others, that it is increasingly common
for Bollywood to tell stories about Indians going to America and trying to
succeed there, he disputed claims that Bollywood is obsessed with the West.
Rather, he pointed to a desire to establish internal order and to provide
Indians with a recognizable vision of themselves that they can endorse. In
unwitting response to Simran's inquiry about India – "Are we going to continue exoticizing it," she asked, "and comparing it to Western society?" –
Kahil ruminated:

> I think one of the biggest lessons that I learned about Indian films – I think
> in the West I always thought that Indian films were – well, not always
> thought, but I thought to some degree that Indian films were sort of like
> what India would be like, you know, people running around in gorgeous
> saris, running around singing and dancing [laughs]. No, more seriously, I
> think you just get the sense that it's a real fantasy world, and then you go
> to India, and you see the reality of India, and it hits you in the face like a
> ton of bricks that it's not a fantasy for those living in the West about what
> they think about India, it's a fantasy for Indians about what they want their
> India to be.

He also addressed accusations that Bollywood mimicked Western styles in
music and clothing, responding that it did add its own touches: "So yes, it's
changed a lot, and yes, it definitely takes inspiration from the West, but I
think it's also made it its own ... it's done in a way that only Indians could
do it. It's Indianized."

Asked whether this Indianized approach was useful in addressing important issues, respondents provided a variety of answers. Nadim praised the
unique quality of Bollywood films and their ability to evoke emotion and
pathos. Some felt that the genre was too melodramatic and simplistic in
nature to really treat any serious topics in a meaningful way. Others compared the Bollywood treatment to the more nuanced approach found in
alternative Indian films, or those described by Desai (2004) as diasporic
films, and again provided different answers. Some found the latter far more
meaningful and serious, whereas others complained that even the most
well-meaning films of this genre still provided cut-and-dried solutions and

promoted some stereotyping. Simran noted appreciatively that Bollywood was now willing to tackle issues it would never have addressed before, such as AIDS or taboo historical questions, a point raised by other participants as well. She did not valorize this genre, but she felt that it deserved credit for raising such topics with an audience that might not otherwise have been prompted to think about them. Asked to compare this treatment to that found in alternative Indian films, she cited *Bend It Like Beckham* (2003) specifically and suggested that it played on stereotypes and did not go far enough to depict the kind of issues it raised.

"It Shook My Soul": Evaluating Bollywood's Significance
There were no simple answers, then, regarding whether one genre was superior to another or whether everyone was affected in the same way by these movies. Even though the diasporic films seemed to elicit high degrees of recognition, particularly those made by Toronto filmmaker Deepa Mehta, they did not garner universal praise, nor did they have the same impact on all viewers. Some saw these types of films as sharing some of the basic problems of Bollywood, namely embedded assumptions, simplistic solutions, and some stereotyping. Two participants commented that they were surprised to find that even diasporic filmmakers experienced such difficulty in fully understanding Indians living in the West, and in particular, they criticized *Bollywood/Hollywood* (2002) for mocking South Asians in a way that they found unnecessary and demeaning. Others felt that they were more likely to relate to these films, which sometimes crossed into transgressive territory, offered more progressive depictions of women, and – most important for some – were filmed in English and set in diasporic settings. Their format and content usually bypassed Bollywood's structural elements cited most often by viewers as common dislikes, including fight scenes, the three-hour length of some films, the high levels of melodrama, and the consistent use of formula. Other dislikes were not by any means universal. One young woman said that she found a type of humour in Bollywood movies that was reflective of her culture and that she could not find elsewhere, whereas a few other respondents criticized the humour as silly and meaningless, something that did not, as Jaya said, give the audience much credit.

There are, of course, other alternatives to Bollywood cinema besides diasporic movies, including mainstream North American films, which most participants watched but did not consider personally affecting or a major source of entertainment. Several commented that the infrequency of their Bollywood viewing should be considered in light of the fact that they did not watch films very much as a general rule, and the critique of formula in Bollywood was applied at times to Hollywood as well. Asked about Pakistani films (sometimes called Lollywood films), the participants who were familiar with them dismissed them as any competition to Bollywood, suggesting that they attempted to follow the same formula but did so poorly, with lower production values. Alma did note that her cousins in the United States watched these films and enjoyed them because they felt a connection to home, but she found them impossible to watch, and Tariq, Alma, and Nimrit all agreed that they had found many viewers in Pakistan who still preferred Bollywood films, which could be accessed through black-market satellite dishes.

The observation is interesting since it seems to offer a response to the young women who complained about the demonization of Muslims and Pakistan in Bollywood, a complaint that Iram addressed by saying, "Well, because they're Indian filmmakers ... they're not Pakistani filmmakers." Evidently, having a Pakistani filmmaker was not in itself enough to woo viewers, although in one case Simran cited the Pakistani-made *Khamosh Pani* (Silent Waters, 2003) as a meaningful film. Complaints about Bollywood notwithstanding, it seemed to retain its appeal and its reach, particularly with the release of major hits. Some viewers were familiar with a wide range of films, but less frequent viewers indicated that they might make time for a film that was considered hugely popular or that otherwise generated positive feedback from family or friends.

Even among those whose viewing patterns differed widely, many of the same film titles were cited repeatedly. Perhaps not surprisingly, the most commercially successful movies were mentioned with corresponding frequency, yet the reasons given for citation were not entirely the same. As conversations unfolded, it became clear that many identified the films they found most entertaining, romantic, or well made, whereas others cited films that had more personal appeal. Like several respondents, Kahil named *Hum Aapke Hain Koun (HAHK)*, *Kabhi Khushi Kabhie Gham* (Sometimes Happy, Sometimes Sad, 2001), and *Veer-Zaara,* and he did note the high production values as a factor in his enjoyment, but he added that he also felt each of those movies "either pushed the limits in some ways" or brought up a modern-day issue that had been previously unexplored, such as the Hindu-Muslim divide in *Veer-Zaara* or family values in *Kabhi Khushi Kabhie Gham*. Having said that, he was even-handed in his praise of various Indian films, including the non-Bollywood variety, for their willingness to tackle topics that Bollywood would not think to approach: "On the other hand, the cultural nuances are really picked up in the Bollywood films: the clothes, again the music, the culture ... I think in that way Bollywood does have its place, as do non-Bollywood films expressing India." Asha also identified an older film but one considered by many to be a classic, the film *Sholay* (Flames, 1975), which she saw as one of the few popular Indian films to provide high levels of entertainment without descending into campiness.

Others identified films that taught them about history, society, or politics, as when Simran cited *Roti Kapada aur Makaan* (Food, Clothing, and Shelter, 1974) as a film that had a big influence on her, an impact that she summarized simply by saying, "It shook my soul for some reason." She then elaborated on the importance of the film, which chronicled the inability of youth to obtain education or employment, despite the grand promises of the future following Independence. *Khamosh Pani* also discussed youth and social unrest but with more specific reference to increasing Muslim fundamentalism following a declaration of martial law, as well as the violence against women that followed Partition, a fact that Simran found fascinating as she looked back to the history of her own family and tried to relate their experiences to what was depicted in such films. Nimrit cited *Pinjar* (2003) for similar reasons, and Iram found new meaning and significance in *Mughal-e-Azam* (1960) after learning about the Mughal period, which she perceived as part of her own history. Interestingly, another Muslim participant identified *Mughal-e-Azam* but said that Mughal history was not particularly significant in terms of how he recalled the film; rather, he was struck by the powerful love story and the production values. Similarly, although he named two films that dealt with interreligious marriage, *Bombay* (1995) and *Zakhm* (Wound, 1998), it was not simply the subject matter but also factors such as music that drew his attention.

Nazia, who reported that she prefered those films that have social relevance, cited *Ek Hasina Thi* (2004), which did not provide educational components but which contained quasi-feminist elements in its depiction of a duped woman who seeks revenge on the man who used her. Lalita also said that she preferred films that dealt with social issues, such as the colonial-era epic *Lagaan* [Land Tax]: *Once upon a Time in India* (2001) and *Swades* (2004), a film that speaks to a non-resident Indian's responsibility to help improve the lives of villagers in India. Asha named the original *Umrao Jaan* (1981) for its comments on society, as well as *Heer Raanjha* (1970), mainly because of the fact that it is Punjabi. Clearly, the simple fact of feeling represented played some role in this choice, as with the choice of the film *Gadar* (2001), another post-Partition film that dealt with a Sikh-Muslim romance, praised by the commentators for its depiction both of a Sikh character and of the events that took place during that time.

Others had even more personal reasons for selecting the films that they did. Jaya commented on *HAHK* as a film that she watched repeatedly with her family while staying in India, noting that the film was associated with that period in her memories. Alma offered a bit of a twist on this reminiscence, saying that *HAHK* resonated with her because the weddings and rituals depicted in the film reminded her of events that she had attended while visiting Pakistan. Iram linked her choice to her feeling of sadness following the diagnosis of a chronic disorder:

Mine is *Dosti* [Friendship, 1964] ... the older version, the black-and-white one ... It was about this orphan that was blind and he met this other boy who wasn't ... and the other friend gave him that confidence, that regardless of your disability ... you can take the talent that you have and make somebody of yourself. He was a singer, he had this amazing, amazing voice ... So it was that voice that ended up giving out the message to the rest of them that just because I have a disability, or because I don't have parents, I'm an orphan, just because I have these misfortunes, it doesn't mean that I'm not normal. I can live a normal life and it truly hit me because I watched it when I was – I think it was about two years ago, when I was diagnosed with my ... disorder and at that point I was feeling helpless and whatnot, and when I watched it, it truly showed me that there are people out there that are going to be able to look at you as a normal person regardless of your disability ... It made me feel better to know or to believe that there were people in – like, Indian people quote unquote that could be like that.

Clearly, some viewers remembered films in a way that was highly personal, which often made the memory favourable. By comparison, Suhil and Asha mentioned *Devdas*, which stirred vivid memories because both were repelled by its depiction of women. Suhil in particular was strongly affected by a scene in which the title character strikes his childhood love to mark her as his prior to her marriage to another man. Similarly, Nimrit clearly did not like the negative depiction of Indians living in the diaspora in *Salaam Namaste*, but she returned to this film repeatedly because she felt that it broke new ground, going so far in some respects that she could not relate but also moving into territory that she felt had to be addressed. I did expect some degree of personal reminiscence when naming films of importance, but I was interested in the fact that the viewers criticized certain elements in a general way – unfair depictions of South Asians living in the diaspora as well as skewed representations of women and particular religious or ethnic groups – without these observations always entering into their comments about a specific film, even one where these viewpoints would be quite relevant.

For instance, a number of young people complained about the way that diasporic individuals were represented, a trend that some critics felt was addressed in complex and transformative ways in *Dilwale Dulhania Le Jayenge* (*DDLJ*; The Lover Takes the Bride, 1995). Several ranked this as an important film, citing the romance, the music, and the production values, but none – even Nadim, who spoke several times about unrealistic depictions of diasporic life – made reference to the diasporic themes embedded so clearly within this movie. One participant named *Pardes* (Foreign Land, 1997) as an important film without making any reference to its clearly negative portrayal of diasporic Indians. *Swades,* a strongly pro-nationalist Indian film that returns to the familiar treatment of the heroine as the preserver of culture and tradition, was cited favourably by two participants, both of whom described themselves as feminists, one of whom was Pakistani. For the most part, the judgment seemed to be simply that Bollywood was far behind where it should be in terms of speaking to the diasporic audience, although attempts at increasing representation of marginalized religious and cultural groups did elicit cautious praise. Asked to name films that she saw as significant, Zara spoke positively of *Namastey London* (2007), a story about an assimilated British woman of South Asian origin: "I mean, I didn't necessarily agree with the way she acted, but I think she expressed a kind of confusion that we all feel." *Veer-Zaara* did not seem to be universally popular, and its treatment of the two main characters was seen as rather fantastical and caricatured in some ways, but two or three respondents suggested that its subject matter indicated a willingness on Bollywood's part to move beyond constructed rivalries and to suggest that all South Asians have commonalities and should seek unity.

Thus there were some obvious contradictions that recurred throughout the study, some of which may be attributed to a lack of critical insight on the part of viewers, yet I believe that this was not necessarily the case, at least not in a frequent or protracted way. For the most part, respondents gave thoughtful, perceptive answers, but they also indicated that their lives and their habits have come to be characterized by contradiction. Some of the young women complained about sexism in Bollywood and then continued to watch; similarly, complaints about inaccurate religious or ethnic depictions did not cause cessation in viewing. These movies could still satisfy a need for these viewers, who were aware of the shortcomings of Bollywood cinema but extracted the elements that were meaningful to them.

This was why context and situational positioning seemed most important for some when they were asked whether they would find any benefit in screening these films one day for their children. The heaviest viewers agreed that they would do so despite their criticisms of the genre, linking the experience to family and culture, and one young man who very rarely watched said that he would also show his children those films as a way of preventing further erosion of Indian culture than he had experienced himself. Another light viewer commented that he saw definite value in using the films to promote a sense of cultural identity and affinity similar to what he himself felt when watching Bollywood, however rarely he did so. Alma, who frequently referenced her comments by offering comparisons to other countries or to the past, answered the question by returning to the evolution of Toronto into a truly diverse city, in contrast to other parts of North America, and also by indicating, as did many others, that Bollywood was one of the less authentic ways to explore South Asian culture:

I think it would depend where I live. If I lived in the States, where again it's like it was here maybe ten years ago, where there's not a huge community and you wouldn't see yourself or your culture reflected in the places and the people around you, then yeah. I've noticed that, I have family there, like cousins and such, and besides having specialty channels, they really don't have anywhere to explore their desi culture. I find in Toronto, it's becoming a lot more like London, where it's become a lot more mainstream, everyone knows about it, you can easily explore yourself there on any given night. You can do it in a very specific way as well, if you only want to do a certain part of it, it's so easy now. So if I was living in Toronto that's different. I'd rather have them experience the real culture as it is.

Diversity, Diaspora, and Media

In explaining what they saw as the "real" culture, several individuals described scenarios where their parents' beliefs regarding nationalism or culture might be quite different from theirs, but parents and children alike had learned to respect each other's choices even though neither side was above promoting its own ideas where applicable. Unlike the informant in Maira's (2002, 133) study who saw himself as diluted because he was separated from the authenticity supposedly found within South Asia, the young adults here did speak of practising culture and religion differently, but they did not necessarily consider this less authentic. Some noted that living outside of South Asia, where religions and cultures were less likely to be questioned, had prompted them to search for the meaning of these entities, a search that led to an understanding that they saw as entirely authentic because it was relevant and valuable to them. For those respondents, the diaspora is indeed, as Mandaville (2001) might suggest, a place that provides the possibility of more incisive exploration and understanding of faith. Their parents may have had a stronger sense of ethnic and religious identity because they lived in places where these were rarely questioned, hence adding to their sense of immutability and permanence, but these young people, living in a place where they are surrounded by various understandings of ethnicity and faith, are more likely to ask questions and to make comparisons. This does not always – or often – translate into a weakening of traditions and beliefs. However, it means that the traditions that remain are ones whose meanings have been interrogated and whose significance is thus better understood and perhaps even more valued.

Nonetheless, some participants did speak in terms of loss, particularly as this encompassed language. As Murji and Hébert (1999) point out, language is an important component of ethnicity, and this was referred to at several points over the course of the project. Language did appear to provide some participants with an increased sense of closeness to their culture, although this was not an exact predictor of strong identification with a particular ethnic community. The hybrid nature of language and community was reflected often in these comments, as one woman noted that an increasing move globally toward interpreting Islam as a religion that is most authentic when couched in Middle Eastern, Arabic terms marginalized those Muslims who are fluent in Urdu yet conduct many rituals in a language that is not native to them. This dilemma arose for other Muslims more than for any other group, although something related did arise for a Gujarati Hindu whose ability to speak Hindi was acquired through a variety of means, partly because she was surrounded by it so often in media aimed at South Asians. Young people who were raised in Gujarati-, Kutchi- or Punjabi-speaking homes sometimes did become relatively competent in other languages, including Hindi and Urdu, because so much South Asian media content called for this, and they learned to switch between languages or even to mix them with ease. However, even those who had good comprehension of other languages sometimes expressed regret that they were not more fluent speakers, and they made reference to the eventual loss of some of these linguistic capabilities. This loss was happening rapidly in some cases, as one might expect from reading Murji and Hébert (1999), who seem to indicate a swift generational change, but as with Jiwani's (1989) informants, those who were losing their command of South Asian languages, or who saw this occurring among others, were juxtaposed with individuals who were highly fluent in at least one South Asian dialect, if not more. Moreover, whereas the informants who did possess this linguistic competency saw its value and expressed pleasure, those who did not speak other languages were not always regretful, at least not openly.

There was a kind of spectrum in these matters, among others, that unfolded over the months during which I conducted my interviews. In the case of Bollywood, for instance, some participants distanced themselves as much as possible from popular Indian films, whereas others were utterly immersed. Nonetheless, there was not a single interviewee who had never seen a Bollywood movie, indicating, perhaps, the industry's enormous reach or the consistent use of these films by South Asians living in the diaspora. Moreover, some of the most devoted or most long-standing viewers were Muslim, an interesting discovery given this study's emphasis on the confluence of Bollywood viewing and identity construction among Canadian Muslims. It was also true, however, that even the avid viewers were not wholly uncritical of the industry; nearly all saw shortcomings, beginning with a melodramatic treatment of serious issues and moving on to stereotypical or unappealing depictions of women, Muslims, Sikhs, and people living in the diaspora. Muslim viewers were well aware of the problematic depictions of themselves and their rituals in these films, yet many continued to watch or to retain some vestige of affection for them. Several saw them as integral to their upbringing and to their understanding of South Asia, a sentiment that they did not express toward the movies made by Pakistan's film industry, Lollywood. This may speak partly to Bollywood's hegemonic authority, to a perceived lack of quality in Lollywood films, and/or to the fact that young people who have lived many years in a society where they rarely see themselves depicted may come to depend on even the most absurd portrayals of South Asian life as long as some representation does exist. Whatever the exact reason, it appears that even those respondents who could not trace their roots directly to India still felt the influence of its media, a point also noted in Jiwani (1989), where some youth who seem unaware of – or unwilling to acknowledge – their Indian heritage make reference to their enjoyment of Indian movies and music.

A related point in terms of the films' appeal seems to demonstrate how a medium described by participants and critics as superficial and purely entertainment-driven can affect viewers' everyday actions and self-esteem. Asked whether Bollywood had influenced the kind of person she now is, one young woman replied that she felt it had helped to increase her comfort level when she wore Indian clothes in public, a response that was echoed by others in different ways. Although this may seem trivial to some, I think the recurrence of this theme – the shame associated with marking oneself as South Asian in public – in Gillespie (1995) and Handa (2003) demonstrates its significance and also emphasizes the degree to which individuals may internalize shame and discomfort over their race and ethnicity rather than attributing negativity to those who single them out as different. With the possible exception of one very light-skinned, light-eyed participant, the young adults in this study were always already marked as South Asian, but choosing to wear South Asian fashions indicated, as Gillespie's and Handa's informants claim, a willingness to demonstrate a South Asian identity in public. This demonstration could result in marginalization not only from the mainstream but also from other young South Asians who felt that such identity markers were best confined to the private sphere whenever possible.

One group of interviewees raised a similar point, noting that Bollywood and Indian popular culture had become mainstream, increasing the acceptability of wearing such fashions or *mendhi* (henna) in public, an acceptability that had been withheld from them as children growing up in a society more multicultural in name than in action at that time. Yet the same informants indicated the inherent contradiction in this, debating whether their culture had simply become appropriated and whether they should feel offended rather than proud. Indeed, there was an ambivalence, if not explicitly stated, toward the global flow of capital, which has helped to shape diasporas through the movement of people and goods. This capital flow has increased

Bollywood's visibility and elicited recognition from non–South Asians, but at the same time it has also simplified the public image of South Asian culture in a way that some participants found troubling.

Those who subscribed to that image might have been familiar only with a few very popular movies that were consumed, at some level, for purely escapist purposes, somewhat similar to major Hollywood hits. Echoing Durham's (2004) respondents, my participants explained that Bollywood still carried a ring of cultural familiarity and that this inspired a considerable affection for Indian films that they were unlikely to transfer to Hollywood. Some of the respondents who knew Indian cinema more intimately – although interestingly, few of the Hindu interviewees – pointed to Bollywood as an alternate system of education about their cultural and religious history. Many scoffed at the amplified nationalism running through many of the films, especially if this concerned a conflict between India and Pakistan or India and the diaspora, but several suggested that they had gathered information about South Asian history through selected films. Similar to Raj's (2003, 47) Hindu Punjabi interviewees, who are intimately acquainted with those aspects of their parents' history of immigration that have compelled respect and filial obedience, although not necessarily with every detail, the young people in this study found it difficult to extract the background they would have found most beneficial. Respondents in one particular group complained about an inability to obtain information about their culture and history through community associations or family, further remarking that formal education had not only helped to fill in some of the gaps but had also intensified their understanding of selected Bollywood films.

Participants such as these expressed themselves in emotive terms that initially surprised me. Although these comments were specific to Bollywood, several young adults brought emotion and feeling to their descriptions of nationalism and their efforts to bridge cultures. Based on Gillespie's (1995) observations about Punjabi youth who use television programs – usually mainstream ones – as a way of initiating conversation with their parents on sensitive topics, I had expected that movies might be relevant in some respect to real-life issues, but I did not anticipate the level of emotion and personal identification that occurred in selected cases.

There is one point about the consumption of Bollywood cinema that I found increasingly interesting as I transcribed interviews, and in a sense this may be the most significant point. There was clearly some level of dissonance present for several of the young people, particularly those who were Muslim or Sikh. Nearly all of the viewers, especially casual ones, described a frothy world of escape that meant very little. At the same time, Muslim and Sikh viewers were entirely conscious of the religious and cultural archetypes that circulated in these films, and they expressed their dislike of this circulation. Similarly, several participants demonstrated equally intense repugnance when discussing the depiction of women, and last but certainly not least, a large number indicated awareness that pro-Indian discourses could easily be read as narratives that excluded South Asians in the diaspora, especially those born outside of South Asia. This consciousness was perhaps expressed most fervently by three young women who were frequent viewers and who had no intention of relinquishing this activity; in fact, very few of the individuals in this study contemplated doing this entirely, which is a telling point in itself.

Discussion

The intention of this study is not to establish the overriding importance of Bollywood but to understand its significance in the lives of diasporic viewers, who increasingly seem to form the target audience for some of the biggest films. This significance appears mixed, but it was there for a number of viewers, although I think that the percipience of these same viewers might take some Bollywood producers by surprise. Nonetheless, some of the hybrid elements in Bollywood film were greeted by participants with exasperation, but others did appear to capture the imagination in some ways. The attempt at capturing a new modernity in films such as *Hum Aapke Hain Koun* and *Kuch Kuch Hota Hai* did not go unnoticed, although equally strenuous attempts at speaking to previously neglected groups, such as Punjabis or Muslims, were greeted with criticism if they did not go far enough. Moreover, the overwhelming nationalist sentiment in popular Indian films seemed to leave many viewers cold. Some noticed it, especially in films such as *Kabhi Khushi Kabhie Gham, Veer-Zaara*, and the older *Mother India*, and one or two did comment on it favourably, but there were also instances where many complained that the pro-India themes were utilized at the expense of another, equally important group – diasporic individuals such as themselves who were capable of respecting cultural and religious values while also declaring fidelity to their own country. Films such as *Kal Ho Naa Ho* (Tomorrow May Not Come, 2003), which does depict people settled in the United States and even displays an American flag prominently in the background of one dance sequence, and *Dilwale Dulhania Le Jayenge*, which reverses the anti-diaspora sentiment, were mentioned as favourites but with little reference to these themes. In the case of *DDLJ*, Nadim did see the emphasis on India as a point of return for diasporic peoples, but he added thoughtfully that this type of nostalgia for a motherland was largely irrelevant for his generation:

> Nowadays, young educated Indians are far more mobile, they're less drawn to our homeland, they're jet setting, they're ready to go anywhere and start fresh. They don't have that same link to their home country that gives them their identity that their fathers or forefathers might have. And it's funny, you see that in a lot of movies as well, you can go anywhere you want but

India's your home [names *DDLJ* and *Kabhi Khushi Kabhie Gham* as examples].
It's probably comforting to the masses but in reality I think you've got a lot
of young, professional, well-educated Indians that are quick to move on.

Although Nadim veered between a matter-of-fact attitude and a critical one,
several of the participants were more likely to express intense dislike of the
portrayal of South Asians living in the diaspora. In their minds, Bollywood
left very little room for compromise, and compromise was essential to individuals who made no attempt to deny their South Asian heritage but
mainly refused to be identified as anything other than Canadian.

If Bollywood has generally been seen as a kind of hybrid beast, one that
works to provide a niche for nearly everyone, this is rarely viewed as the
innovative hybridity that Bhabha (1994) has endorsed enthusiastically in
the past. The term "hybrid culture" recurs frequently in discussions of Indian
cinema as a pejorative, as when Dharker (1997, 400) states that the "trouble
with hybrids, especially when they are too deliberately forced to adapt to
another culture, is that they don't work" (see also Barnouw and Krishnaswamy 1980, 157; Dickey 1993, 58). The observations of participants in this
study seemed to endorse at least part of that perspective; hybrids themselves
are not the problem, but forcing one culture on another creates tension and
hinders success. The same, in fact, may be said of the young people I cite
here; in one instance after another, they suggested that the reason they could
make their composite identities work was because they lived in a society
that encouraged them to do just this.

Kraidy (1999, 459) echoes the belief of several participants that the hybridization of cultures has been occurring as an actual practice for far longer
than many have admitted, such that any attempt to distinguish clearly
between local and global spaces "glosses over years of osmosis between different national and cultural entities." This process is referred to by García
Canclini (cited in Kraidy 1999, 460) as "cultural reconversion," in which
local cultures accommodate the influence(s) of the global "without being
destroyed because tradition is re-articulated in modern processes." Bollywood, then, may be simply one element where tradition is being rearticu-
lated, although the viewers here were correct to point to its flaws. However,
I think they may also have been justified in continuing to negotiate the
meaning and significance of these films, not just for themselves but as a way
of communicating with parents or others. It was not possible for most of
the young adults here "to exclusively belong to one or the other of what
they saw as two irreconcilable worldviews" (Kraidy 1999, 464), so they took
the tools they had at their disposal, used them as best as they could, and
supplemented them where necessary.

Tensions such as these clearly demonstrate that the creation of a hybrid
culture is a tenuous and imperfect process, one that never really concludes.

Several participants did suggest that they had found creative and meaningful ways to form a lifestyle that embodied elements of old and new, North and South, but no one went so far as to deny the fissures and contradictions within. Some, in fact, seemed to realize the complexities of their positioning as they considered different questions and scenarios. Most felt, as Mandaville (2001) and Bhabha (1994) would perhaps suggest, that migration had given them a kind of freedom to explore knowledge and culture that differed from what their parents had possessed, but at the same time, they also felt that exposure to different settings and forms of education meant that their understanding of many cultural elements, including cinema, would always be tinged with frustration. Diaspora, then, was a meaningful space for these young people, allowing for syncretic melding of elements and beliefs, but it was also a space where freedom was intertwined with constraint and paradox.

Along those lines, nearly all of the participants agreed that Indian cinema did nothing to project a more realistic view of Indian society. Several were disappointed that Bollywood depicted both India and the West in a skewed manner, doing little to promote a positive image of the genre or the industry. Others were less critical, dismissing such films as mere entertainment with a limited role to play in terms of education. Some participants noted, with a certain amount of nostalgia, that Indian films, as Gillespie (1995) suggests, had indeed educated them about their culture. More than one person explained that these films had been the only source of information they received regarding Partition and the history of inter-ethnic discord.

In short, in the case of those I interviewed, even Bollywood's rampant nationalist tendencies did not manage to call these young people home in any literal way, not least because they clearly identified with the home they already had. However, films had helped them to maintain some sense of continuity and connection to South Asia from within the diaspora, and it was a sense unlikely to be broken now or in the future. Even when viewers expressed outright rejection of what they saw onscreen, very few contemplated the possibility of leaving these films behind entirely. Flaws and all, Bollywood offered a reflection of a struggle these individuals lived daily: an attempt to reconcile competing cultures in a way that made sense to them in the context of their own upbringing and ambitions for the future. This attempt had never met complete success but it had to be undertaken. South Asia may not have called them home for good, but it lived within each of these young people, and the possibility, the promise, and the obligation of their plural identities were not aspects that they were willing or able to ignore.

10
Beyond Futility: The Future of Young Canadians of South Asian Origin

This is what her note said: "My name is Pratiti Kaka. As a child I
learned dancing, and my mom thought I'd grow up to be a dancer of
renown. I soon joined skating classes. She assumed I'd break Olympic
records. When I started swimming, she hoped I'd swim across the
English Channel someday. But all her dreams crash-landed when I grew
up to be an ordinary, amiable girl with varied interests. After managing
an office, I married a wonderful man of my choice and am enjoying life.
Just the other day, someone told Mom, 'I want my daughter to be like
yours.'" The confidence in the unexceptional, rather, the dream of being
part of the ordinary, is also indicative of the process of the immigrant
becoming a citizen. You don't stand out, or stick out, anymore. You
are like any other American. (Kumar 2002, 180)

Never studied properly because they are so numerous and undefinable ...
immigrant children seem to be the major source of wealth and entrepre-
neurship in Canada. They dominate most innovative academic fields.
They seem to run every business. Even a cursory examination of Canada
will tell you that it is a country being built not by struggling immigrants,
but by their fluently literate, culturally integrated, wealth-generating,
numerous children. (Saunders 2003, F2)

I opened this research by asking what role Bollywood cinema plays in the
construction of identity for young Canadians of South Asian origin, particularly Muslims. Despite the protestations of one participant that media were
not very influential in her life, and the comments of others that media may
not have been the most important aspect of identity formation, film did
seem to have a role, although the nature of this role varied significantly.
Nearly all of the interviewees identified problems with Bollywood cinema,
and several detected shortcomings in its representations of nation and culture,

elements that were presumably intended to speak to people such as themselves. All the same, many continued to consume it, although this viewership
was sometimes sporadic and often critical. Bollywood seemed to satisfy, at
minimum, a need to see South Asian individuals and rituals depicted onscreen, yet those whose specific realities were portrayed more peripherally,
as was the case for Muslims, perceived a tendency for popular Indian cinema
to stereotype or marginalize them, much like North American media.

A sense of being ignored by popular media and by mainstream society
made Bollywood more valuable for some participants, a feeling that had
generally tended to diminish as South Asian populations increased in Canada and as some markers of South Asian culture became accepted more
generally in mainstream society. These young adults charted changes in
Canada, in their own ethnic and religious communities, and in their families
that had sometimes been negotiated through the use of media, particularly
popular Indian cinema. As these informants explained and as this book
suggests, a variety of factors, including media, contribute to identity formation. It would be overstating the case to imply that media alone create
identity, but it would also be saying too much to argue that most young
people are entirely oblivious to the influence of media. Some of the individuals in this study pointed out changes in the media that had affected them
throughout their lives while also describing their own transformation into
adults, a growth that involved evaluating a number of influences. Watching
Indian cinema was undoubtedly among these influences for some of the
respondents, and the reasons for this are worth evaluating.

Bollywood provides viewers with images that purport to be like them,
and however far-fetched these images might seem, they signify an attempt
at representation. As interviewees noted, the options available to them had
improved over the years, and they did have more ways of seeing themselves,
but Bollywood can sometimes exercise an ameliorative effect in societies
where South Asians feel that their rituals, activities, and faiths exist on the
margins. It was clear that some participants distinctly remembered a time
when a South Asian identity made one the target of racism and ostracism
and that they remained aware of the ways they were still marked as different.
Diasporic media can offer a vehicle to address a sense of difference. Indian
cinema's increasing acknowledgment of the fact that one of its key markets
lies outside of South Asia and is centred more specifically in an entity as
amorphous as the diaspora, demonstrates the importance that diasporic
peoples can have in the maintenance of a nation-state and its chief industries.
Bollywood is perhaps unique in its ability to speak – however inaccurately
or inappropriately – to the diaspora, to feed it nationalist discourse, and to
benefit from diasporic capital at the same time. Once this relationship pros-
pered on the basis of nostalgia, but if the responses given in this study are

any indication, such nostalgia is unlikely to persist for the second generation of immigrants and may be unthinkable for the third generation.

The young people in this study saw themselves as Canadian, not in terms of a piece of paper that marked them as such or because they appeared integrated, but because Canada was the home they had known for most of their lives. Like the children of immigrants described by Saunders at the beginning of this chapter, they are indeed the building blocks of Canada, a Canada whose plurality is a factor that resonated considerably for these participants. Even when they did not meet with full acceptance, they expressed their right to it, and were willing to do battle over and over again to claim those rights. Deeply conscious of the massive transition their parents or other family members made in coming to Canada, they have attempted to integrate into Canadian society without fully assimilating, seeking to maintain knowledge of their origins and – for the most part – respecting those of others. This was not a perfect process, occurring at a different pace and in different ways for those undergoing it. This finding does echo some of the integration found among Haji-ar-were's (2006) Australian and Thai subjects, as well as the complicated acculturation taking place among Maira's (2002) South Asian American ones. However, the assertion among participants here that their right to belong was something enshrined in Canadian policy, and something they would not surrender, is perhaps unique to this study and to the avowed multiculturalism of the host society in this case.

Participants spoke of a variety of exclusionary and racist practices that they had encountered, even though they rarely attached these labels to them, and it appeared that these experiences were formative in each individual's sense of self. Indeed, it was interesting to note that many young people made implicit reference to racial stereotyping and ignorance on the part of other Canadians, yet only a few spoke frankly of racism and its deleterious effects, including a sense of shame attached to their origins that had lasted throughout childhood. Several were inclined to use diplomatic and optimistic language reminiscent of that accompanying policy claims to multiculturalism and diversity, avoiding most commentaries around race as it related to them, although there were references to the prejudice experienced by other South Asians and by Muslims around the world, a prejudice whose existence seemed so palpable that few expanded on it, merely speaking of it as an accepted fact. Moreover, a few participants were quick to note that Canada is itself the result of a colonial project that displaced the First Nations who lived on these lands for millenia and who continue to fight for their rights as indigenous peoples. Thus, those who describe themselves as truly Canadian, by virtue of English or French heritage, are no more indigenous to the land than recent immigrants. Nearly all raised the issue of being asked frequently about their origins and described meeting this inquiry with acceptance, indifference, or anger.

Indeed, their refusal to give any quarter when their Canadian nationality was challenged could speak either to their ability to resist prejudice or to their willingness to adapt themselves to a place that may never fully accept them. In spite of recurring reminders that not all Canadians viewed them as Canadian, most of these young people maintained their insistence that they were as Canadian as anyone else. The level of insight that emerged in response to Canadian and South Asian nationalist discourses indicates that numerous influences enter into acculturation, many of which these individuals appeared to be capable of evaluating critically and confidently as they continued fostering not only their identity but also that of a diverse new Canada.

Part of the Ordinary? Young Minorities and Integration
In terms of answering the study's main questions, the participants provided thoughtful and diverse commentary. Methodologically, there may be some value in conducting more interviews with non-Muslim participants in order to make better comparisons and to examine specific depictions of or pressures on non-Muslim South Asians in more depth. Some of the most poignant commentary on racism, marginalization, and a search for belonging came from non-Muslim participants, and there were other consistent concerns, such as gender inequality, that were mentioned by a number of participants, regardless of religious affiliation. Although the findings are not generalizable to all South Asians or all Muslims, they still display certain recurring themes, confirming the conclusions of others while indicating the way that a later generation, as well as an older sample, than that found in Jiwani (1989) might show some maturing and consolidating of the insights provided in Durham (2004) and Maira (2002). All of the respondents in these studies indicated that they had pondered the definition of their identity; many of the participants in this specific study seemed to have arrived at an answer about their identity that they could live with. Jiwani's respondents provided mixed responses and appeared occasionally unsure of how they view themselves, signifying some uncertainty about their place in Canadian society, while the American informants in Durham and Maira walked a fine line between considering themselves American and Indian all at once. Most participants here offered a position on nationality that was almost unequivocal, even if they felt they were constantly made to account for their ethnic origin and/ or religious background, which most described as lending considerable richness to their life and upbringing. This richness, of course, was occasionally complicated by the challenge of juggling multiple identities and of having to translate oneself to others (Costantino 2008, 133). Muslims and Sikhs seemed particularly conscious of the burden of explaining themselves to others and especially aware of skewed representations of their communities in media (with regard to Muslims, see also Khan 2009b).

Although the fact of the 11 September 2001 attacks was hinted at in some Muslim respondents' remarks, particularly when they spoke of the way others perceived them, no such demarcating event was identified by Sikh participants, who appeared to be referencing a long history of discrimination. Although the emphasis in this study is on Muslims, whose responses did seem to indicate a high degree of consciousness around identity formation and expressions of that identity in a society most saw as biased, Sikhs gave answers that were similar in some respects. This fact, combined with the very close coherence between these Sikh participants' answers and the ones provided in Desai (2005), suggests to me that a study on Sikhs might be equally warranted if one wanted to narrow the scope of participants. This may be because Muslims and Sikhs experienced a similar sense of marginality as diasporic Canadians; Muslims appeared to express awareness of a global trend toward intense scrutiny of Islam, and Sikhs also implied that they had long been the subject of stereotyping, in media and elsewhere. Despite their small numbers, I was struck by the consistent nature of the observations made by the Sikh respondents. Any of these religious groups, in fact, deserves further examination in the context of identity construction, and this type of research need not be done by an insider.

Indeed, I am unsure whether my identity as a Canadian Muslim of South Asian origin played a significant role here. It may have helped me to interpret interview comments, but I think that this process was also theoretically informed to a large extent. If my identity did play an ameliorating role, it may have been in the sense that participants seemed to speak to me with ease, perhaps feeling that I might recognize the kinds of observations they made. In retrospect, I think that reflexivity did not affect the results of the research, but it could have done. The temptation to voice my own opinions or to share experiences was strong, and occasionally I did share an experience if I felt it might illustrate a point better, but for the most part I tried to act more as a researcher than as a deeply involved participant, preferring to hear these young people speak in their own voices without notable interference. In choosing to follow this path, I came across findings that I had not anticipated: whereas some participants were indifferent to the possibility of racism in Indian cinema or in society at large, others were not and had spent considerable time grappling with this issue. I was impressed and occasionally surprised by the resolute, clearly argued assertion of a Canadian identity grounded in state-mandated principles of diversity. I was not necessarily surprised that gender was an important issue, but I was rather taken aback by the fact that this question surfaced over and over again, brought to the forefront by men and women alike. This was true even though perceptions of gender were not addressed in my research questions, demonstrating that gender inequality continues to be salient in studies of film and/or South Asian culture and a real source of discontent as well as a catalyst for change.

In fact, young people are a source of fascination to many academics because of the role they will play in shaping the future. This study provides a glimpse into what thought processes and behaviours may arise following adolescence or the very early stages of adulthood for those second-generation immigrants who have been largely raised in Canada but who are still affected by their parents' experiences of migration or by their own memories of this. Studies of immigration sometimes suggest, in alignment with the responses provided here, that first-generation immigrants are more likely to nurse beliefs in the immutability of the society left behind, whereas their children, whose chief or initial source of exposure is often the oral history provided by parents, may eventually rebel against imposed mores that they see as outdated and meaningless, only to learn later that these are indeed out of date everywhere except in the diaspora. Participants in this research simultaneously endorsed the importance of their upbringing in providing a sense of ethnic identity, and they critiqued the contradictions found in the practices of their relatives. Moreover, they made predictions regarding the way their own children would be less affected by some traditions and practices, predictions whose outcomes might be useful to monitor.

Despite their own awareness of change, however, it is not possible to say that the young people in this study were immune to the lure of the countries in which they or their parents were born. It is not at all uncommon for immigrants to embark on return trips, sometimes even with the intent of settling down permanently. Some return for personal reasons, others for economic ones, although there are those who carry out a limited return, establishing a home but maintaining multiple citizenship to facilitate frequent travel or to allow overseas alternatives for the schooling of their children. This does occur and, indeed, is among the practices currently being encouraged by the Government of India as it seeks to benefit from diasporic human capital.

The young people in this case, however, may maintain considerable interest in the countries where they or their parents were born and may even pursue relevant travel or study of their own accord. Unlike the frequent flyers in Ong (1999), however, very few suggested any possibility of moving back and forth constantly between these places, and even fewer hinted at any permanent settlement in the place(s) of their parents' birth. Several did note that they had taken trips to these places, trips that some saw as a form of homecoming and others as tourism and still others as career development, but if any saw such trips as the first step in a circular process of return, they did not say so. More often, these young adults suggested that places like India, Pakistan, or East Africa were still not ones where they fully belonged, and very few used the language of "going back," a constant refrain among Maira's (2002, 112-13) participants, many of whom are second-generation immigrants who have never been to India. Having been educated and raised in Canada, with extensive familial, professional, and/or peer networks and with an emotional investment in their Canadian citizenship, my own respondents found it difficult to adopt a mentality that would see their parents' home countries as their own. Some remarked sentimentally on these places and felt affection for them, but they did not comment on them as home.

This may hearken back to what appeared to be a widespread belief that Canada was a place where they could balance the multiple layers of their identities, a departure from the British youth of Pakistani/Kashmiri origin in Cressey (2006), who are divided between those who dislike Pakistan and Kashmir intensely and those who finally find a belonging there that they think will never be possible in Britain. In contrast, Canada seems to be a place where Muslims and South Asians continue to seek a new home. As observed throughout this book, both Muslims and South Asians are significant contributors to immigration growth in Canada, especially in major cities. As a 2007 poll conducted by Environics and CBC indicates, many Muslims living in Canada acknowledge the presence of hostility or prejudice, but for the most part they are happy to live in Canada, wish to fit into mainstream society, and demonstrate higher levels of satisfaction than that displayed by Muslims in other parts of the world (Canada's Muslims 2007). For the young people in the present study, the difference from Canada was not the only aspect that struck them when they embarked on trips to their place(s) of ethnic origin. Some were also well aware that they were seen as fundamentally foreign from locals, a fact that they thought was unlikely to change, even if they worked constantly to acquire the correct linguistic skills, dress, or behaviours.

Some, similar to the young people in Maira's (2002) study, may have continually sought out those avenues of cultural retention that they believed to be the most genuine, despite the fact that this intensity was likely unmatched in South Asia. As one of Maira's interviewees observed, those who live in South Asia are more likely to take cultural and religious practice for granted, whereas those living in the diaspora, continually reminded of the possibility of loss, may approach these matters from the perspective of work or obligation. For instance, Maira (2002, 146) notes that some of her participants have worked hard to ensure they are speaking the most technically correct Hindi possible in order to appear optimally authentic, even when employing terms that are generally Anglicized by Indians living in India. The young people I interviewed had widely varying approaches to language and culture, similar to the diversity exhibited by participants in Gillespie (1995) or in Maira (2002). Some were fluent in South Asian dialects, others not at all, whereas many occupied a hazy middle ground that they admitted would leave them unable to pass on any linguistic skills in this area to their children. However, not all of them saw this as a genuine loss. There was deep regret among a few and acceptance among others, as well as a suggestion that other languages would prove to be more useful to them in their Canadian settings. Whereas some embraced the fact that they could communicate with their parents and eventually their children in South Asian dialects, others saw this as a convenience but not a necessity. Indeed, some had acquired proficiency in Hindi or Urdu independently of any urging from their parents, learning this skill almost accidentally while watching Hindi films.

Overall, there were numerous differences between the young adults in this study in the ways they saw the retention of language, culture, and religion. Compared to their parents, some were less likely to engage in related rituals, others continued to seek seemingly authentic methods of practice, and most tended toward a rather selective approach where they did not feel bound to all the rituals that were important to their parents but continued to observe those that carried meaning for them. Unlike the participants in Maira (2002), who seem to experience some pressure to fit into South Asian communities where failure to conform is condemned, these young people appeared to feel more free to move in and out of different social circles, including South Asian ones, and they were able to find places for themselves in each, echoing the observations of Handa (2003). Most seemed to feel that evolution was natural; the loss of linguistic skills or cultural memories was unfortunate in some respects, but they were working to forge new cultural opportunities, doing so in a way that had been unavailable to their parents. If one culture was unfamiliar, most engaged with it as a learning experience, whereas others saw these experiences as interesting but not crucial to their identity.

The participants here defined that identity differently in terms of ethnicity or religion, but most found common ground in their national identity. National identity was seen as separate from ethnic identity, countering Howard-Hassman's (1999) reasoning for seeing these as the same. This distinction may well explain the considerable disparity between the findings here and those of Reitz and Banerjee (2007), who claim that second-generation immigrant youth, including South Asians, are unlikely to self-identify as Canadian. Reitz and Banerjee (2007, 539) explain the process they used in trying to discover whether these youth saw themselves as Canadian:

"What is your ethnic or cultural identity?" This was asked following the series of questions on ancestry, and for which the respondent was read the statement: "I would now like you to think about *your own* identity, in ethnic or cultural terms. This identity may be the same as that of your parents, grandparents or ancestors, or it may be different. (Original emphasis)

The inability of the researchers in this case to acknowledge the difference between nationality and ethnicity leads them to conclude that these youth are improperly integrated and that each generation of visible minorities is less likely to see themselves as Canadian. In actual fact, Reitz and Banerjee's (2007) study is simply one more example of the ways that the complex identities of minority youth are misunderstood and misrepresented. For the most part, my own informants were likely to articulate a belief that nationality may have a connection to ethnicity and religion, but they did not see these as the same (for related findings, see Khan 2009b).

It is true that some Muslims in the current study, like the European Muslims cited in Saunders (2007), placed their religion first when summarizing their identities, whereas others spoke of their cultural origins, but in several cases they also indicated that they did this because their self-identification as Canadian was so often seen as insufficient by others. In the case of Muslim informants, their awareness that Islam was the subject of both scrutiny and criticism may have contributed to their emphasis on religious identity. It was clear that several had been led to consider their religious identity, and the positioning of Islam within various societies, more carefully because of a perception that their religion was misunderstood. Although this misunderstanding may have intensified in the wake of 11 September 2001, it did not arise simply out of the events that occurred that day. Several participants were able to identify long-standing problems of religious representation in media and among their acquaintances, problems that are hinted at even by the informants in Jiwani (1989). The young people in this study, many of whom operated from a position of relative privilege because they were middle class and/or educated, knew what it meant to be excluded from society for a protracted period of time, and they had developed techniques for addressing this. Some used these moments as teaching experiences for those who would question their identity, whereas others were dismissive, but none seemed to feel shaken in their beliefs regarding their nationality or their right to claim it. Unlike the young South Asian women in Durham's (2004) study, who have their own methods of creating hybrid identities but also indicate a kind of outsider status in American society, the respondents here were more likely to exhibit resistance to any attempts to confine them to the margins.

As detailed by Hoodfar's (2003) and Khan's (2000) interviewees, marginalization and resistance can come from several sources, encompassing acts both large and small. One approach assumed by some of the young women in Hoodfar (2003) is to educate themselves about their culture and religion, in order to answer the criticisms of others, while simultaneously refusing attempts to exile them to the private sphere or to otherwise silence them. The young people in this study evidenced something similar, rejecting attempts to downgrade or deny their citizenship. Is Kumar's description of the process of becoming a citizen, cited at the beginning of this chapter, too simplistic? Perhaps. It can be read as valorizing the assimilative functions of such a process, but at the same time it may also speak to an eventual diminishing of the emphasis on Canadians of South Asian origin as something other than Canadian. The young people in this study made clear that they had often been singled out as different, and sometimes this marking occurred both in Canadian society and in the communities or countries that might be identified as places of ethnic communality. At the same time, however, they also indicated their refusal to accept this categorization, at least in terms of their national identity. Asked repeatedly over the years about their origins or their "real" nationality, each had developed his or her strategies for answering such questions from strangers, but few seemed to find it necessary to ask these questions of themselves. They were and remain Canadian, citizens rather than immigrants, as Kumar summarizes.

It may be too much, however, to say that Kumar's prognosis is entirely accurate. These young people did stand out, even when they had been born and educated here and spoke English, sometimes exclusively. At the same time, they saw – or wanted to see – their society as a place in which they were free to stand out in any number of ways. Their Canadian birthright, as several of them described it, was to embrace the cultures or religions in which they had been raised without shedding one ounce of their national pride or sense of belonging. They were exceptional but not by choice. They sketched a picture of a society that has yet to fully understand them and their positioning, but they also recognized its promise. Confirming Anderssen and Valpy's (2003) suggestion in their article on young Canadians in their twenties, the respondents here were conscious of having been raised in a country where multiculturalism is enshrined in law, and they attempted to make the most of that right.

All of them acknowledged their origins but in different ways. Some of them problematized their culture and their religion, whereas others accepted these legacies with apparent ease. Even when an interviewee did acknowledge tensions with ethnic or religious communities, this did not necessarily translate into a repudiation of either, perhaps because, like the participants in Bhimani's (2003) study, they realized the extent to which cultural and religious dictates have been matters of interpretation rather than representing something intrinsic and static. They seemed to indicate an awareness of others and where they fit into society – Canadian, diasporic, or otherwise. More than two decades have passed since Jiwani's (1989) interviewees expressed some puzzlement over their ethnic identity and their relationship to other South Asians. In that time, Canada has become increasingly diverse, and the world has seen the social and political consequences of failing to bridge cultural clashes. These young people, like those in Maira (2002) and Desai (2005), had given a great deal of thought to who they were, and who they wanted to be, in part because they felt that ignoring their heritage and identity was simply not an option. This attention to identity dovetailed with efforts by the Canadian state to acknowledge them, as well as the consistent attempts from diasporic industries to market to them as a loosely grouped global community. Many of these themes emerged in their interviews, as discussed in the following passages.

A range of issues and points were covered in the interview recordings and transcripts. First, the diversity of the respondents' thoughts and opinions was sufficiently pronounced to demonstrate that there are no definite factors that can simply and predictably dictate the way that young people will internalize their thoughts about culture, faith, and nationality. I opened this book by making reference to various studies, some by the *Globe and Mail* (cited in Anderssen and Valpy 2003) and one by Reitz and Banerjee (2007), that made differing claims about the nature of nationality for Canadian youth, and I suggested that I hoped to add the perspectives of my own participants to such claims. The sample was too small and possibly too specialized to allow for broad generalizations, but the respondents provided rich and complex data, demonstrating apparent contradictions that appear to be the hallmarks of cultures, societies, and people in flux. Many of these results, however different in detail, had links to previous studies: the young adults here indicated the generally confident sense of self cited in Handa (2003), but they also noted their awareness of and occasional vulnerability to pressures from a variety of sources, such as those chronicled in Khan (2000), Maira (2002), and Hoodfar (2003). Moreover, even their most confident assertions were sometimes undermined by their descriptions of upbringing or everyday life. The findings regarding media and nationalism were similar in some respects to those in Jiwani (1989), Gillespie (1995), Maira (2002), Durham (2004), and Desai (2005), where informants are often aware of attempts to impose patriotic readings on them but generally resist these, instead embracing an enhanced sense of ethnic self. It was clear that the period in time as well as the geographical location of the participants in this study were definite factors in establishing a sense of nationalism and a particular reading of media.

Although this research project was constructed around media, particularly Bollywood, as the central concern, I was also interested in assessing the other factors that had contributed to identity construction. No one factor seemed to indicate the reason for the strong national identification that emerged as the first finding of this study. Some participants did identify themselves using hyphenated terminology, such as "Indo-Canadian" or "Pakistani-Canadian," but most identified as Canadian to some degree. A significant number identified only as Canadian. Many were Canadian-born and pointed out that they had no other home to which they could make such definite reference, even if parents or strangers attempted to emphasize their role as outsiders in Canadian society. Few consciously identified as members of a South Asian or Muslim diaspora, but when they did comment on their relationships with states, industries, or individuals in a diaspora, this was almost always in the context of ethnic or religious identity, not as national subjects.

Socialization in Canadian educational institutions appeared to be a key factor in helping with the construction of a Canadian identity, although participants named different aspects of this experience. One pointed to official rituals such as learning and performing the national anthem, whereas others spoke more to the acquisition of a kind of cultural capital – interaction with other Canadians from different walks of life had helped them to understand the forms of behaviour, language, and dress deemed normative by the mainstream. Some also described the more formal learning that takes place in such institutions, commenting on the significance they attached to the history of the country, its politics and laws, and in some sense, its linguistic legacies. One participant, seeking to denote the extent to which his parents had distanced themselves from their former country, explained that they wanted him to be fully Canadian and to settle into that society in every way, including developing advanced capability in the country's two official languages. Although creating a sense of nationalism is not a primary purpose for educational institutions, such sentiment seems to arise informally, even if it is not the impassioned patriotism found elsewhere. Participants did occasionally note instances of discrimination or reminders of difference from their childhood experiences of school, but several cited it as a place that helped them to acculturate into Canadian society and to succeed there. Other, less formal activities also contributed to this acculturation, including the formation of a diverse circle of friends and acquaintances as well as simple engagement with the neighbourhoods in which they lived.

If the public sphere was the place where these young people learned how to feel Canadian in (nearly) every way, the private sphere was more often the space where ethnic practice was learned and maintained. Parents were often cited as a cultural influence, rarely as a national one. One young woman did describe an upbringing in which her father reminded her constantly that she was not truly Canadian since their family was from Pakistan, but for the most part parents appeared to emphasize ethnic and religious identity more than the notion that their nationality was other than Canadian. Parental influence is hardly surprising, and the importance of extended family and community was also emphasized. Some individuals, especially young women, pointed to rather traditional expectations imposed on them by their parents, and they did discuss not always being able to relate to their parents in the same way that they might relate to friends or others. However, the extreme code-switching described by Maira (2002), in which American youth of South Asian origin transformed themselves in radical ways when leaving the familial domain and entering the social scene, was not mentioned here. It is possible that it had taken place, but it was not referenced by any of the participants. The different scope of this study may account for this – Maira's study is specific to a particular manifestation of South Asian culture, one built around parties and clubs in New York City, whereas this research mainly restricts itself to identity and the interpretation of media.

Other possible reasons for this difference in behaviour do come to mind, if indeed there is a significant disparity. Contrasting Muslims in Canada with those in the United States, two participants suggested that for the latter, an intense pressure to retain traditional ways of thinking was at war with an equally strong compulsion to assimilate into American society. If this is the case, it might not be that unusual for youth who feel the necessity of appearing comfortable in both cultures to switch, as Maira (2002) describes, between the two by wearing conservative clothing and appearing demure with family and then moving to the other extreme by donning either women's clothing that is more seductive or men's clothes that are often associated with hip-hop culture. The young people in this study were hardly immune to clashes with their parents or others in their communities, but they seemed to have negotiated compromises in some respects and acceptance in others.

The use of media involved other compromises. Despite some level of dissonance and even occasional repugnance, many of the participants continued to view Bollywood films. The simple explanation for this might be that the activity of watching Bollywood films was seen as meaningless in many respects for those participants who singled out problematic aspects, including those that denigrated them, and yet continued watching. Possibly, they thought the significance of these films was minimal. However, it seems to me that their own responses indicated otherwise. One woman, who actually did try to limit the films she watched to those that satisfied her principles and beliefs, pointed out that experience and education had helped her to discard some of the ideas she had earlier internalized from Bollywood films regarding romance, gender, and beauty, but she considered it important to note that she had once been influenced by these ideas, and she was likely not alone. Another woman, one who was familiar with a broad range of Indian films but also expressed notable dislike of the representation of gender in Hindi movies, voiced a concern about many young South Asian women who appeared susceptible to the notions of star-crossed love found in these films. Notions of gender that were perceived as distorted were crucial to the way that some viewers judged these movies, which also spilled over into a distaste for increasingly explicit costumes on women as well as an emphasis on sexuality, a finding whose recurrence was both unexpected and notably pronounced.

This emphasis on sexuality was seen as distasteful in part for the way women were portrayed but also because it seemed to speak to a perceived belief about the values of viewers, especially the purportedly liberal ones living in the South Asian diaspora. This belief is stated more explicitly by a respondent in Brosius (2005, 221), who is at a loss to explain such scenes to her daughters, having previously used Indian and Pakistani cinema to model demure behaviour:

> In the Pakistani films, I used to tell them, look we Muslim people *we don't do that,* okay? I didn't mind if the kiddies watched Pakistani movies, because it was *really* clean. But *now,* even in the Pakistani movies, they're showing them [women] with half-sleeve dresses and their scenes are really vulgar. So I don't even bring that anymore! Because that was our way of telling the kiddies, listen, this is our culture, do you see anything in the movies like that!? But you can't even do *that* anymore. So I think it's the same thing with the Indian movies. (Original emphasis)

Participants here saw the suggestion that they would be open to viewing sexually explicit scenes both as a personal insult and as a way of depriving them of family-friendly entertainment that they could otherwise enjoy safely with elders. According to their interpretation, then, there was a genuine possibility of being influenced by Bollywood cinema in a variety of ways, even when one focused on the themes that were seen as being most frivolous.

If we dismiss the possibility that these films have no significance, what compelled these critical young viewers, who had numerous entertainment options available to them and who indicated themselves that watching a Bollywood film involved a considerable investment of time, to continue watching? Even if that viewing was infrequent, it remained a fact. Based on the interviewees' comments, I am inclined to conclude that Bollywood does in fact play some role in the constitution of identity. The role may be largely negative, inspiring resistance to the social paradigms alluded to in the films, or it may be minimal, but it does exist, and in several cases, the role was significant. Despite placing emphasis on a variety of factors, a number of young people did see meaning in Bollywood films, at least in part because of the context in which they consumed these films and because of their ability to see themselves represented in some form, however caricatured or unrealistic this depiction might be. Many of them saw the strong nationalism in popular Indian cinema and the concurrent marginalization of themselves as diasporic subjects, but they professed to be largely unaffected by this, except in the sense that they did sometimes see it as insulting. Media were not seen as having a significant effect on a sense of nationalism, although some did take pride in the Indian film industry itself.

Given that the concept of resistance and its accompanying limitations formed part of the framework of this study, I am interested in the fact that resistance was a recurring theme and yet not fully realized in some respects. As Raby (2005) notes, resistance can take a variety of forms, ranging from collective, organized action against a dominant power, to the production of alternative discourses, to simple refusal to engage in particular activities. As she points out, it is difficult to fully conceptualize resistance without accounting for power and agency. If this is so, it is unclear what kind of resistance is truly occurring here, particularly because the young people in this study encountered a number of dominant powers, and may, at times, have occupied positions of power themselves based on their class, education, and the cultural capital they had acquired. Without wishing to be overly sanguine about the complexities underlying the lives of these individuals, I argue that resistance can be found here in several ways and on differing levels. Participants refused to surrender their sense of identity in the face of external challenges, and they offered critical readings of many of the media under discussion, rejecting interpretations that marginalized them in terms of gender, geography, or religion, sometimes going so far as to use these readings to initiate difficult and controversial discussions with family members. They were invested in a belief that Canada was a pluralist and accepting place but were not necessarily naive about this. Most were prepared to educate those who would question or criticize their cultural heritage or their place either in their host society or in their ethnic and religious communities.

At the same time, there was a distinct ambivalence to their understanding of nationality, an ambivalence that was perhaps less troubled than that of the respondents in Cressey (2006) or Maira (2002), where racism and prejudice are invoked openly, but it was ambivalence nonetheless. If there was not outright acceptance of racism, it is clear that some participants saw a minimal level of discrimination as a fact of life and had learned to tolerate it. In the same way, some did attempt to resist what they saw as outdated social norms from family or community members, but it was evident that a few had been scarred by expectations around gender, beauty, or relationships that they could not possibly fulfill. Related to this, in the reading of Bollywood films, there was enormous ambiguity in the way they approached the very thematics they identified. Concerns about gender, diasporic portrayals, religious stereotyping, and Westernization were debated, sometimes hotly, and informants displayed a keen eye for contradictions or prejudices in the films under discussion. Nonetheless, many continued to consume some of these films and to speak of their favourites in ways that did not always reflect the insightful critique they displayed elsewhere. Although their readings were clearly oppositional at times, it was not obvious whether those readings had translated into meaningful change in their lives. Perhaps outright resistance was not taking place in the way that some critical researchers define it – there was no boycott of these films in response to problematic themes and no attempt to restructure an industry that exercises totalizing control over vulnerable competitors, and only a few had disengaged from the enormous market for consumer goods that is connected to this industry.

However, these participants were people who faced hegemony on many levels, so they showed resistance as they deemed appropriate rather than withdrawing utterly from the consumption of any and all media, or all forms of daily existence, that may have been problematic in some respects. As many pointed out, Bollywood is fraught with issues, but it does provide an alternative for an ethnic group that is otherwise largely ignored or side-lined in most media. These young people may have been working toward a place of acceptance and comfort in Canadian society, but they were not – and perhaps may never be – operating wholly at its centre. At the same time, very few operated as solely South Asian subjects. Living in the diaspora had shaped them far too substantively, and this thought occupied the minds of many informants as they explained how they viewed themselves and the media that claimed to address them. Criticisms of diasporic portrayal aside, very few referred to the positive depictions of the diaspora in some films, such as *Dilwale Dulhania Le Jayenge* (The Lover Takes the Bride, 1995), pre-ferring instead to comment on its romantic themes and its production values. Stated rejections of supposedly Western, consumerist themes warred with a cautious affection for films that were seen to be modern and more interesting than older films with darker storylines and fewer special effects. However, some were open about the guilty complicity they felt with such media; they did not always agree with what they saw, yet they continued to watch Bollywood cinema. They would have preferred a better alternative, but none was available. Some of the same sense of unwilling complicity also slips into the responses of participants in Desai (2005) and Maira (2002), for whom Bollywood has become one of the few options for seeing oneself on screen, even if it is in a limited way. The hybrid, transitory strategies for cultural survival that are seen in the way this study's young people assert identity are also seen in their consumption of media; their reading of Bolly-wood texts cannot be understood as wholly passive or oppositional but rather as part of a multi-layered, contradictory, partially satisfactory phil-osophy of identity building.

Conclusion:
You Really Are Global Citizens:
Resistance and Reconciliation

> *Most find comfort and solace in nationalism; it is an indication of home, comfort, and friends. To be an exile is to be without a nation, a nationality, a home, and security. Nationalism, in [Edward] Said's estimation, is a God that always fails because it reduces human experience and lines of solidarity between people to territories and borders that in reality carve up the world in unproductive and destructive ways. To be an exile is to relate to all people regardless of their country of citizenship or place of birth. (Abraham 2006, 139)*

The use of Bollywood as a means for identity construction, including that use in combination with other socializing agents, suggests that, similar to the young women in Durham (2004), the respondents in this study were capable of drawing on myriad cultural elements in coming to terms with who they were. None aligned themselves entirely with one identity, preferring instead the richness of the many selves available in a pluralist society. I commented earlier that a kind of chameleon-like quality exhibits itself in some young minorities who have learned to move between worlds, a tendency documented as well by Roger Ballard in his study of South Asian Britons (cited in Patel 2006, 158) and less consciously by the participants in Ali (2003, 140):

> Those who feel tied by "blood" to particular countries of parents' origin can argue for their inclusion of this part of their hyphenated identity. Yet they may shift this to become British when "needed" or, indeed, wanted. Recent migrants, and "monoracial" children who are second or third generation settlers, also show this ability, and in many ways it is more marked with them.

This ability might not have been overt in all of the individuals studied here, and the ease of this movement undoubtedly varies, but there did seem to be a flexibility in terms of their willingness to engage with a host of elements. Indeed, that engagement seemed consonant with a wish to mine the best of Canadian culture, whose plurality they viewed as imperfect yet necessary and highly desirable. As diversity has become more embedded in Canadian society, it has also become less necessary to move so constantly between worlds and more possible to combine them. Although this study was not intended to examine romantic relationships, it is interesting to note that several participants made reference to non-South Asian partners and to the ways they might introduce their culture to those partners. Others noted that they engaged in a variety of cultural activities, South Asian and otherwise, encompassing different religious traditions, as their social circles presented them with the opportunity to learn about others and to demonstrate mutual respect.

In a scenario such as this, which echoes Anderssen and Valpy's (2003) portrayal of a society marked by increased melding of groups and traditions (also see Anderssen 2003), Kraidy's (1999, 472) notion of hybridity becomes ever more relevant, with his description of "re-formulating intercultural and international communication beyond buoyant models of resistance and inauspicious patterns of domination." This is not to say that resistance and domination do not take place. Bollywood itself is a medium that embodies, rather curiously, domination, resistance, and hybridity all in the same venue. Despite running roughshod over less powerful competitors and drowning out regional voices, it works to establish South Asian pride in the face of foreign media conglomerates, particularly American ones, whose global hegemony is challenged all too rarely. Bollywood does hew to standard formulas and it does endorse many aspects of the very culture it critiques, such as consumerism and excess, but at the same time, it has bent slightly in acknowledgment of the changing needs of diasporic South Asians. According to the respondents in this research and to my own analysis, this attempt at change is often misguided, representing the diaspora in ways that indicate only its physical and intellectual distance, yet the effort is there to speak to a number of cultures. In many respects, the hybridity that is thus achieved only validates Araeen's (2000, 15) criticism that victory for Bhabha's (1994) hybrid Other means "a triumph of neo-liberal multiculturalism, a part of the triumph of global capitalism."

Undoubtedly, one does not want to romanticize the kind of messy, contradictory, simplified creolization found in these films, aptly called "masala films" by some for their combination of disparate elements. However, it is a hybridity that allows many in, even if some are accorded more belonging than others. Araeen (2000) comments critically on Bhabha's belief that the hybrid Other is destined to exist on the margins or in an altogether new space rather than moving freely from the periphery to the centre. The young people in this study seemed somehow to have reconciled the two, bypassing notions that a hybrid space is the same as an exilic space; despite the resistance they had encountered when they positioned themselves in the centre, they had continued to attempt to move into that area, even as they maintained an awareness of what it was like to exist on the periphery.

In the analysis these participants offered, the new space they had created could be found simultaneously in the centre and on the margins. Muslims in particular seemed to feel that they were asked to exist on the margins, but that did not stop any of the young people in this study from pushing back against such attitudes, similar to the kind of defiance exhibited by some of the subjects in Hoodfar (2003) and Khan (2000). As in those studies, some tended to gain confidence by assimilating into Canadian society, minimizing as many ethnic markers as they could, whereas others tried as much as possible to hold onto ethnic and religious traditions, but nearly all moved toward a complicated middle ground. They researched their options, educated themselves, and attempted to teach others about difference. In fact, although Abraham's (2006) observations at the beginning of this chapter refer to the plurality and sensitivity to difference exhibited by exiles, these young people demonstrated some of those same traits while refusing to be classified as exiles. Naturally, this came with its own set of contradictions: they had concerns that stretched well beyond the borders of Canada or their own ethnic or religious communities, but many of them did fall back on the solace of finding home in Canada, at least the Canada they envisioned. Referring to the willingness of migrants to see vast promise and hope in an imagined America, Harzig and Hoerder (2006, 44) describe a place that is "neither the United States nor Canada but a transnational image of potentialities." The potentialities these young people seemed to glimpse were touched, as Joseph (1999) suggests in her discussion of nomadic identities, with "incomplete desires of community and allegiances" (19), but their citizenship was not really nomadic given its performance across and within boundaries (17).

Citizenship is a concrete entity, as is nationalism. It places demands on the self, of course, and these are demands that must be weighed against the equally pressing demands of ethnic and religious communities. Citizenship, in this formulation, is work, as is identity construction, and neither can be denied. The young people here suggested that they had devoted much thought to who they were and how they wanted to live but not necessarily to where they wanted to live. Having been raised in Canada, they had considered how to carve out their existence there, even if they lived with memories or stories of other places. The complexity of living such an existence, actually inhabiting that transnational vision of potentialities, may have seemed burdensome, and no doubt it had been at times. Undoubtedly, there was a form of labour involved here, yet it was a labour that appeared to offer considerable rewards and that could not be neglected if one wished to continue the process of societal and communal change. The creation of hybrid selves appeared to be a natural process in some ways, one bound to occur over time and across space. Some young people seemed to refer to this rather casually, accepting it as a fact of life. In their specific comments about their influences and about their mediated interpretations and perceptions of nationalism and ethnicity, however, they indicated that creation of the self was work and that the self was an ongoing construction. Overall, the methods that these individuals used to blend resistance, assimilation, and integration, sometimes all at once, were testaments to their ability to continue building not just their selves but also the Canadian and global society that they envisioned, a space of extensive diversity and acceptance.

Although my initial desire to explore the participants' feelings toward citizenship and civic engagement soon moved into the background, comments regarding citizenship did filter into a few of the interviews, demonstrating that the young adults here had indeed, as predicted, been devoting thought to their place in Canadian society and the obligations and rights attached to their citizenship. Interviewed at a time when dual citizenship and multiculturalism had experienced protracted attack for their failure to integrate minority Canadians (DiManno 2006; Ford 2006), nearly every respondent here indicated a belief that they were Canadian and that Canada was their home, regardless of any messages received to the contrary from any source. They took Canada's claims to multiculturalism seriously, and expected their country and their fellow citizens to live up to these claims. In their conviction that this was possible, many found a sense of belonging, however uneasy.

This very uneasiness, this awareness of possible unsettlement, might be the reason that nationalism did not translate here into parochialism or assimilation. The respondents took the subject of their origins seriously and seemed to feel a certain global consciousness in relation to this. The global citizenship, the constant travel, the feeling of belonging to nowhere or nothing – informants were aware of these but not necessarily defined by them in the same way as the individuals described in Joseph (1999) and Ong (1999). Global citizenship was abstract for some and a serious concept for others, and cosmopolitanism was something they endorsed rather loosely. Nearly all indicated a home base and a distinct national identity, which they combined with a sense of solidarity with others in the South Asian diaspora, for instance. Many of the participants were well travelled and several were multi-lingual. It would be stretching the point to suggest that all of these young adults were cosmopolitan in every sense or even in most senses, but their dedication to pluralism did align with the notion of cosmopoliteness, "the degree to which an individual is oriented outside his immediate social system" (Rogers 1969, 147), "motivated to look beyond his environment, when most others are content to maintain a localistic frame of reference" (149).

Asked whether he would use Bollywood films to acculturate his children in the same manner that his parents had employed, Kahil said that he would but that he would also seek to provide a balanced experience, incorporating other foreign films, for instance. His comments here serve as perhaps the best summary regarding the participants' attitudes, as well as the role they will undoubtedly play in Canada's present and future:

> Because I think we're living in a world and a time now where you do have to be in touch with your own identity, otherwise you seem to lack one and it's tougher to keep up with that when you have so many different – not necessarily conflicting – but different influences. With that said though, I think there's a need to be much more aware of the larger world, so knowing your own is important but knowing others is important as well, because you really are global citizens.

The global citizenship described here is a state of mind, an acknowledgment of obligation. It is not a political manifestation of cosmopolitanism or world citizenship (Heater 1996, 1999) but an outcome of growing up in an environment where transnationalism is a known fact: "Cosmopolis meant viewing the whole of the universe and all its inhabitants as if they were a social entity. A cosmopolite was one who recognised his membership of this cosmopolis. It meant little more in human social terms than accepting all men as brethren" (Heater 1996, 181). Various forms of transnationalism and diaspora had been witnessed by these young people and others during their upbringings. Even when constant movement, remittances, or transnational communication were not directly part of their experience, they were aware of such practices and may have been further reminded by flows of media and goods.

Transnationalism and diaspora are undoubtedly more real to some people than to others. Some might argue that the individuals in this study were particularly privileged ones. Although they possessed varying educational levels and backgrounds and may have been different in terms of class, their time in Canada had provided them with linguistic and social capabilities that more recent immigrants or older immigrants might have struggled to obtain. These informants were less likely than some of their parents or grandparents to have spent many years making significant adjustments to Canadian life. At the same time, this was part of the history that some of these young people shared, and it gave them an insight into a transnational or a diasporic existence. This insight may also have arrived at least in part due to their awareness that a transnational reality was inscribed onto their bodies by those who saw them; non–South Asians saw them as immigrants, regardless of how hard they had worked to adapt to Canadian society, and South Asian Canadians might have been equally inclined to view them as outsiders on a variety of levels: they could be insufficiently South Asian, they might not have subscribed to the same beliefs, and/or they were simply among those who did not belong to the mainstream. At the same time, governments such as that in India, as well as a number of Indian industries, make clear their belief that individuals of South Asian origin belong to a transnational economic network, and they attempt to speak to them as members of a global family or market.

There is work involved in the construction of identity, then, and a number of factors enter into this work. Some factors are the purview of the state, others of media or upbringing, but ultimately every individual will combine these factors differently in arriving at a space that allows for a workable combination of nationality, ethnicity, and religion, a blend that can be explained to the self and to others. Identity was a work in progress for several participants, although some acknowledged this fact frankly from the very beginning and others seemed to arrive at that conclusion once they had interrogated their own beliefs further. There is nothing simple about the identity of the Canadian nation, the one with which these young people primarily identified, nor is there anything simple about creating an identity that allows one to live in multiple worlds without sacrificing a sense of unified self.

Hybridity is not an easy solution, nor is it the only one. However, even the most optimistic participants interviewed here knew the impossibility of simply stepping outside of the socializing institutions they described and entering mainstream Canadian society as fully fledged and completely accepted. Marked from the very beginning as different, placed under additional pressure when stereotypes and generalizations had been imposed on them following events involving Muslims or South Asians, they had needed to find a way to cope. Each person in this study subscribed, unconsciously or not, to some degree of hybridity as a result. Most sought to bridge the differences between their various social networks, introducing non-South Asian friends to their culture and lives.

Whether or not they were equipped for the task, they found themselves, as Kumar (2002, 178) suggests, performing the roles of cultural interpreters, facing the need to educate themselves and then translate their experiences for people whose own experiences might not have been as broad. For the latter, the unfamiliar act of inhabiting one space while drawing – at least mentally – on the influences of many others may seem like an impossibility, an impingement on citizenship and nationalism. All the same, this is the choice with which diasporic individuals, especially those whose difference is as marked as that of South Asians and Muslims, are faced. In a space that simultaneously was and was not displacement, that was home and not home, that was both acceptance and exclusion, these young people were freed from instinctive commitments to unitary identities and accepted beliefs, but such apparent liberty was accompanied by the requirement to apply conscious thought and effort to new identities, to bridge building, and to cultural, religious, and societal transformation.

The glorious optimism expressed by Valpy and Anderssen (2003), in which immigrant youth come to change the face and the future of Canada, may be going too far, but if diasporic individuals do maximize the possibility of the liminal space they inhabit, they may well transform the communities and institutions in which they dwell. The participants in this study were well aware of the considerable obstacles attached to effecting such evolution, in which difference becomes the norm, yet most refused to shy away. Surrounded by various pressures, conscious of their responsibilities and rights, they nonetheless saw themselves as capable of undertaking the challenges of a hybrid, fluctuating, not entirely definable identity. To have avoided doing so would have been, like unthinking resistance, simply futile.

Appendix:
Films Cited by Participants

Bollywood films cited by participants

Film title	Times cited	Description
Dilwale Dulhania Le Jayenge	7	1995 film hugely successful both in and outside of India. For perhaps the first time, a couple raised outside of India but with true Indian values finds happiness and returns to England to live their lives
Hum Aapke Hain Koun	6	1994 film described as one of the most successful of all time; a lavish love story that shows two families going through the rituals of marriage and childbirth, among others. Believed to mark the beginning of a youth-oriented, modern era in Bollywood
Kabhi Khushi Kabhie Gham	6	2001 star-studded movie about marriage opposed by a patriarch and the resulting discord, which drives part of the family to exile in London, only to return to India in the end for a happy reunion
Devdas	4	2002 remake of a popular classic in which the title character sinks into alcoholism after his family prevents his marriage to his childhood love
Kuch Kuch Hota Hai	4	1998 love story that, like Hum Aapke Hain Koun, attracted many youth back to Bollywood, possibly because of high production values and depiction of popular brands
Veer-Zaara	4	2004 film about cross-border romance between an Indian man and a Pakistani woman
Black	3	2005 film that won major accolades for Rani Mukherjee as a blind and mute woman

▶

Film title	Times cited	Description
Bombay	3	1995 Tamil film about a Hindu-Muslim romance and the turmoil visited upon the couple's sons during intercommunal rioting in Bombay
Hum Tum	3	2004 romance between two long-time friends
Kal Ho Naa Ho	3	2003 film in which the protagonist helps the dejected heroine learn how to love and live anew
Lagaan	3	2001 film nominated for Best Foreign Film Oscar; depicts a makeshift cricket team playing to oppose an unfair tax by the British
Baghban	2	2003 film about children's neglect of loving parents
Dil	2	1989 love story
Gadar	2	2001 romance between a Sikh man and a Muslim woman during post-Partition chaos
Mughal-e-Azam	2	1960 classic about doomed romance between a prince and a courtesan; notable for its lush depictions of the Mughal era
Qurbani	2	1980 film renowned partly for its music; features a love triangle and an intricate criminal plot
Salaam Namaste	2	2005 film about an unmarried couple in Australia coping with unplanned pregnancy
Swades	2	2004 movie in which the star is convinced to leave his prestigious job in the United States and apply his talents toward improving an Indian village
Amar Akbar Anthony	1	1977 hit about three brothers separated and raised as Hindu, Muslim, and Christian, respectively
Amar Prem	1	1971 movie about a young woman sold into prostitution
Banjaran	1	1991 movie of star-crossed love
The Burning Train	1	1980 thriller about a train designed to be the best in India and an attempt to foil its inaugural run
Dhoom	1	2004 action-packed film that led to a sequel
Dosti	1	1964 film about two friends beset by misfortune
Dus	1	2005 action film about an attempt to foil a terrorist plot
Ek Hasina Thi	1	2004 movie in which the heroine is framed and sent to jail, where she plots her revenge

▶

Film title	Times cited	Description
Heer Raanjha	1	1970 Punjabi romance (a number of other versions exist)
Judai	1	1997 film based loosely on *Indecent Proposal;* a wealthy non-resident Indian woman attempts to buy a married man's companionship
Kalnayak	1	1993 film about, as the title says, a "bad man" who eventually finds a type of redemption through the very people who sought to imprison him
Khamosh Pani	1	2003 film depicting a widow's fears for her son in a Pakistan transformed by martial law and fundamentalism; also raises history of women's experiences following Partition
Mohabbatein	1	2000 movie about a music teacher who honours his dead love by encouraging romance at the school where his lover's father is the stern principal
Mother India	1	1957 classic about poverty and harsh living conditions in India
Namak Halal	1	1982 comedy-drama in which the main character moves to the big city, only to become embroiled in a plot involving family and crime
Namastey London	1	2007 film about an assimilated woman in England
Pardes	1	1997 film about an Indian woman who travels to the United States to stay with her fiancé's family, only to discover that life there is cold, corrupt, and dissolute
Parineeta	1	2005 movie set in 1960s Kolkata; depicts a love triangle
Pinjar	1	2003 movie that depicts the mistreatment of women of various backgrounds as a way to settle scores during the partitioning of the Punjab
Raja Hindustani	1	1996 romance between a wealthy woman and a poor man
Ram aur Sham	1	1967 movie where mistaken identity fuels a complicated series of events
Roti Kapada aur Makaan	1	1974 film depicting the despair of youth who cannot obtain employment
Sholay	1	1975 classic revenge drama with romantic elements
Umrao Jaan	1	1981 tragic romance about a courtesan named Umrao Jaan

►

Non-Bollywood films cited by participants

Film title	Times cited	Description
Water	6	2005 film completing Deepa Mehta's trilogy; Oscar-nominated story about a group of widows condemned to poverty
Bollywood/Hollywood	5	2002 film set in Toronto; Deepa Mehta's comedic take on a Bollywood-themed romance
Monsoon Wedding	5	2001 film about preparations for a wedding where family secrets are revealed
American Desi	2	Comedy released in 2001; one of the first films to explore being an American-Born Confused Desi (ABCD), someone who battles his or her Indian identity
Earth	2	1998 film by Deepa Mehta about inter-communal conflict following Partition
Bride and Prejudice	1	Perhaps best known as Aishwarya Rai's crossover vehicle, this 2004 film remakes *Pride and Prejudice* as an American-Indian romance
Guru	1	2003 comedy about an Indian immigrant in New York who finds success posing as a sex guru
Mississippi Masala	1	Mira Nair's 1992 breakout film about inter-racial romance in the Deep South and a family's struggle to integrate following their departure from Uganda
Murder Unveiled	1	2005 film based on the real story of an Indo-Canadian woman murdered for refusing to marry into a higher caste
Bend It Like Beckham	*	2003 comedy about young British woman of Punjabi origin who aspires to be a soccer star in the face of parental opposition

* Not cited in questionnaires but discussed

References

Aamir. 2008. Dir. R. Kumar Gupta. UTV Spotboy Motion Pictures.

Abraham, M. 2006. History, memory, and exile: Edward Said, the New York intellectuals, and the rhetoric of accommodation and resistance. *Journal of the Midwest Modern Language Association* 39, 2: 133-55.

Abu-Laban, Y., and D. Stasiulis. 2000. Constructing "ethnic Canadians": The implications for public policy and citizenship: Rejoinder to Rhoda Howard-Hassman. *Canadian Public Policy* 26, 4: 477-87.

Abu-Lughod, L. 1991. Writing against culture. In *Recapturing anthropology: Working in the present*, ed. R.G. Fox, 137-62. Santa Fe, NM: School of American Research Press.

Ackah, W., and J. Newman. 2003. Ghanaian Seventh Day Adventists on and offline: Problematising the virtual communities discourse. In *The media of diaspora*, ed. K.H. Karim, 203-14. London: Routledge.

Agnew, V. 2007. Introduction. In *Interrogating race and racism*, ed. V. Agnew, 3-31. Toronto: University of Toronto Press.

Ahmed, L. 1982. *Women and gender in Islam: Historical roots of a modern debate*. New Haven, CT: Yale University Press.

–. 1999. *A border passage: From Cairo to America – a woman's journey*. New York: Farrar, Strauss and Giroux.

Alessandrini, A.C. 2001. "My heart's Indian for all that": Bollywood film between home and diaspora. *Diaspora* 10, 3: 315-40.

Ali, S. 2003. *Mixed-race, post-race: Gender, new ethnicities and cultural practices*. Oxford, UK: Berg.

Allemang, J. 2005. The limits of tolerance. *Globe and Mail*, 24 September, F6.

Alvi, S., H. Hoodfar, and S. McDonough, eds. 2003. *The Muslim veil in North America: Issues and debates*. Toronto: Women's Press.

Amar Akbar Anthony. 1977. Dir. M. Desai, Hirawat Jain, and Company. M.K.D. Films and Manmohan Films.

American Desi. 2001. Dir. P.D. Panya. Secausus, NJ: Eros Entertainment.

Anderson, B. 1983. *Imagined communities: Reflections on the origin and spread of nationalism*. London: Verso.

Anderssen, E. 2003. Two weddings, one marriage. *Globe and Mail*, 7 June, F1, F3-7, F12.

Anderssen, E., and M. Valpy. 2003. Face the nation: Canada. *Globe and Mail*, 7 June, A10-11.

Ang, I. 2001. On the politics of empirical audience research. In *Media and cultural studies keyworks*, ed. M.G. Durham and D.M. Kellner, 177-97. Malden, MA: Blackwell.

Appadurai, A. 1991. Global ethnoscapes: Notes and queries for a transnational anthropology. In *Recapturing anthropology: Working in the present*, ed. R.G. Fox, 191-210. Santa Fe, NM: School of American Research Press.

–. 1996. *Modernity at large: Cultural dimensions of globalization*. Minneapolis: University of Minnesota Press.

Araeen, R. 2000. A new beginning: Beyond postcolonial cultural theory and identity politics. *Third Text* 50: 3-20.

Aubry, J. 2007. Study finds Canadians dubious of dual citizenship. *CanWest News,* 24 July, 1.

Awaara. 1951. Dir. R. Kapoor. All India Film Corporation and R.K. Films.

Baghdadi, R., and R. Rao. 1995. *Talking films.* New Delhi: Indus.

Bandit Queen. 1994. Dir. S. Kapoor. Channel Four Films and Kaleidoscope Entertainment.

Barnouw, E., and S. Krishnaswamy. 1980. *Indian film.* New York: Columbia University Press.

Basch, L., N. Glick Schiller, and C. Szanton Blanc. 1994. *Nations unbound: Transnational projects, postcolonial predicaments, and deterritorialized nation-states.* Postfach, Switzerland: Gordon and Beach.

Beck, U. 1994. The reinvention of politics: Towards a theory of reflexive modernization. Trans. M. Ritter. In *Reflexive modernization: Politics, tradition and aesthetics in the modern social order,* ed. U. Beck, A. Giddens, and S. Lash, 1-55. Stanford, CA: Stanford University Press.

–. 2000. The cosmopolitan perspective: Sociology of the second age of modernity. *British Journal of Sociology* 51, 1: 79-105.

Bend It Like Beckham. 2003. Dir. G. Chadha. Fox Searchlight Pictures.

Bhabha, H.K. 1994. *The location of culture.* London and New York: Routledge.

Bhaji on the Beach. 1993. Dir. G. Chadha. Channel Four Films and Umbi Films.

Bhimani, H. 1995. *In search of Lata Mangeshkar.* New Delhi: Indus.

Bhimani, S. 2003. *Majalis al-ilm: Sessions of knowledge – Reclaiming and representing the lives of Muslim women.* Toronto: TSAR.

Bissoondath, N. 2002. *Selling illusions: The cult of multiculturalism in Canada.* 2nd ed. Toronto: Penguin.

Blanchfield, M. 2002. Canadian attitudes toward Muslims, immigration harden in wake of Sept. 11. *Montreal Gazette,* 21 December, A1, A12.

Bollywood/Hollywood. 2002. Dir. D. Mehta. Bollywood/Hollywood Productions, Different Tree Same Wood, Fortissimo Films, and iDream Productions.

Bombay. 1995. Dir. M. Ratnam. Amitabh Bachchan Corporation and Madras Talkies.

Booth, G.D. 1995. Traditional content and narrative structure in the Hindi commercial cinema. *Asian Folklore Studies* 54, 2: 169-90.

Boyarin, D., and J. Boyarin. 2003. Diaspora: Generation and the ground of Jewish identity. In *Theorizing diaspora: A reader,* ed. J. Evans Braziel and A. Mannur, 85-118. Malden, MA: Blackwell.

Brah, A. 1996. *Cartographies of diaspora: Contesting identities.* London and New York: Routledge.

Braziel, J.E., and A. Mannur. 2003. Nation, migration, globalization: Points of contention in diaspora studies. In *Theorizing diaspora: A reader,* ed. J. Evans Braziel and A. Mannur, 1-22. Malden, MA: Blackwell.

Brender, N. 2009. If we're going to talk citizenship, let's have a principled debate. *Globe and Mail,* 8 April, A19.

Bride and Prejudice. 2004. Dir. G. Chadha. Miramax.

Brosius, C. 2005. The scattered homelands of the migrant: Bollyworld through the diasporic lens. In *Bollyworld: Popular Indian cinema through a transnational lens,* ed. R. Kaur and A.J. Sinha, 207-38. Thousand Oaks, CA: Sage.

Bryman, A. 1988. *Quantity and quality in social research.* London: Unwin Hyman.

Cairns, A. 1995. *Reconfigurations: Canadian citizenship and constitutional change.* Toronto: McClelland and Stewart.

Campbell, C. 2007. The Lebanon evacuation: The bill is in. *Maclean's,* 7 May, 24.

Canada's Muslims, an international comparison. 2007. CBC News, http://www.cbc.ca/news/background/islam/muslim-survey.html.

Carens, J.H. 2000. *Culture, citizenship, and community: A contextual exploration of justice as evenhandedness.* Oxford, UK: Oxford University Press.

Cesari, J. 2002. Islam in France: The shaping of a religious minority. In *Muslims in the West: From sojourners to citizens,* ed. Y.Y. Haddad, 36-51. New York: Oxford University Press.

Chakravarty, S.S. 1993. *National identity in Indian popular cinema, 1947-1987.* Oxford, UK: Oxford University Press.

Chatterji, S. 1998. *Subject cinema, object woman – A study of the portrayal of women in Indian cinema*. Calcutta: Parumitam.

Chhalia. 1960. Dir. M. Desai. Subhash Pictures.

Chopra, A. 2005. Bollywood's good girls learn to be bad. *New York Times*, 24 July, Section 2, 1, 9.

Chowdhry, P. 2000. *Colonial India and the making of empire cinema: Image, ideology and identity*. Manchester, UK: Manchester University Press.

Clifford, J. 1997. *Routes: Travel and translation in the late twentieth century*. Cambridge, MA: Harvard University Press.

Cohen, R. 1997. *Global diasporas: An introduction*. Seattle: University of Washington Press.

Comedy Network Presents Russell Peters. 2007. TV, Comedy Network, 1 April.

Costantino, M. 2008. Emerging from the linguistic divide: Wayson Choy's self-translation into the other in paper shadows: A Chinatown childhood. *ARIEL: A Review of International English Literature* 39, 1-2: 129-46.

Cottle, S., ed. 2000. *Ethnic minorities and the media: Changing cultural boundaries*. Buckingham, UK: Open University Press.

Crash. 2004. Dir. P. Haggis. Bob Yari Productions, DEJ Productions, Blackfriars Bridge, Harris Company, ApolloProScreen Filmproduktion, and Bull's Eye Entertainment.

Cressey, G. 2006. *Diaspora youth and ancestral homeland: British Pakistani/Kashmiri youth visiting kin in Pakistan and Kashmir*. Boston: Brill.

Dayan, D., and E. Katz. 1992. *Media events: The live broadcasting of history*. Cambridge, MA: Harvard University Press.

Dei, G.J.S. 2008. *Crash* and the relevance of an anti-racism analytical lens. In Crash *politics and anti-racism: Interrogations of liberal race discourse*, ed. P.S.S. Howard and G.J.S. Dei, 13-23. New York: Peter Lang.

Desai, J. 2004. *Beyond Bollywood: The cultural politics of South Asian diasporic film*. New York and London: Routledge.

–. 2005. Planet Bollywood: Indian cinema abroad. In *East Main Street: Asian American popular culture*, ed. S. Davé, L. Nishime, and T.G. Oren, 55-71. New York: New York University Press.

Deutsch, K.W. 1966. *Nationalism and social communication: An inquiry into the foundations of nationality*. 2nd ed. Cambridge, MA: MIT Press.

–. 1969. *Nationalism and its alternatives*. New York: Alfred A. Knopf.

–. 1974. *Politics and government: How people decide their fate*. 2nd ed. Boston: Houghton Mifflin.

Devdas. 2002. Dir. S.L. Bhansali. Eros Entertainment.

Dhareshwar, V., and T. Niranjana. 2000. *Kaadalan* and the politics of resignification: Fashion, violence and the body. In *Making meaning in Indian cinema*, ed. R.S. Vasudevan, 191-214. New Delhi: Oxford University Press.

Dharker, A. 1997. *Sorry, not ready: Television in the time of PMdarshan*. New Delhi: HarperCollins.

Dickey, S. 1993. *Cinema and the urban poor in South India*. Cambridge, MA: Cambridge University Press.

Diebel, L. 2007. When rights collide with freedoms. The Toronto Star, 28 May, A19.

Dil Se. 1998. Dir. M. Ratnam. India Talkies and Madras Talkies.

Dilwale Dulhania Le Jayenge. 1995. Dir. A. Chopra. Yash Raj Films.

DiManno, R. 2006. Since when is covering women's faces feminism? *Toronto Star*, 25 October, A2.

Do Bigha Zameen. 1953. Dir. B. Roy. Bimal Roy Productions.

Dossa, P. 1988. Women's space/time: An anthropological perspective on Ismaili immigrant women in Calgary and Vancouver. *Canadian Ethnic Studies* 20, 1: 45-65.

Dosti. 1964. Dir. S. Bose. Rajshri Productions.

Durham, M.G. 2004. Constructing the "new ethnicities": Media, sexuality, and diaspora identity in the lives of South Asian immigrant girls. *Critical Studies in Media Communication* 21, 2: 140-61.

Dwyer, R. 2000. *All you want is money, all you need is love: Sexuality and romance in modern India*. London: Cassell.

Earth. 1998. Dir. D. Mehta. Cracking the Earth Films.

East Is East. 1999. Dir. D. O'Donnell. Assassin Films, BBC, and Film Four.

Ek Hasina Thi. 2004. Dir. S. Raghavan. S.K. Sera Sera, S.R.B. Films, and Varma Corporation.

Engber, D. 2005. What are the rules of Bollywood? *Slate*, 2 June, http://www.slate.com/id/2120162.

Fanaa. 2006. Dir. K. Kohli. Yashraj Productions.

Ferguson, L. 2007. A one-year chronology of the province's "reasonable accommodation" controversy. *Montreal Gazette*, 3 February, A9.

Ferguson, S.D. 2002. A cacophony of voices: Competing for the future. In *Civic discourse and cultural politics in Canada: A cacophony of voices*, ed. S.D. Ferguson and L.R. Shade, 3-14. Westport, CT: Ablex.

Fernandes, L. 2000. Nationalizing the "global": Media images, cultural politics and the middle class in India. *Media, Culture and Society* 22, 5: 611-28.

Finlay, L. 2002. Negotiating the swamp: The opportunity and challenge of reflexivity in research practice. *Qualitative Research* 2, 2: 209-30.

Fire. 1996. Dir. D. Mehta. Kaleidoscope Entertainment and Trial By Fire Films.

Fiza. 2000. Dir. K. Mohammed. UTV Motion Pictures.

Fleras, A., and J.L. Kunz. 2001. *Media and minorities: Representing diversity in a multicultural Canada*. Toronto: Thompson.

Ford, T. 2006. We're changing our ideas on national purpose. *Winnipeg Free Press*, 2 October, A11.

Gadar: Ek Prem Katha. 2001. Dir. A. Sharma. Zee Telefilms.

Gagnon, L. 2006. The kirpan decision isn't welcome in Quebec. *Globe and Mail*, 13 March, A15.

Garam Hawa. 1973. Dir. M.S. Sathyu. Unit 3 mm.

Gardner, D. 2006. Lessons from Holland. *Ottawa Citizen*, 28 October, B1.

Ghafour, H. 2006. Terrorism cases strikingly similar. *Globe and Mail*, 10 June, A16.

Ghuman, G. 2006. The Muslim as the "Other" in Bollywood. *Countercurrents*, 21 February, http://www.countercurrents.org/arts-ghuman210206.htm.

Gillespie, M. 1995. *Television, ethnicity, and cultural change*. London and New York: Routledge.

Gilroy, P. 1993. *The black Atlantic: Modernity and double consciousness*. Cambridge, MA: Harvard University Press.

Glazer, N., and D.P. Moynihan. 1963. *Beyond the melting pot: The Negroes, Puerto Ricans, Jews, Italians, and Irish of New York City*. Cambridge, MA: MIT Press.

Gokulsing, K.M., and W. Dissanayake. 1998. *Indian popular cinema: A narrative of cultural change*. New Delhi: Orient Longman.

Gopal, S., and S. Moorti. 2008. Introduction: Travels of Hindi song and dance. In *Global Bollywood: Travels of Hindi song and dance*, ed. S. Gopal and S. Moorti, 1-62. Minneapolis: University of Minnesota Press.

Gottschalk, P. 2000. *Beyond Hindu and Muslim: Multiple identity in narratives from village India*. New York: Oxford University Press.

Guru. 2007. Dir. M. Ratnam. Madras Talkies.

Haji-ar-were, S.R. 2006. Muslim diasporas in a modern world: A study of strategies of adaption. PhD diss., Department of International Communication, Macquarie University.

Hall, S. 1980. Encoding/decoding. In *Culture, media, language*, ed. S. Hall, D. Hobson, A. Lowe, and P. Willis, 128-38. London: Hutchinson.

–. 1994. Cultural identity and diaspora. In *Colonial discourse and postcolonial theory: A reader*, ed. P. Williams and L. Chrisman, 392-403. New York: Columbia University Press.

Handa, A. 2003. *Of silk saris and mini-skirts: South Asian girls walk the tightrope of culture*. Toronto: Women's Press.

Hansen, T.B. 2005. In search of the diasporic self: Bollywood in South Africa. In *Bollyworld: Popular Indian cinema through a transnational lens*, ed. R. Kaur and A.J. Sinha, 239-60. Thousand Oaks, CA: Sage.

Hare Rama Hare Krishna. 1971. Dir. D. Anand. Navketan International Films.

Harzig, C., and D. Hoerder. 2006. Transnationalism and the age of mass migration, 1880s to 1920s. In *Transnational identities and practices in Canada*, ed. V. Satzewich and L. Wong, 35-51. Vancouver: UBC Press.

Heater, D. 1996. *World citizenship and government: Cosmopolitan ideas in the history of Western political thought*. London: Macmillan.

–. 1999. *What is citizenship?* Cambridge, UK: Polity Press.

Heer Raanjha. 1970. Dir. C. Anand. Himalaya Films.

Henna. 1991. Dir. R. Kapoor. R.K. Films and Studios.

Hiebert, D., and D. Ley. 2006. Characteristics of immigrant transnationalism in Vancouver. In *Transnational identities and practices in Canada*, ed. V. Satzewich and L. Wong, 71-90. Vancouver: UBC Press.

High Level Committee on the Indian Diaspora. 2001. *Report of the High Level Committee on the Indian Diaspora*. New Delhi: Ministry of Overseas Indians Affairs, Government of India.

Hoodfar, H. 2003. More than clothing: Veiling as an adaptive strategy. In *The Muslim veil in North America: Issues and debates*, ed. S. Alvi, H. Hoodfar, and S. McDonough, 3-40. Toronto: Women's Press.

hooks, b. 1994. *Outlaw culture: Resisting representations*. New York: Routledge.

Howard-Hassman, R.E. 1999. "Canadian" as an ethnic category: Implications for multiculturalism and national unity. *Canadian Public Policy* 25, 4: 523-37.

Hum Aapke Hain Koun. 1994. Dir. S.R. Barjatya. Rajshri Productions.

Husaini, Z. 1990. *Muslims in the Canadian mosaic: Socio-cultural and economic links with their countries of origin*. Edmonton: Muslim Research Foundation.

Isin, E.F., and M. Siemiatycki. 2002. Making space for mosques: Claiming urban citizenship. In *Race, space and the law: The making of a white settler society*, ed. S. Razack, 185-209. Toronto: Between the Lines.

Jagte Raho. 1956. Dir. A. Mitra. R.K. Films.

Jiménez, M. 2007. How Canadian are you? *Globe and Mail*, 12 January, A1.

Jiwani, Y. 1989. Situating identity. Unpublished raw data.

–. 1993. By omission and commission: "Race" and representation in Canadian television news. PhD diss., Department of Communication, Simon Fraser University.

–. 2006. *Discourses of denial*. Vancouver: UBC Press.

Johnson, B.D. 2007. Blazing a northern passage to India. *Maclean's*, 5 February, 55.

Joseph, M. 1999. *Nomadic identities: The performance of citizenship*. Minneapolis: University of Minnesota Press.

Kabbani, R. 1986. *Europe's myths of Orient: Devise and rule*. London: Macmillan.

Kabhi Alvida Naa Kehna. 2006. Dir. K. Johar. Dharma Productions.

Kabhi Khushi Kabhie Gham. 2001. Dir. K. Johar. Dharma Productions.

Kabir, N.M. 1999. *Talking films: Conversations on Hindi cinema with Javed Akhtar*. New Delhi: Oxford University Press.

Kal Ho Naa Ho. 2003. Dir. N. Advani. Dharma Productions.

Kalam, A.P.J.A. 2007. Address by the President of India at Pravasi Bharatiya Diwas. http:// presidentofindia.nic.in/presentation/splangnewPDF%20Format948.pdf.

Karim, K.H. 1997. The historical resilience of primary stereotypes: Core images of the Muslim Other. In *The language and politics of exclusion: Others in discourse*, ed. S.H. Riggins, 153-82. Thousand Oaks, CA: Sage.

–. 1998. From ethnic media to global media: Transnational communication networks among diasporic communities. Ottawa: Department of Canadian Heritage, Government of Canada.

–. 2000. *The Islamic peril: Media and global violence*. Montreal: Black Rose Books.

–. 2002. Crescent dawn in the Great White North: Muslim participation in the Canadian public sphere. In *Muslims in the West: From sojourners to citizens*, ed. Y.Y. Haddad, 262-77. New York: Oxford University Press.

–. 2003. Mapping diasporic landscapes. In *The media of diaspora*, ed. K.H. Karim, 1-17. London: Routledge.

–. 2010. At the interstices of tradition, modernity and postmodernity: Ismaili engagements with contemporary Canadian society. In *The modern history of the Ismailis*, ed. F. Daftary. London: I.B. Tauris.

Karma. 1986. Dir. S. Ghai. Mukta Arts.

Katz, E. 1987. Communications research since Lazarsfeld. *Public Opinion Quarterly* 51: S25-S45.

Kaur, R., and A.J. Sinha. 2005. Bollyworld: An introduction to popular Indian cinema through a transnational lens. In *Bollyworld: Popular Indian cinema through a transnational lens*, ed. R. Kaur and A.J. Sinha, 11-32. Thousand Oaks, CA: Sage.

Kellner, D. 1995. *Media culture: Cultural studies, identity and politics between the modern and the postmodern*. London and New York: Routledge.

Khamosh Pani. 2003. Dir. S. Sumar. Vidhi Films and Flying Moon Filmproduktion.

Khan, D-S. 2004. *Crossing the threshold: Understanding religious identities in South Asia*. London and New York: I.B. Tauris, in association with the Institute of Ismaili Studies.

Khan, S. 1995. The veil as a site of struggle: The *hejab* in Quebec. *Canadian Woman Studies* 15, 2: 146-51.

–. 2000. *Muslim women: Crafting a North American identity*. Gainesville: University of Florida Press.

–. 2009a. Nationalism and Hindi cinema: Narrative strategies in *Fanaa*. *Studies in South Asian Film and Media* 1, 1: 85-99.

–. 2009b. Reading *Fanaa*: Confrontational views, comforting identifications and undeniable pleasures. *South Asian Popular Culture* 7, 2: 127-39.

Kolar-Panov, D. 2003. Video and the Macedonians in Australia. In *The media of diaspora*, ed. K.H. Karim, 105-18. London: Routledge.

Kraidy, M.M. 1999. The global, the local, and the hybrid: A native ethnography of glocalization. *Critical Studies in Mass Communication* 16: 456-76.

Kuch Kuch Hota Hai. 1998. Dir. K. Johar. Yash Raj Films.

Kumar, A. 2002. *Bombay-London-New York*. London and New York: Routledge.

Kymlicka, W. 2001. The new debate over minority rights. In *Democracy and national pluralism*, ed. F. Rèquejo, 15-39. London: Routledge.

Lagaan: Once upon a Time in India. 2001. Dir. A. Gowariker. Aamir Khan Productions.

Lakshmanan, I.A.R. 1999. Hooray for Bollywood: India's film industry doubles Hollywood's annual output. *Hamilton Spectator*, 27 March, W3.

Lamhe. 1991. Dir. Y. Chopra. Yashraj Films.

Larkin, B. 2003. Itineraries of Indian cinema: African videos, Bollywood, and global media. In *Multiculturalism, postcoloniality, and transnational media*, ed. E. Shohat and R. Stam, 170-92. New Brunswick, NJ: Rutgers University Press.

Lee, J., and J. Lutz, eds. 2005. *Situating "race" and racisms in time, space, and theory: Critical essays for activists and scholars*. Montreal and Kingston: McGill-Queen's University Press.

Leonard, K. 2002. South Asian leadership of American Muslims. In *Muslims in the West: From sojourners to citizens*, ed. Y.Y. Haddad, 233-49. New York: Oxford University Press.

Lorimer, R., and J. McNulty. 1996. *Mass communication in Canada*. 3rd ed. Toronto: Oxford University Press.

Lyall, S., and I. Fisher. 2006. Many Muslims in Britain tell of feeling torn between competing identities. *New York Times*, 13 August, Section 1, 6.

Maa Tujhe Salaam. 2002. Dir. T. Verma. Eros International.

Macbeth, D. 2001. On "reflexivity" in qualitative research: Two readings, and a third. *Qualitative Inquiry* 7, 1: 35-68.

MacFarquhar, N. 2007. Iraq's shadow widens Sunni-Shiite split in U.S. *New York Times*, 4 February, Section 1, 1, 22.

Mahtani, M. 2004. Interrogating the hyphen-nation: Canadian multicultural policy and "mixed race" identities. Toronto: Centre of Excellence for Research on Immigration and Settlement (CERIS).

–. 2008. How are immigrants seen – and what do they want to see? Contemporary research on the representation of immigrants in the Canadian English-language media. In

Immigration and integration in Canada in the twenty-first century, ed. J. Biles, M. Burstein, and J. Frideres, 231-51. Montreal and Kingston: McGill-Queen's University Press.

Maira, S.M. 2002. *Desis in the house: Indian American youth culture in New York City.* Philadelphia: Temple University Press.

Malkani, G. 2006. Sounds of assimilation. *New York Times*, 19 August, A15.

Mamdani, M. 2004. *Good Muslim, bad Muslim.* New York: Pantheon Books.

Mandaville, P. 2001. *Transnational Muslim politics: Reimagining the umma.* London and New York: Routledge.

Mann, J. 2001. Hooray for Bollywood. *Vancouver Sun*, 5 January, F3.

Manning, E. 2003. *Ephemeral territories: Representing nation, home, and identity in Canada.* Minneapolis: University of Minnesota Press.

Martin, M. 1997. *Communication and mass media: Culture, domination, and opposition.* Scarborough, ON: Prentice Hall Allyn and Bacon Canada.

Masala Trois Collective. 2003. Foreplay. In *Desilicious*, ed. D. Barretto, G. Singh Jolly, and Z. Wadhwani, 11-13. Vancouver: Arsenal Pulp Press.

McCorkel, J.A., and K. Myers. 2003. What difference does difference make? Position and privilege in the field. *Qualitative Sociology* 26, 2: 199-231.

Mere Huzoor. 1968. Dir. V. Kumar. Movie Mughals.

Miladi, N. 2003. Mapping the Al-Jazeera phenomenon. In *War and the media: Reporting conflict 24/7*, ed. D.K. Thussu and D. Freedman, 149-60. Thousand Oaks, CA: Sage.

Miller, M.J. 2005. Introduction: Creating a classic in television history. In *Growing up Degrassi: Television, identity and youth cultures*, ed. M. Byers, 13-27. Toronto: Sumach Press.

Mishra, V. 2002. *Bollywood cinema: Temples of desire.* New York: Routledge.

Mission Kashmir. 2000. Dir. V.V. Chopra. Vinod Chopra Productions.

Mississippi Masala. 1991. Dir. M. Nair. Black River Productions, Channel Four Films, and Mirabai Films.

Mitra, A. 1999. *India through the western lens: Creating national images in film.* New Delhi: Sage.

Moghissi, H. 2006. Introduction. In *Muslim diaspora: Gender, culture and identity*, ed. H. Moghissi, xiv-xxv. London and New York: Routledge.

Mohammad, A.T. 2001. Relationships between Muslims and Hindus in the United States: *Mlecchas* versus *Kafirs*? In *Community, empire and migration: South Asians in diaspora*, ed. C. Bates, 286-308. New York: Palgrave.

Monsoon Wedding. 2001. Dir. M. Nair. IFC Productions and Mirabai Films.

Morley, D. 1980. *The* Nationwide *audience: Structure and decoding.* London: British Film Institute.

–. 2000. *Home territories: Media, mobility and identity.* London and New York: Routledge.

Morley, D., and K. Robins. 1995. *Spaces of identity: Global media, electronic landscapes and cultural boundaries.* London and New York: Routledge.

Mother India. 1957. Dir. M. Khan. Mehboob Productions.

Mughal-e-Azam. 1960. Dir. K. Asif. Sterling Investment Corp.

Munro, D. 2005. Is multiculturalism on its deathbed? *Toronto Star*, 18 August, A27.

Murji, R., and Y.M. Hébert. 1999. Collectivized identity among Shi'a Imami Ismaili Muslims of Calgary: Implications for pluralism and policy. Paper presented at the conference Youth in the Plural City: Individualized and Collectivized Identities, May 1999, Rome.

Naficy, H. 1993. *The making of exile cultures: Iranian television in Los Angeles.* Minneapolis: University of Minnesota Press.

–. 2001. *An accented cinema: Exile and diasporic filmmaking.* Princeton, NJ: Princeton University Press.

Namastey London. 2007. Dir. V.A. Shah. Blockbuster Movie Entertainers.

Nandy, A. 1983. *The intimate enemy: Loss and recovery of self under colonialism.* New Delhi: Oxford University Press.

–. 1995. *The savage Freud and other essays on possible and retrievable selves.* Princeton, NJ: Princeton University Press.

Nayar, S. 1997. The values of fantasy. *Journal of Popular Culture* 31, 1: 73-90.

–. 2003. Dreams, dharma, and Mrs. Doubtfire: Exploring Hindi popular culture via its "chutneyed" Western scripts. *Journal of Popular Film and Television* 31, 2: 73-81.

Nikaah. 1982. Dir. B.R. Chopra. B.R. Films and United Productions.

Noorjehan. 1923. Dir. J.J. Madan. Madan Theatre.

Ogan, C.L. 2002. Communication and culture. In *Global communication,* ed. Y. Kamalipour, 207-28. Belmont, CA: Wadsworth.

Oommen, M.A., and K.V. Joseph. 1991. *Economics of Indian cinema.* New Delhi: Oxford and India Book House Publishing (IBH).

Ong, A. 1999. *Flexible citizenship: The cultural logics of transnationality.* Durham, NC, and London: Duke University Press.

Orona, C.J. 1997. Temporality and identity loss due to Alzheimer's disease. In *Grounded theory in practice,* ed. A.L. Strauss and J. Corbin, 171-96. Thousand Oaks, CA: Sage.

Pakeezah. 1972. Dir. K. Amrohi. Mahal Pictures and Sangeeta Enterprises.

Pardes. 1997. Dir. S. Ghai. Mukta Arts.

Partition. 2007. Dir. V. Sarin. Montreal: Seville Pictures.

Patel, D. 2006. The Maple-Neem nexus: Transnational links of South Asian Canadians. In *Transnational identities and practices in Canada,* ed. V. Satzewich and L. Wong, 150-63. Vancouver: UBC Press.

Patriquin, M. 2006. Canadians out of convenience. *Maclean's,* 20 November, 42-43.

Pendakur, M. 1990. India. In *The Asian film industry,* ed. J.A. Lent, 229-52. London: Christopher Helm.

–. 2003. *Indian popular cinema: Industry, ideology and consciousness.* Cresskill, NJ: Hampton Press.

Perigoe, R. 2006. Mediating diversity: Muslim representations in *The (Montreal) Gazette* newspaper post 9/11. *International Journal of Diversity in Organizations, Communities and Nations* 4: 1089-99.

Phool. 1944. Dir. K. Asif. Famous Films.

Pinjar. 2003. Dir. C. Dwivedi. Lucky Star Entertainment.

Pipes, D. 2001. This American feels safer. *Globe and Mail,* 3 October, A15.

Pipes, D., and L. Hedegaard. 2002. Muslim extremism: Denmark's had enough. *National Post,* 27 August, A14.

Poole, E. 2002. *Reporting Islam: Media representations of British Muslims.* London: I.B. Tauris.

Prasad, M.M. 1998. *Ideology of the Hindi film: A historical construction.* New York: Oxford University Press.

–. 2000. Signs of ideological re-form in two recent films: Towards real subsumption? In *Making meaning in Indian cinema,* ed. R.S. Vasudevan, 145-67. New Delhi: Oxford University Press.

Purab aur Pachhim. 1970. Dir. M. Kumar. V.I.P. Films.

Pyaasa. 1957. Dir. G. Dutt. Guru Dutt Films.

Pyke, K., and T. Dang. 2003. "FOB" and "Whitewashed": Identity and internalized racism among second generation Asian Americans. *Qualitative Sociology* 26, 2: 147-72.

Raby, R. 2005. What is resistance? *Journal of Youth Studies* 8, 2: 151-71.

Radhakrishnan, R. 2003. Ethnicity in an age of diaspora. In *Theorizing diaspora: A reader,* ed. J. Evans Braziel and A. Mannur, 119-31. Malden, MA: Blackwell.

Radway, J. 1984. *Reading the romance: Women, patriarchy, and popular culture.* Chapel Hill: University of North Carolina Press.

Rai, A.S. 2003. Patriotism and the Muslim citizen in Hindi films. *Harvard Asia Quarterly* 7, 3: http://www.asiaquarterly.com/content/view/136/40.

Raj, D.S. 2003. *Where are you from? Middle-class migrants in the modern world.* Berkeley: University of California Press.

Rajadhyaksha, A. 1996. Strange attractions. *Sight and Sound* 6, 8 (August): 28-31.

–. 2000. Viewership and democracy in the cinema. In *Making meaning in Indian cinema,* ed. R.S. Vasudevan, 267-96. New Delhi: Oxford University Press.

Ramadan, T. 2002. Islam and Muslims in Europe: A silent revolution toward rediscovery. In *Muslims in the West: From sojourners to citizens,* ed. Y.Y. Haddad, 158-66. New York: Oxford University Press.

Ray, M. 2001. Bollywood down under: Fiji Indian cultural history and popular assertion. In *Floating lives: The media and Asian diasporas*, ed. S. Cunningham and J. Sinclair, 136-84. Lanham, MD: Rowman and Littlefield.

–. 2003. Nation, nostalgia and Bollywood: In the tracks of a twice-displaced community. In *The media of diaspora*, ed. K.H. Karim, 21-35. London: Routledge.

Razack, S. 1998. *Looking white people in the eye: Gender, race, and culture in courtrooms and classrooms.* Toronto: University of Toronto Press.

Reitz, J.G., and R. Banerjee. 2007. Racial inequality, social cohesion, and policy issues in Canada. In *Belonging? Diversity, recognition, and shared citizenship in Canada*, ed. K. Banting, T.J. Courchene, and L. Seidle, 489-545. Montreal: Institute for Research on Public Policy.

Rogers, E. 1969. *Modernization among peasants: The impact of communication.* New York: Holt, Rinehart and Winston.

Roja. 1992. Dir. M. Ratnam. Hansa Pictures.

Roti Kapada aur Makaan. 1974. Dir. M. Kumar. V.I.P. Films and Vishal Productions.

Rushdie, S. 2005. In defence of multiculturalism. *Toronto Star*, 15 December, A27.

Said, E. 1978. *Orientalism.* New York: Vintage Books.

Salaam Bombay. 1988. Dir. M. Nair. Cadragee, Channel Four Films and Doordarshan.

Salaam Namaste. 2005. Dir. S. Anand. Yashraj Films.

Salim Langde Pe Mat Ro. 1989. Dir. S.A. Mirza. National Film Development Corporation of India.

Sarfarosh. 1999. Dir. J.M. Matthan. Cinematt Pictures.

Sassen, S. 2006. *Territory, authority, rights: From medieval to global assemblages.* Princeton, NJ: Princeton University Press.

Saunders, D. 2003. The kids are all right. *Globe and Mail*, 7 June, F2.

–. 2007. Why the fear of a "Muslim tide" makes too much of a splash. *Globe and Mail*, 14 April, F3.

Schensul, J.J. 1999. Focused group interviews. In *Enhanced ethnographic methods: Audiovisual techniques, focused group interviews, and elicitation techniques*, ed. J.J. Schensul, M.D. LeCompte, B.K. Nastasi, and S.P. Borgatti, 51-114. Walnut Creek, CA: Altamira Press.

Seale, C. 1999. *The quality of qualitative research.* Thousand Oaks, CA: Sage.

Sevunts, L. 2002. Poll shocks immigrants, refugees. *Montreal Gazette*, 21 December, A12.

Shoemaker, P., and S. Reese. 1996. *Mediating the message: Theories of influence on mass media content.* 2nd ed. White Plains, NY: Longman.

Shohat, E., and R. Stam. 1994. *Unthinking Eurocentrism: Multiculturalism and the media.* London and New York: Routledge.

–. 2003. Introduction. In *Multiculturalism, postcoloniality, and transnational media*, ed. E. Shohat and R. Stam, 1-17. New Brunswick, NJ: Rutgers University Press.

Sholay. 1975. Dir. R. Sippy. Sippy Films Pvt.

Shri 420. 1955. Dir. R. Kapoor. R.K. Films.

Shukla, S. 2003. *India abroad: Diasporic cultures of postwar America and England.* Princeton, NJ, and Oxford, UK: Princeton University Press.

Siddiqui, H. 2006. Muslim-bashing dilutes our democratic values. *Toronto Star*, 11 June, A17.

Sidhva, S. 1996. Hollywood nudges in on India's movie market: India has the world's keenest moviegoers, and the U.S. wants a piece of the action. *Financial Post*, 18 July, 49.

Sinclair, J., and S. Cunningham. 2001. Diasporas and the media. In *Floating lives: The media and Asian diasporas*, ed. S. Cunningham and J. Sinclair, 1-34. Lanham, MD: Rowman and Littlefield.

Sinclair, J., A. Yue, G. Hawkins, K. Pookong, and J. Fox. 2001. Chinese cosmopolitanism and media use. In *Floating lives: The media and Asian diasporas*, ed. S. Cunningham and J. Sinclair, 35-90. Lanham, MD: Rowman and Littlefield.

Singh, M. 2007. Address by the Prime Minister of India at Pravasi Bharatiya Diwas. http://pmindia.nic.in/speeches.htm.

Slumdog Millionaire. 2008. Dir. D. Boyle. Celador Films, Film 4, and Pathé Pictures International.

Smith, J.I. 2002. Introduction. In *Muslims in the West: From sojourners to citizens*, ed. Y.Y. Haddad, 3-16. New York: Oxford University Press.

Sreberny-Mohammadi, A., and A. Mohammadi. 1994. *Small media, big revolution: Communication, culture, and the Iranian revolution*. Minneapolis: University of Minnesota Press.

Statistics Canada. 2003a. *Canada's ethnocultural portrait: The changing mosaic*. Ottawa: Government of Canada.

–. 2003b. *Religions in Canada*. Ottawa: Government of Canada.

Stillar, G.F. 1998. *Analyzing everyday texts: Discourse, rhetoric, and social perspectives*. Thousand Oaks, CA: Sage.

Sun, W. 2002. *Leaving China: Media, migration, and transnational imagination*. Lanham, MD: Rowman and Littlefield.

Swades. 2004. Dir. A. Gowariker. Ashutosh Gowariker Productions.

Taal. 1999. Dir. S. Ghai. Mukta Arts.

Tamale, S.A. 1996. The outsider looks in: Constructing knowledge about American collegiate racism. *Qualitative Sociology* 19, 4: 471-93.

Thien, M. 2003. But, I dream in Canadian. *Globe and Mail*, 27 December, A13.

Thobani, S. 2007. *Exalted subjects: Studies in the making of race and nation in Canada*. Toronto: University of Toronto Press.

Thoraval, Y. 2000. *The cinemas of India*. New Delhi: Macmillan India.

A Touch of Pink. 2004. Dir. I.I. Rashid. London and Toronto: Martin Pope Productions and Sienna Films.

Tsaliki, L. 2003. Globalisation and hybridity: The construction of Greekness on the Internet. In *The media of diaspora*, ed. K.H. Karim, 162-76. London: Routledge.

Turner, B.S. 2000. Liberal citizenship and cosmopolitan virtue. In *Citizenship and democracy in a global era*, ed. A. Vandenberg, 18-32. New York: St. Martin's Press.

Ujimoto, K.V. 1990. Studies of ethnic identity and race relations. In *Race and ethnic relations in Canada*, ed. P.S. Li, 209-30. Toronto: Oxford University Press.

Umrao Jaan. 1981. Dir. M. Ali. Integrated Films.

Valpy, M., and Anderssen, E. 2003. 10 ways the 20s will challenge us. *Globe and Mail*, 1 July, A6.

Van den Bulck, H., and L. Van Poecke. 1996. National language, identity formation, and broadcasting: The Flemish and German-Swiss communities. In *Globalization, communication and transnational civil society*, ed. S. Braman and A. Sreberny-Mohammadi, 157-77. Cresskill, NJ: Hampton Press.

van Dijk, T.A. 1988. *News analysis: Case studies of international and national news in the press*. Hillsdale, NJ: Lawrence Erlbaum.

–. 1991. *Racism and the press*. London and New York: Routledge.

–. 1993. Stories and racism. In *Narrative and social control: Critical perspectives*, ed. D.K. Mumby, 121-42. Newbury Park, CA: Sage.

–. 1996. Discourse, power and access. In *Texts and practices: Readings in critical discourse analysis*, ed. C.R. Caldas-Coulthard and M. Coulthard, 84-104. London and New York: Routledge.

–. 1998. *Ideology: A multidisciplinary approach*. Thousand Oaks, CA: Sage.

Vanity Fair. 2004. Dir. M. Nair. Focus Features.

Vasudevan, R.S. 2000. Shifting codes, dissolving identities: The Hindi social film of the 1950s as popular culture. In *Making meaning in Indian cinema*, ed. R.S. Vasudevan, 99-121. New Delhi: Oxford University Press.

Veer-Zaara. 2004. Dir. Y. Chopra. Yash Raj Films.

Virdi, J. 2003. *The cinematic imagination: Indian popular films as social history*. New Brunswick, NJ: Rutgers University Press.

Walton, D., and P. Kennedy. 2002. Muslims feel doubts linger. *Globe and Mail*, 7 September, A5.

Warah, R. 1998. *Triple heritage: A journey to self-discovery*. Nairobi: Colour Print.

Water. 2005. Dir. D. Mehta. Mongrel Media.

Wente, M. 2001. Tiptoeing through Islam. *Globe and Mail*, 2 October, A17.

Wiwa, K. 2005. Workers of the word world, unite! *Globe and Mail*, 27 August, A15.

Worthington, P. 2006. Working stiffs pay bills. *Toronto Sun,* 23 September, A15.
Yaadein. 2001. Dir. S. Ghai. Mukta Arts.
Yelaja, P. 2006. South Asian youth rebrand for a new era. *Toronto Star,* 27 October, A1.
Zakhm. 1998. Dir. M. Bhatt. Pooja Bhatt Productions.

Index

Dhoom, 220
diaspora
"Brown Atlantic," 42, 67, 68
choice of host country as colonial
  legacy, 42-43, 61-63, 71, 106
citizenship and (*see* citizenship; global
  citizenship)
complexity of multiple identities, 50-53,
  214-15
concerns regarding second-generation
  immigrants, 33-34
cultural identity and preservation in
  diasporic communities, 53-57
definitions and notions of, 34-38
  affiliation with cultural or religious
    collectives as response to alienation
    in host country, 36-37, 48-49, 56, 81,
    150-51
  characterization by what diasporas are
    not, 35-36
  connections to the "old country," 36,
    105
  diasporas as imagined communities, 35
diversity of, 42
experience of, for different generations
  of immigrants, 216-17
experience of, for first-generation
  immigrants, 40, 216-17
experience of, for second-generation
  immigrants, 39-41, 195, 216-17
idealized vision of homeland, 44-45,
  156-57, 183
impact on identity construction, 45-46
India's marketing to, 43-44
media and, 89-91, 104
media technologies' role in maintaining
  cohesiveness and attachment to
  homeland, 35, 41, 43-44, 86
on Muslims as religious, 59, 71
pro-assimilation discourses, 33-34, 51-52
See also diaspora, Indian; diaspora,
  South Asian
diaspora, Indian
ascendance of Hindu Indian identity, 65
attempts at segregation on religious,
  linguistic, or caste grounds, 64-65
history of, 61-62
influence of colonialism, 62-63, 69
Sikhs portrayed as different from
  Hindus, 65
size of, 42, 60-61
diaspora, South Asian
affiliation with cultural or religious
  collectives as response to alienation
  in host country, 36-37, 48-49, 56, 81,
  150-51

ascendance of Hindu Indian identity, 65
attempts at segregation on religious,
  linguistic, or caste grounds, 64-65
"Brown Atlantic," 42, 67, 68
diversity of, 8-9, 58, 60-61, 62
ethnic diaspora, 59
ethnic enclaves and citizenship
  identities, 63-65
hybridity and accommodation vs
  existing rivalries, 66-67
influence of colonialism, 62-63, 69
integration in Canada compared with
  United States, 152-53, 208
on leadership positions of South Asian
  (rather than Middle Eastern)
  Muslims, 81-82
multiple migrants (from South Asia to
  more than one country), 62-63
relationship to film, 13, 103, 181, 193
size and extent, 60
diasporic films
comparison with Bollywood films,
  101-2, 106
nationalism and Indian values as
  consistent focus of films, 107-11,
  112, 129, 193-94
themes relevant to diasporic audiences,
  91, 100-2, 106-7, 183-84, 185-86
Dil, 220
Dil Se (From the Heart), 122
Dilwale Dulhania Le Jayenge (The Lover
  Takes the Bride) *(DDLJ)*
appeal to diasporic youth, 3, 170
description, 219
diasporic film with theme of nationalism
  and Indian values, 108, 109-10, 112,
  129, 193-94
earnings and success, 22, 24
portrayal of diasporic individuals, 13-14,
  110, 187, 193, 211
Dissanayake, W., 21, 23, 24, 26, 29, 30,
  31, 115
Do Bigha Zameen (Two Acres of Land), 29
Dossa, P., 74
Dosti (Friendship), 187, 220
Durham, M.G.
identity concerns regarding second-
  generation immigrants, 17
influence of Bollywood on identity
  construction, 16, 192, 206
study on second-generation viewers,
  130, 199, 204, 212
Dus, 220
Dwyer, Rachel
on cultural influences on Indian film,
  21, 23

in diasporic films, 107-11, 112, 129, 193-94
double and triple migrants and, 89
to an imagined community, 86
media as conveyors of nationalist and cultural sentiment, 84, 85-89
media technologies' role in maintaining cohesiveness and attachment to homeland, 35, 41, 43-44, 84, 88
nation-states' use of media to promote nationalism, 85-89
See also nationalism as Bollywood theme
nationalism as Bollywood theme
amorality and corruptive influence of the West, 109-10, 112-13
challenge to American-dominated international film, 19
"Hindutva" or Hindu supremacy, 14
legacy of colonialism, 112-13
Muslim themes in era of Hindu fundamentalism, 120-27, 128-29
Muslims and Islam, role in films, 12, 14, 116-20
nationalist focus of films, 7, 10, 14, 22-23, 107-8, 182-83, 193, 197
portrayal of South Asians in diaspora, 108-12, 113, 178, 181-82, 187-88, 210
role of nationalist political parties in film industry, 113
theme consistent with government initiatives, 13
"third space" occupied by those with dual cultures, 114-15
nationality
implied arguments of Canadian nationality for white Canadians, 151-52
nationality and ethnicity as separate identities, 147-53, 157, 198-99, 203-5, 206-7
second-generation's identification as Canadian, 147-53, 157, 198-99, 203-5, 206-7, 214-15
See also citizenship
Nationwide (television show), 97-98
The Nationwide Audience (Morley), 98
Naushad, 119
Nayar, S., 20, 26, 111, 115
Nehru, Jawaharlal, 21
Newman, J., 90
Nikaah (Marriage), 120
Niranjana, Tejaswini, 23, 40, 115
Noorjehan, 117

Ong, A., 41, 88, 201, 215

Orona, C.J., 136-37
Ottawa
choice of participants in study, 15, 131, 133-34
South Asian population, 159

Pakeezah (Pure of Heart), 120
Pakistan
control over importation of Indian films, 13
Lollywood, 24, 102, 184-85, 191
Pardes (Foreign Land)
description, 221
subject of living in two cultures, 32, 108-9, 110, 187
theme of nationalism and identity, 109, 110, 111, 128
Parineeta, 221
Partition, 96
Patel, D., 58, 82
Pendakur, M.
on censorship, 13, 29, 120, 122
on films addressing living in two cultures, 108
on gender, 27, 28
on imperialist nature, 11
on multilingual nature of Indian films, 20-21
on operations of Bollywood, 22, 23, 26
on viewing films as Indian family activity, 141
Peters, Russell, 106
Phool, 117
Pinjar, 186, 221
Pinto, Freida, 94
Prasad, M.M., 10-11, 20, 26
Purab aur Pachhim (East and West), 108, 109, 111
Pyaasa (Eternal Thirst), 29
Pyke, K., 54, 69, 135

Quebec and the *hijab*, 8, 73
Qurbani, 220

Raby, R., 209-10
racism
affiliation with cultural or religious collectives as response to alienation in host country, 36-37, 48-49, 56, 81, 150-51
in Bollywood films, 91, 94, 123
in Canada vs in the United States, 152-53
as catalyst to work through identities, 82
common denominators of identity, 17
cultural enclaves as response to, 36

Printed and bound in Canada by Friesens
Set in Stone by Artegraphica Design Co. Ltd.
Copy editor: Robert Lewis
Proofreader: Kate Spezowka
Indexer: Pat Buchanan